POLITICS
IN
LIBERIA

POLITICS
IN
LIBERIA

THE
CONSERVATIVE
ROAD TO
DEVELOPMENT

MARTIN LOWENKOPF

HOOVER INSTITUTION PRESS
STANFORD UNIVERSITY, STANFORD, CALIFORNIA
1976

The Hoover Institution on War, Revolution and Peace, founded at Stanford University in 1919 by the late President Herbert Hoover, is a center for advanced study and research on public and international affairs in the twentieth century. The views expressed in its publications are entirely those of the authors and do not necessarily reflect the views of the staff, officers, or Board of Overseers of the Hoover Institution.

Hoover Institution Publications 151
© 1976 by the Board of Trustees of the
   Leland Stanford Junior University
All rights reserved
Printed in the United States of America
International Standard Book Number: 0-8179-6511-4
Library of Congress Catalog Card Number: 75-27010

Contents

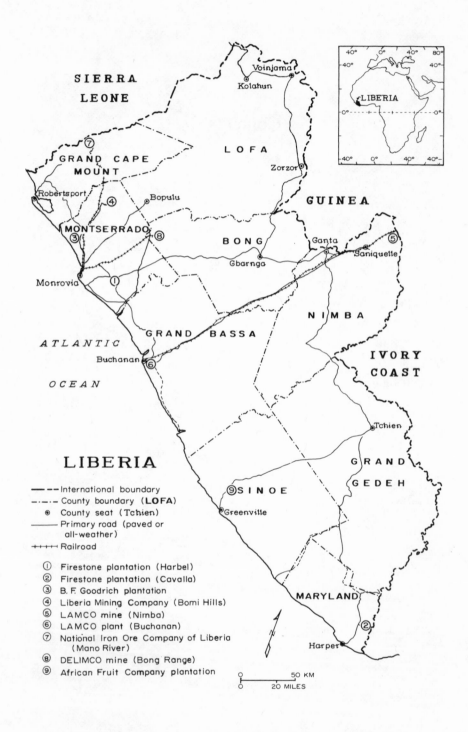

SIERRA
LEONE

Voinjama

Kolahun

LOFA

GRAND CAPE
MOUNT

⑦

Robertsport

Bopulu

④

Zorzor

GUINEA

MONTSERRADO

③

⑧

BONG

Ganta

⑤

Saniquelle

Gbarnga

Monrovia

①

NIMBA

ATLANTIC

GRAND BASSA

Buchanan

⑥

IVORY

COAST

OCEAN

Tchien

LIBERIA

- - - International boundary
- · - · County boundary (**LOFA**)
◉ County seat (Tchien)
——— Primary road (paved or
     all-weather)
+++++ Railroad

① Firestone plantation (Harbel)
② Firestone plantation (Cavalla)
③ B. F. Goodrich plantation
④ Liberia Mining Company (Bomi Hills)
⑤ LAMCO mine (Nimba)
⑥ LAMCO plant (Buchanan)
⑦ National Iron Ore Company of Liberia
   (Mano River)
⑧ DELIMCO mine (Bong Range)
⑨ African Fruit Company plantation

⑨ SINOE

Greenville

GRAND

GEDEH

MARYLAND

②

Harper

50 KM

20 MILES

Preface

This study was written because I felt some explanation was needed about how Liberia, long governed by a small elite class, had remained politically stable during the 1950's and 1960's, a time of massive economic and social change. It escaped the disruption that has afflicted Africa because in the early 1950's Liberia began to develop a political system that would bring new members into the elite and allow more ordinary Liberians to have a choice in determining how they would live their lives and how they would be governed. It also began to develop an economic system that was both more productive and capable of a somewhat fairer distribution of goods.

In seeking to find out how this came about, I came to the second focus of this study: modernization. Although modernization is not a solution to regressive traditionalism, to tribal, caste, religious, and class divisions, or to economic backwardness, and although it does not ensure the development of democratic government, it may nevertheless confer a capacity to overcome unproductive practices, to organize society in a way that engenders a sense of national identity, and to avail to more people a broader choice of personal goals (through education and jobs, for example) and goals for their society.

Modernization has not led to democratic government in Liberia. But few, if any, African nations are democratic. Apart from those under military dictatorships, a number are "developing" under single party systems, most of them dominated by one so-called charismatic leader, and via several variants of "socialism" that are not democratic, much less socialist. I believe that students of Africa would do well to suspend judgment about democracy and measure political development with concepts that allow more objectivity, by using the concept of modernization. That is what I have tried to do.

President W. V. S. Tubman died during the writing of this study, shortly after my last visit to Liberia in 1971. Though his death wrenched the hearts of the people of Liberia, it had an almost negligible effect upon Liberia's political development. The "Tubman era," which had begun in 1944, was, in effect, already over. Indeed, Tubman's last term was marked by a political as well as economic turnabout: economic growth had slowed considerably, and some sour notes of political repression had been sounded. The administration of William Tolbert appears to have resumed, with modest alterations, Liberia's modernization processes. A brief postscript on Tolbert's presidency concludes this study.

I have sought to keep rough chronological divisions in tracing the background to, and the several periods of, the Tubman administration. However, I have found it convenient and useful to analyze the processes of modernization by sector. Economic and social developments and the political consequences of these processes are discussed separately. Owing to the dearth of available official records and other data, a chronological discussion would have suffered serious gaps. I have frequently been warned by my sources, and warn the reader in turn, about the unreliability of the economic data. Demographic data, too, are sparse, and the early ones unreliable. The first census ever, for Monrovia, took place in 1956. Moreover, there is a paucity of historical and sociological studies. Merran Fraenkel's *Tribe and Class in Monrovia,* based on fieldwork in 1958-59, is the only published in-depth urban study. While it provides insights into the lives of some of the inhabitants of the capital city, there has been no sociological development of Fraenkel's basic findings, and no comparable research at the Firestone and Goodrich rubber plantations, at the iron ore mines, or at the larger Liberian-owned rubber estates.

This study has been so long in preparation—beginning with a visit to Liberia in 1964 for the Department of State and the Agency for International Development—that it is difficult to recall all the persons and institutions whose assistance should be acknowledged. For financial and other forms of direct help, I wish to thank the Research and Publications Committee, University College of Dar es Salaam, Tanzania; the Hoover Institution and the Committee on African Studies, Stanford University; and Franklin and Marshall College. At Hoover, I received moral as well as editorial support from Peter Duignan and Lewis Gann; and from Betty Smith, editor of this book, invaluable criticisms and saving corrections. At Stanford, a young Liberian scholar, C. Zamba Liberty, was an invaluable sounding board for and critic of my ideas. Richard Mendoza, of AID, has been a tireless source of support and of the economic statistics which, we both hope, give order to an otherwise hazy picture of economic change in Liberia. I am indebted to Svend Holsoe for the map of tribal and language areas. None of these people, of course, is responsible for the matter or manner of this book. My wife Effie is, for without her, nothing . . .

M.L.

— 1 —

Introduction

Liberia is unique in Africa. The history of the 127-year-old West African republic seems so far removed from the supposed mainstream of African political development as to exempt it from comparative analysis. The differences between Liberia and most other African states are fundamental. Liberia has never had a foreign colonial ruler.[1] It has not experienced a populist movement aimed at driving out foreign colonizers and stripping away an alien culture. Nor did its independence come at a time when socialist and egalitarian ideologies were considered to be the appropriate motor forces moving the new nations. Indeed, Liberian leaders have sought to preserve their historical political system rather than to uproot or transform it. And notwithstanding its efforts to become part of African regional and continental associations, Liberia still looks first to the United States and the Western world for protection, technology, investment and management, trade and aid, and cultural inspiration.

For these and other reasons, Liberia is still vulnerable to the malignity and the romanticization it experienced from writers a generation ago; it is still occasionally caricatured as a hybrid of the antebellum American South and precolonial Africa. Liberia seems to defy dispassionate analysis by either foreigners or Liberians. Indeed, it is sometimes regarded as a model for what the newer nations of Africa should *not* be doing, in spite of its enormous economic growth and the expansion of its social infrastructure since World War II; twenty-eight years of stability under one elected president and an orderly transfer of power upon his death; significant development of both central and local governmental institutions; and widening popular participation and representation in the political processes of the nation.

Two contemporary studies focus on Liberia's modern characteristics, and in so doing correctly treat Liberia as something more than a political artifact.[2] In dispelling some old myths, however, they have introduced a new, highly critical perspective. The crux of their case is that substantial economic *growth* after World War II has not produced commensurate or broadly shared *development*—economic, social, or political—and that this growth has, instead, strengthened the political system which permits the fifteen thousand descendants of nineteenth-century black American settlers to maintain an often oppressive and exploitative domination over the 1.5 million indigenous tribal Liberians.[3]

According to this view, Liberia consists of two distinct and virtually separate societies: the Americo-Liberians, as the settlers and their descendants came to be called, and the indigenous tribal peoples. There has been some assimilation into the dominant group, particularly among coastal tribes, but the few assimilated tribesmen were required to deny their traditional identities and values and to embrace those of the dominant group. Implicit in this description is the assumption that these relationships are relatively static in nature.

Liberia is, in fact, a loosely integrated nation. The great majority of its people remain, for the most part, outside the modern sector, which encompasses the active members of the polity and society. This state of affairs is sometimes regarded as a product of the calculated exclusion of tribal people from the central political arena and its attendant benefits. This is only partially true. Elitism in Liberia tends to restrict vertical mobility, but not the horizontal movement of people into the modern sector, where they might also participate in national political life. What hinders national integration and modernization in Liberia is not so much repression as it is the inherent traditional conservatism and parochialism of the tribal Liberians and, in some respects, of the ruling class. In the case of the rural population, at least, Liberia resembles other underdeveloped nations of the Third World.

A more profitable way of examining political modernization and integration in Liberia would be to ask: Is the separation of the coastal settlers (and assimilated tribesmen) from the hinterland tribal peoples being bridged in such a way as to bind them together in complementary activities and institutions? Are common views and interests evolving? And, is the political system capable of absorbing the new stresses that accompany wider membership?

Since the 1950's the barriers to integration, which had kept most tribal people outside the central arena of Liberian life since the formation of the Republic, have been falling fairly rapidly. The need for wage laborers to man the growing mining industry and large rubber plantations has taken more than one-fourth of the tribal people physically out of the bush and into modern economic enclaves. The establishment of industries has also brought about the economic interdependence of the coastal and hinterland sections of the country.

Roads linking the country to the capital city, Monrovia, have provided hinterland farmers the opportunity to get their crops to markets. Traders have seized the opportunity to bring to the interior Western-type consumer goods, thus increasing two-way commerce between the hinterland and the coast. The radio, newspapers, new post offices, telephone links, and airports, covering the farthest reaches of the country, have reinforced the important new roadway communications. Public education and other social services, which in a sense also followed the roads, have afforded, for the first time, a shared experience within common national institutions to many hinterland and coastal peoples.

Tribesmen from every region of Liberia have entered wage employment as unskilled workers, many on a permanent basis. Foreign firms have trained workers for skilled, semiskilled, and clerical positions. Young Liberians of tribal origin have formed voluntary associations in Monrovia, usually based upon ethnic affinities, but oriented to the modern values, norms, and challenges of urban existence. As traditional tribal values clashed with modern, secular ones, the former began giving way. Labor unions opened the way for inter-ethnic association to an important segment of the work force.

A number of the more progressive and educated tribal people have pursued their fortunes in modern commerce and in the government. The civil service has become an important meeting ground for a new breed of young, educated Liberians representing all elements of the country. Their shared experiences and outlooks have brought together men whose fathers had been separated by cultural, ethnic, and class barriers. Finally, a growing number of the more highly educated tribesmen who have assimilated Western cultural values and behavior have been admitted into the ranks of the ruling elite.

Owing to the penetration of the hinterland by roads from the capital, the authority of the central government has become a more immediate factor in the lives of the hitherto relatively autonomous tribal peoples. Executive Councils of Chiefs, appointed local government officials and "public relations officers" (presidential agents and informers) of tribal origin, new county and district branches of the True Whig Party, a nearly universal franchise, and broader representation in the central legislature—all have extended Monrovia's control of the hinterland. At the same time, the government began to bring the hinterland under unified laws and regulations. Thus, in 1963, some sections of the laws which applied exclusively to the tribes were amended,[4] and a distinguished British legal scholar was invited to visit Liberia to help further unify the nation's laws.[5]

Nevertheless, thirty years after the inception of the Unification Policy launched by President Tubman in 1944, most tribal people still do not have access to the citadels of political and economic power, or easy and open social association with the ruling elite (and they do not necessarily desire either). Deep and persistent differences in culture and values continue to separate tribal Liberians from the descendants of Americo-Liberians. Yet these differences tend to diminish where educated tribal people and coastal people meet—for the former almost invariably adopt the behavior of the "civilized" group.

There are few analogies in Africa to this type of development, except perhaps in the assimilation policies of the French and the Portuguese during the colonial era. Yet, the manner of development does not set Liberia far apart from other African states. Like most of them, Liberia is poor, suffers a dearth of skilled manpower, and uses its scarce resources wastefully and distributes them inequitably. It lacks linguistic and societal unity (its people speak twenty-eight tribal languages; there is about 24 percent literacy in English, the official language). And its essentially export-oriented, two-product economy is highly vulnerable to fluctuations in international markets. Because there is a paucity of domestic saving and investment, Liberia relies upon foreigners for investment capital as well as for economic aid, technical skills, and business management (as do even those African states pursuing policies of self-reliance).

More important, Liberia shares the agonies of political modernization now besetting most African states. Neither its unique history, its ostensibly dual social structure, nor its superficial appearance as a black Western enclave in Africa, insulates Liberia from the external influences and domestic stresses associated with modernization. The indicators of social mobilization—population movements, new economic activities, and new forms of association—the incidence of widely supported strikes in every major industry, and serious (the government has called it "seditious") discord at the principal institutions of higher learning clearly suggest that Liberia's political system is experiencing such stresses.

Even Liberia's social structure resembles those of most of its African neighbors. At the top of the modern sector is a small, urban-based, Western-oriented group which has political power and material comforts comparable to those found in some of the most developed societies; at the bottom of the subsistence sector is a largely tradition-bound rural population, remote from the political arena. Attempting to hold the two loosely related sectors together is a narrowly representative, highly centralized government, whose leaders are one with a single party. Opposition, though legal, is harassed or, if potentially strong, suppressed.

Like most other African nations, Liberia has not made much progress in developing democratic institutions and practices or in drawing its citizenry into the national political arena. But nations which have been most vigorous in trying to do so have either suffered the upheavals of the "participation explosion," or have developed more or less authoritarian regimes of which sporadic repression, not effective leadership, has been the hallmark.[6] Liberia differs from the mobilization-type systems, though only in degree. Participation is growing in Liberia, but hardly explosively. And while the government has developed certain authoritarian mechanisms, they do not penetrate all strata of society.

Finally, in spite of almost precipitous economic and social change, Liberia is relatively stable. This book seeks to describe and analyze both the stresses the system faces and the capabilities and responses it has developed to contend with them. To do so, it is necessary first to revise the customary and oversimplified way of looking at Liberia's social structure— that is, as if it were two discrete cultures, one of which dominates the other through a repressive state system—and second to explore theories of modernization that may illuminate the kind of development occurring in Liberia, and that may be applicable to other nations of the Third World.

The Liberian Social Structure

In order to portray the Liberian social system in concrete terms, we may view it as consisting of two hierarchically organized sectors: the modern Western-oriented sector, and the traditional, tribal sector, in which subsistence agriculture predominates (chart, p. 11). At the apex of the modern sector is the "inner elite," enjoying political power, economic dominance, and the fruits of both, in what can best be described as conspicuous—and at times voracious—consumption. At the base of the traditional sector is the mass of illiterate, barely self-sustaining, rural tribal peoples. They are plagued by tuberculosis, intestinal parasites, malaria, high infant mortality, and short life expectancy.[7] A third component, not included in the chart, may be considered as a bridge between the two sectors. It consists of tribal people who are venturing into cash farming and occasional trading and wage labor. While they are still attached to their tribal lands, they have begun the physical and psychological transition to membership in the modern sector.[8]

This portrayal of Liberia's social system as three partially overlapping sectors may serve several purposes: (1) it permits a description of the flow of individuals and groups between and within the conceptually discrete but interacting sectors of society; (2) it distinguishes the modern sector, which is where the relevant political activity is, from the subsistence, tribal sector; and (3) it helps to measure in broad terms the openness of the modern sector and the degree of freedom of entry into it from other sectors, one basic indicator of modernization and integration.

How do we empirically test such concepts as societal sectors and modernization? We are talking about people; and they move physically and socially within and among the several sectors, altering both the composition of the sectors and personal and sectoral relationships. Moreover, there are different strata within each social sector. For example, we may speak of the people who occupy the rural hinterland as being part of the traditional sector in view of their apartness from the modern sector. But their apartness and even their "ruralness" are relative. Similarly, the modern sector is not wholly modern, owing to the multifarious linkages of most of its members with the traditional or tribal sector. Thus the two sectors do not constitute a dichotomy. Yet they are more than conceptually discrete owing to the differing impact and relevance of modern and tribal institutions.

Modernizing influences can also be rendered geographically — radiating from Monrovia or advancing inland from the Atlantic coast. Tribal people who have lived longest in proximity to the coastal towns and other modern enclaves are generally better educated, better paid, and healthier than Liberians of the interior. But participation in the economic, political, and social life of the relatively modern sector was limited to a very small number of tribesmen until World War II, owing principally to the economic weaknesses of — and hence the only mild attraction exerted by — that sector, and only secondarily to the exclusivity of the Americo-Liberians. Traditional social norms, therefore, remained the most important cultural referent for the majority of tribal people whether near the coast or deep inland.

Although the movement of tribal people into the modern sector will be treated as part of the processes of modernization and integration, the sectors cannot be identified solely in terms of ethnicity or by posing the tribal "masses" against the Americo-Liberian "ruling class." The tribal people are not a coherent group; moreover, their modern leaders and most of their higher ranking chiefs are, in effect, part of the ruling class. On the other hand, the Americo-Liberians, though relatively more unified, are not the sole rulers, nor do they possess such a clearly defined identity or cohesion as they did — or appear to have done — in the past. Thus, while we may speak of "Americo-Liberianism" as reflecting the values of the early settlers, the attendant power and privilege no longer are the sole preserve of their descendants.

Foreigners in Liberia

Although they are prohibited from becoming citizens of Liberia, white European and American businessmen and technical advisers occupy a place at the apex of the social structure, alongside the ruling group. Ostensibly in alliance with the political leadership, foreign concessionaires and professional and technical cadres have in fact altered the very socioeconomic relationships which formerly secured Americo-Liberian dominance. Foreigners have introduced new economic activities, wage labor, and roads, and new standards of efficiency for government and business management; and they have helped to draw many Liberians out of subsistence agriculture into the modern, cash sector of the economy.

Foreign business activity is crucial to Liberia's economic life. Rubber and iron ore production, almost completely foreign-owned and managed, constituted 80 to 90 percent of all Liberian exports, and provided approximately 50 percent of government revenues over the past five years. (Rubber farming also is a profitable activity for a number of prominent Liberians.) The business climate and terms of concession agreements are quite favorable to foreign investors. Foreign concessionaires are generous, in turn, to political leaders. The Firestone Plantations Company, for example, provides politicians (and other Liberians) with technical advice and equipment, and rubber tree seeds and clones at cost. Firestone, Alan T. Grant, and B.F. Goodrich have often purchased Liberian-grown rubber at market prices even when the quality was wanting.

The approximately 4,700 Lebanese who reside in Liberia dominate retail trade and are active as well in marketing cash crops. (Muslim Mandingoes, and lately a small but growing number of Liberians, also engage in commerce.) Since the Lebanese enjoy this bounty at the sufferance of the ruling group, they measure their fortunes with those of Liberia's rulers. Their own position in Liberian society, however, is more precarious than that of other foreign businessmen and managerial personnel who usually are not permanent residents. A reputation for sharp business practices, cultural separateness, and monopolization of trade in even the most remote hinterland villages have won the Lebanese little affection in Liberia. (Non-Liberian Africans too have had a part in Liberian history; it is discussed in Chapter 2.)

Political Modernization

A generally acceptable and useful definition of modernization is elusive, in spite of a large number of studies in the field.[9] Few scholars would reject Samuel P. Huntington's description of the *characteristics* of the processes of political modernization, which are the focus of this study. They entail:

1. "The rationalization of authority," that is, the assertion of national sovereignty vis-à-vis the external world and domestic local and regional powers; and the integration and the centralization of power in recognized national institutions.[10]

2. "The differentiation of new political functions and the development of specialized structures to perform these functions," in
which "office and power are distributed more by achievement and
less by ascription."
3. "Increased participation in politics by social groups throughout
society" and "the development of new social institutions, such as
political parties and interest associations, to organize this participation."[11]

It is important to note here that Liberia's modernization, like that of
other African countries, is not a "relentless process" of which the political
leaders are the instruments. It is more often a political "response" to
dynamic changes in the economy and society, and to the consequent
transformation of both.[12]

The genesis of modernization in the Third World might be stated: in
the beginning was a modern economic sector; then there was political
modernization. In the former dependent territories, the colonial rulers
concentrated their administrative and commercial energies in one or two
hub towns, in export-oriented marketing centers, or on plantations and in
mines. In Latin America, according to Charles W. Anderson, economic
growth, particularly in the production of primary goods for the world
market, precipitated economic and social differentiation which, in turn,
produced "new and increased demands upon the powers and resources
that the state could allocate."[13] The response of the political authority that
wished to survive was to modernize.

New nations respond in different ways to the stress of change, both in
their rhetoric and in their actions. All of them—Liberia included—are
beset with the struggle for sheer physical and political survival. The key to
such survival remains elusive, as Africa's record of instability, coups, and
assassinations in the 1960's and 1970's so clearly indicates. Who can doubt
any longer that *all* the new nations, as they modernize, are susceptible to
chronic political instability? The question is how to mitigate it.

Here, Liberia's experience as a modernizing nation may prove in-
structive. That experience illustrates a "conservative" way to modernization, characterized by the adaptation of traditional institutions to the functions of a modern state, and the maintenance of the bonds of the antecedent
social and political order during the transition to a more modern one. This
kind of development involves structural and institutional adaptation rather
than the uprooting or "smashing" of the existing social structure.[14] And it
suggests a strategy of integrating the diverse ethnic, regional, and cultural
groups and tendencies into the political system, as opposed to mobilizing
all elements of a population into a monolithic party-state system.

Integration

National integration is a crucial part of the modernization process. But it also is a separate subject. Descriptions of integration range from definitions, for example, the "ability of a unit or system to maintain itself in the face of internal and external challenges,"[15] to prescriptions of the appropriate processes, for example, "how to build a single coherent society from a multiplicity of 'traditional societies'; how to increase cultural homogeneity and value consensus; and how to elicit from the individual deference and devotion to the claims of the state."[16] If the first definition is too broad in simply requiring that a system not fall apart, then the latter may be too demanding of the fragile political systems which contain multi-ethnic societies. Karl Deutsch, who emphasizes complementarity and mutuality of views and interests,[17] seems to have a better way of describing the real world, developing and developed. Implicit in his approach is the notion "that wholes can consist of different types of parts related in many possible ways"; and, to go a step further, that integration "does not do away with ethnocentrism; it merely modernizes it."[18]

Cultural and other interest groups need not reject the political framework constituted by the nation, but may become rivals for political power in the new, non-tribal setting; old and traditional institutions need not be "smashed," but may be adapted to new goals and consequent new functions.[19] This is not to deny the possibility that one-party mobilization systems may effectively overcome the drag of traditionalism and permit politically organized men to force change.[20] But political men may do just as well—and perhaps more peacefully and enduringly—in a political system which is more open and tolerant of plural interests. Robert Graves aptly summarizes the costs of suppressing plural interests: "[Alexander] brought the whole of Greece under his autocratic rule and broke the ancient principle of individuality and diversity in the name of national cohesion."[21]

In any event, we have not yet tallied up all the human costs of either the mobilization or the evolutionary modes of modernization in the newer nations. The success of one is not more assured than that of the other.

Democracy?

The establishment of democratic norms and procedures is, if anything, a later development and is not a certain consequence of political modernization and integration. Political participation, which connotes "the spread of potential political power to wider groups in society,"[22] is surely a keystone of democracy. But participation as measured by voter turnouts or by the size of membership in political parties and their ancillary organizations may have very little to do with potential political power. This is true especially in nations where illiteracy prevails, where communications with the political center are infrequent and obscured by distance and the perceptions of local purveyors of news and directives, and where the educational and income gaps between the minuscule modern population and the much larger traditional population have not begun to be bridged.

The prospects for democratic development in Liberia are quite faint at this time. Nevertheless, the tolerance of pluralism, the construction and adaptation of governing institutions to serve wider groups in society, and the engagement of more people in modern economic and political activities suggest that at least the *opportunity* to democratize is in the offing.

This claim may come into doubt as the reader negotiates the route I have laid out. The problem is not so much uncertainty about the process as ambivalence about the consequences. Is modernization "good" as well as necessary? Certainly not, if it means the establishment of authoritarian regimes in which a "national bourgeoisie"[23] or ethnic- or caste-based politicians freeze themselves in and others out of power. Such regimes may not be so easily overturned when the "right" historical moment has arrived. This phenomenon recalls the preindependence game in colonial Africa in which colonial officials warned the world that a handful of self-seeking nationalists were misleading the "ignorant masses," who were "not ready for self-government." But who is ever ready for freedom, for democracy? What may matter most at this stage of development are the procedural ground rules that are being established. These will in turn have a great deal to do with the ensuing political culture.

In any case, I have not sought to excise the unresolved ambiguities from this study. One can write dispassionately of corruption, inequitable distribution of wealth and power, and the use of repression by the political authorities—and should be required only to point out its dysfunctionality to sustained and progressive development, not that it is also repulsive to his values. One can equally dispassionately conclude that these political practices might even facilitate modernization by making change and reform more tolerable to old power-holders. One may hope, however, that if given free play, the processes of modernization will lend themselves to the democratization of a society.

In my own mind, Liberia's development is a synthesis of inherited oligarchic rule and the rational, reformist, and participatory forces of modernization. It is my hope simply to provide some of the answers to Albert O. Hirschman's seminal question: "How can good government arise out of bad, reform out of reaction, and progress out of stagnation?"[24]

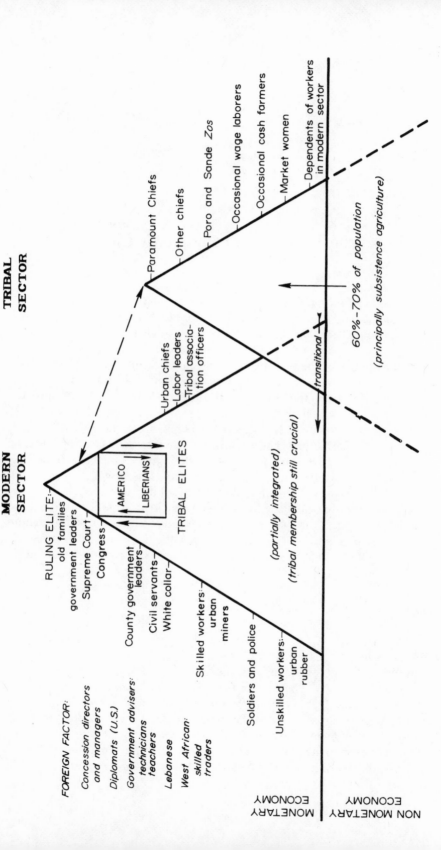

MODERN SECTOR

TRIBAL SECTOR

FOREIGN FACTOR:

Concession directors
and managers

Diplomats (U.S.)

Government advisers:
technicians
teachers

Lebanese

West African:
skilled
traders

RULING ELITE:
old families
government leaders

Supreme Court

Congress

County government
leaders

Civil servants

White collar

Skilled workers:
urban
miners

Soldiers and police

Unskilled workers:
urban
rubber

AMERICO

LIBERIANS

TRIBAL ELITES

Urban chiefs

Labor leaders

Tribal associa-
tion officers

Paramount Chiefs

Other chiefs

Poro and Sande Zos

Occasional wage laborers

Occasional cash farmers

Market women

Dependents of workers
in modern sector

transitional

(partially integrated)

(tribal membership still crucial)

60%–70% of population

(principally subsistence agriculture)

MONETARY
ECONOMY

NON MONETARY
ECONOMY

— 2 —

The History and People of Liberia

If definitions of modernization and integration are arbitrary, so are chronological divisions of history. It is more than a covenience, however, to describe 1820 to 1900 as the period of settlement and consolidation of the colony at the coast; 1900 to 1944 as the period during which the central government established its rule over the entire country; and 1944 to 1971, the Tubman era, as the period of economic, social, and political modernization, and the fuller integration of the tribal people into the Liberian political system.

Since the subject of this book is the Tubman era, the first two periods will be treated as history. This treatment will necessarily be brief. Liberian history is still being compiled, and no definitive published studies yet exist.[1] Hence, an adumbrated history is unavoidable as well as convenient. The first step in tackling nineteenth-century political and economic history is to identify those who made it. Although the North American settlers had important contacts with tribal people, especially near the coast, throughout the nineteenth century, it was the coastal settlements and intra-Americo-Liberian politics that established the foundations of Liberia's contemporary political system.

The Americo-Liberians

Who are the Americo-Liberians? They are generally regarded as the fifteen thousand descendants of American Negro freemen and ex-slaves and West Africans ex-slaves who settled on the African Grain Coast in the nineteenth century. The first settlers were American Negroes who had been born free. Most of them, of whom perhaps one-third were mulattoes, had resided in larger cities in the eastern United States, both north and south. A second wave of settlers was made up principally of former slaves who had been emancipated on the condition that they emigrate to Africa. They were generally of purer Negro stock—or of darker pigmentation, in any case—than the first group. The third group of settlers were "recaptured" Africans, slaves from the Congo Basin, Nigeria, and other parts of West Africa, including Liberia, who were liberated on the high seas by American naval vessels.

Many of the "Congoes," as the recaptured Africans came to be called, formed communities along the St. Paul River, away from the Americans in Monrovia.[2] Although a number of them mixed and intermarried with indigenous tribal people, the Congoes tended to attach themselves to American settlements, often as agricultural employees. Through emulation of and intermarriage with the Americans, the Congoes came to share the prerogatives—if not quite the status—of the ruling group. A final, small wave of West Indians and Sierra Leone Creoles, generally well-educated, arrived later in the nineteenth century; they fairly quickly joined the Americo-Liberian ruling class.

One writer has described the Americo-Liberians as an interlocking family and regional network that has long controlled most economic, educational, social, and religious structures within the Republic of Liberia, and which runs the government today.[3] Socially and culturally, the Americo-Liberians resemble privileged classes almost everywhere and at every time: they firmly hold the reins of political and economic power, and possess the lion's share of domestically owned wealth. They maintain tenaciously and apply rigorously certain aspects of their Western-derived culture, which they display in "correct" behavior: literacy in English; Western dress; owning large houses and automobiles; practicing the Christian faith; and in the past, at least, by keeping the Anglo-Saxon names they had been given in America. These external trappings and a rather Western style of consumption serve to justify the elite's claim to power and privilege, and to set them apart from potential contenders for these values.[4] At the same time, this elite has reproduced in its culture certain aspects of tribal life, such as extended family relationships, age group associations, secret societies, a form of polygamy involving unofficial, "outside" wives, and politico-religious orders. Indeed, the Liberian use of the word "civilized" applies specifically to those Americo-Liberians and tribal evolués whose mode of life is characterized by this hybrid Afro-Western culture.

How accurate are these descriptions? Most studies available today would tend to confirm them in a broad sense. Yet, as noted in the Introduction, power, privilege, and wealth no longer are the preserve of only the descendants of the nineteenth-century settlers. A brief look at Liberian history also reveals that the Americo-Liberians were not always what they now appear to be.

Founding the Colony

The colony of Liberia was founded in 1822 under the auspices of the American Colonization Society (ACS). Sponsored originally by benevolent missionary and charitable societies, the ACS also enjoyed the support of a number of state and national political leaders as well as prominent southern statesmen and planters. The motives of these disparate supporters ranged from the missionary impulse to bring Christianity to Africa and the humanitarian desire to liberate American Negroes from slavery or second-class citizenship, to the desire on the part of the southerners to rid the United States of the some 150,000 freemen of color whose existence and example, it appeared to them, threatened the institution of slavery. The society also sought the blessing and support of the United States government, which it received from President James Monroe personally, and from the Congress in the form of a $100,000 grant for the resettlement of slaves imported into the United States.

The first ship carrying settlers, the *Elizabeth*, was provisioned by the United States Government and accompanied by a naval brig. The *Elizabeth* carried eighty-six emigrants, all but one free born, to Sherbo Island, off the Sierra Leone coast in 1820. The low-lying, malaria-infested island proved most unsuitable to habitation. The survivors were removed to Freetown, Sierra Leone, the following year. In December 1821, American naval officers negotiated the purchase of Cape Messurrado, near present-day Monrovia, with the local chief and his associates, and planted the American flag. The first settlers arrived in January 1822.[5]

Free-born Negroes constituted the majority of early immigrants (nearly double the number emancipated from slavery). They came predominantly from the eastern seaboard: Virginia, North Carolina, northeastern cities, particularly New York and Philadelphia, and Rhode Island. Some 1,200 free men formed an independent colony down the coast from Monrovia, at Cape Palmas, which was under the auspices of the Maryland Colonization Society between 1832 and 1862.[6] Maryland was annexed by the Republic of Liberia in 1856.

Two smaller independent settlements were also established. Bassa Cove was founded in 1834 by the Young Men's Colonization Society of Pennsylvania and the Colonization Society of the City of New York. Mississippi in Africa was founded in 1836 by the Mississippi State Colonization Society in order to resettle the state's free Negroes in Liberia. Bassa Cove became part of the Commonwealth of Liberia in 1839; Mississippi in 1842.[7]

All together, some 22,000 immigrants settled in Liberia in the nineteenth century.[8] Emancipated slaves ultimately outnumbered the free born Negroes. Most of the settlers had arrived by 1867 (see Table 1).

Detailed information regarding the origin, destination in Liberia, age, occupation, and mortality among the settlers is available, to my knowledge, only for the years 1822–43.[9] I explore these data because they add important insights about the Americo-Liberians. Particularly significant is the fact that of the first 4,571 immigrants, only 1,819 remained by 1843 (the rest had died or gone elsewhere).[10] Of the 1,687 free born settlers who came during those years, between one-half and two-thirds perished; among the emancipated, nearly one-half did not survive. The first recaptured Africans fared little better. Most of these deaths occurred during the first few years after arrival in Liberia. "African fever" (possibly malaria), respiratory diseases, and brain afflictions were the greatest killers. A relatively small number of casualties resulted from conflicts between immigrants and natives.[11] Mortality rates of children were high: by 1843 only 587 children born to immigrants in the colony still lived.

Although data are lacking, it may be assumed that death rates declined somewhat as the settlers acclimatized to the tropical environment. This decline should not be overestimated, however. Medical care and facilities remained poor in Liberia until well into the twentieth century. Thus, it seems fair to surmise that the segment of the population classified today as "Americo-Liberian" must include many people (perhaps as many as one-half) who are not direct descendants of the immigrants from North America.

The significance of this speculation is not in the question of the pure-bloodedness of Liberia's current ruling class—a number of leading families undoubtedly can and do trace their ancestry directly to the settlers. What is important is that owing to intermarriage and extramarital liaisons between settler groups and indigenous Liberians, and to the assimilation of these offspring into the "civilized" community, Liberia's social system has never been entirely closed or rigorously caste-like. Though divisions between settlers and natives existed, socially as well as geographically, the custom that sought to discourage mixing of settler and tribesman was apparently much honored in the breach. For example, children having one immigrant and one native parent, plus those born to native parents and adopted as wards into immigrant families, already comprised 10 percent of the colony-born population in 1843. One hundred and ninety-two of the 562 children attending schools in that year, and 353 of the 1,474 communicants in "institutions for religious improvement," were native Liberians.[12] During the 1880's and 1890's, two to three thousand African children were living in Americo-Liberian homes, often being brought up with the children of those families and attending the same schools and churches.[13]

TABLE 1
LIBERIAN IMMIGRANTS, 1822–1867

Source	Number
American slaves emancipated to go to Liberia	5,957
Recaptured Africans	5,722
Free-born American Negroes	4,541
American Free Negroes settled by the Maryland Colonization Society[a]	1,227
Other emancipated American Negroes	753
West Indians	346
American slaves who purchased their freedom	344
Other	68
Total	18,958

SOURCE: Merran Fraenkel, *Tribe and Class in Monrovia* (New York: Oxford University Press, 1964), p. 6.

[a] 1831–1862.

When we speak of Americo-Liberians today as the ruling elite in Liberia, therefore, it is important to recognize that this element owes a significant portion of its numbers and significant aspects of its social behavior as much to Africa as to nineteenth-century North America.

From Colony to Commonwealth

The legal status of the colony was ambiguous from the outset. A special agent appointed by President Monroe and an agent of the American Colonization Society supervised and administered the colony. The ACS, however, allowed the impression that colonization was solely its work. The Constitution of 1820, drawn up by a committee of the ACS, established the society's responsibility for governing the colony through its agent. But "the entire expedition was at the charge of the American Government. The emigrants went out in the employ of the Government of the United States, and as such were transported and furnished with houses and provisions."[14] Moreover, the pact held that the settlers would be entitled "to all the rights and privileges of the free people of the United States."[15] The Constitution of 1825 affirmed the application of American law and rights, as well as the "sovereign power" of the society's agent within the settlement, subject to the approval of the ACS Board of Managers.[16]

Whatever its legal authority, the American Colonization Society undertook complete responsibility for the government of the colony. It appointed all principal officers. Most agents ruled with a strong hand, assisted by an advisory council consisting of three persons nominated by the colonists and appointed by the agent. In 1834 the council's membership was increased to six, and its responsibilities extended to "all matters affecting the public welfare," and the agent's veto power was somewhat reduced.[17] The black colony was administered by white agents until 1841, when the last white administrator, Thomas Buchanan, brother of the United States President, died in office.

The unresolved legal status of settlements outside Monrovia, and the existence of three independent settlements under separate colonization societies (Bassa Cove, Mississippi in Africa, and Maryland),[18] caused legal disputes among the colonists, and international uncertainty as well. The ACS, finding itself increasingly embroiled in conflicts over political jurisdiction among the several settlements, and suffering financial difficulties at home, began to seek ways to disengage itself from the colony's internal as well as external problems. It proclaimed Liberia a self-governing commonwealth in 1839, a union of all independent settlements except Maryland. In addition to Monrovia, the commonwealth came to include parts of present-day Cape Mount, Bassa, and Sinoe, as well as settlements upriver in Montserrado. A new constitution provided for a greater degree of independence from the ACS. The ACS replaced the agent by a governor who, though appointed and paid by the society, was not the agent of the society but the chief executive officer of the Commonwealth.[19] It expanded the legislative powers of the former colonial council and, in 1849, provided for power to override the Governor's veto. Joseph Jenkins Roberts, from Virginia, became the first nonwhite occupant of that office when he succeeded Governor Buchanan in 1841.

The Economy before Independence

George W. Brown, an economic historian, has suggested that the early economic system created in Liberia reflected the settlers' experience in the plantation economy of the old south.[20] However, the first wave of settlers, which produced the people who were economically and politically dominant until the 1870's, had in fact been mostly artisans and traders in eastern American cities. The great majority of these free born colonists settled in Monrovia and its environs. In spite of inducements offered by the Colonial Agent, such as free land and a premium for agricultural products, few Monrovians overcame their disdain for the unfamiliar African food that the land and climate could nurture. Neither trained for, nor interested in agricultural occupations, they were further deterred from farming by the thin soils around Monrovia. They turned, instead, to petty barter with neighboring tribes, and bought imported foodstuffs with their profits.

While a number of emancipated colonists settled in Monrovia, many of the later arrivals from the deep south, and the Congoes, pursued agricultural and semiskilled occupations outside the capital at such places as Millsburg, on the St. Paul River, and what is now known as Grand Bassa, southeast of Monrovia. Only in the mid-1830's did these colonists begin to pursue agriculture on a commercial scale, producing Indian corn, rice, cassava, sweet potatoes, and pumpkins. By 1843, Grand Bassa had the largest farming community in the colony, and became an important source of foodstuffs to Monrovia. Yet, only 3,482 acres of land were owned and cultivated by the settlers in the commonwealth at that time. And only twenty-four farmers, of whom one-third were in Grand Bassa, were working ten acres or more.[21]

The settlers suffered little from their failure to attain economic self-sufficiency, however. They were sustained by American food and money. The Colonial Agent from 1822 to 1828 "commanded virtually unlimited access to funds set aside by the Slave Trade Act of 1819."[22] The

Agent, Yehudi Ashmun, launched a program of constructing public buildings and built up a well-armed militia as well as a small cadre of salaried assistants. Hence, there were jobs in construction and administration, as well as supplies of foodstuffs from the United States. But according to one American naval officer in 1843, only "a few of the more fortunate and prudent of the American settlers have acquired comparative wealth, whilst others have barely succeeded in securing a decent support."[23]

The colonists' dreams of reproducing the American version of abundance, which they had witnessed but not fully partaken of, were based upon the nineteenth-century "miracle" of economic liberalism, not upon its southern version, agricultural capitalism. The greater interest in Monrovia in readily exportable produce, such as palm oil, camwood, ivory, and turtleshell, turned the attention of the capital and its leaders from settler agriculture to foreign trade. The quest for more trading goods brought the settlers into contact, and conflict, with the tribal peoples. It also engendered ill feelings between Monrovia and the several agricultural settlements.

The Establishment of an Independent Republic

During the 1840's, external challenges beset Liberia. An imbroglio with Great Britain, which did not recognize Liberia as a sovereign state, over the attempt by several settlements to levy imposts on British trading ships; a land dispute on the Sierra Leone border; and threats of French-African territorial aggrandizement at Liberia's expense, precipitated a resolution by the ACS Board of Governors in 1846 that "the time had arrived when it was expedient for the people of the Commonwealth to take into their own hands the whole work of self-government, including the management of all foreign relations."[24]

With mixed feelings—the agricultural settlements in particular questioned the desirability of independence, which would mean their domination by Monrovian commercial interests—the colonists accepted their independence in July 1847, and adopted a constitution patterned after that of the United States.[25] The American Colonization Society continued its work as an emigration agency, assisted in 1857 by the Dred Scott decision, which made emigration from the United States more desirable than ever for many blacks. After another brief upsurge immediately after the Civil War, immigration to Liberia petered out.

Liberia's independence was recognized by most European powers, relieving the new Republic for a few years from threats to her territorial integrity. The United States, however, delayed recognition until 1862, apparently because of resistance to the reception of a black envoy in southern-minded Washington, D.C.

In any case, the United States demonstrated little interest in securing closer ties with Liberia. In spite of lively commerce between the two countries, the American government did not seek to develop Liberia as a raw-material producer for its factories, nor as a consumer for its manufacturers. This lack of interest had its most notable effect on the financial circumstances of the settlers: they received little outside aid and virtually no investment, unlike neighboring areas under colonial rule. The United States did assist the settlers in their efforts to put down the international slave trade. These actions, directed mostly against tribal Liberians engaged in the trade, also served to replace coastal European trading posts with those managed by the colonists. But the United States was beset with its own slavery problem in the 1850's, and was unwilling to intervene further in Liberian affairs.

Liberia did not long enjoy relief from territorial depredations. The British, in Sierra Leone, took a border area by force in 1883. In 1891, France attempted to fix its colonial boundary some 80 miles inside what the Liberians, at least, had considered to be their southeastern territory. In 1911, the French again "re-defined" the Liberia-Guinea border after they had occupied Liberian territory while fighting border tribes. But most territorial disputes were settled on the basis of treaties and consent, however grudgingly the Liberians consented to the further loss of portions of their country.[26]

Politics and Economics among the Americo-Liberians

The agricultural settlements up the St. Paul River and down the coast at Bassa soon were at odds with the Monrovian leadership over government policies that tended to favor the commercial class. Liberia's first President, Joseph J. Roberts, an octoroon and a product of the white, missionary side of the American Colonization Society, led an aristocracy of light-skinned Americo-Liberians whose attitudes and behavior reflected "civilized" Western values. Roberts and his class applied these values rigorously in the political realm as well, making the upper social class one with the political elite.

Many—perhaps half—of the emancipated, darker-skinned settlers and Congoes occupied more outlying regions, but always within a few miles of the coast. Those who lived in Monrovia generally became members of a lower class of semiskilled or unskilled workers, domestics, or petty traders. Hence, occupation, region, and differing skin pigmentation combined to create what some scholars have loosely called a "caste" system among the Americo-Liberians. Whatever it is called, it was the source of political divisions among the Americo-Liberians throughout most of the nineteenth century.

Even when the mulattoes and some darker-skinned settlers found common interests in commerce, the mulattoes hung on to the notion of racial superiority. The True Liberian Party (later the Republican Party) reflected the mulatto dominance in President Joseph J. Roberts's eight-year administration. Roberts was finally passed over in 1855, when the Republicans nominated Stephen Allen Benson, a man of darker pigmentation, for the 1856 presidential race. Yet the mulattoes continued to dominate the Republican Party because it was they who controlled the commercial life of the country. Party leaders employed the government, private organizations, and educational institutions to maintain their preeminence.

The West Indian scholar and statesman, Edward Wilmot Blyden, who settled in Liberia in 1855, broke with the Republican Party in 1867 over educational policies that discriminated against black Americo-Liberians. In a bitter indictment of "mulatto oppression," he called the Masonic fraternity (which is part of World Masonry, and is still powerful in Liberia today) a "marvelous conspiracy to perpetuate the prestige of their class and influence the blacks, a number of whom they seduced into this body."[27]

The accession of black Americo-Liberians to positions of importance in commerce and the government, and the relatively diminishing number of mulattoes, contributed to the decline of the old upper class. Yet, an American visitor to Liberia in 1881 still found that "race discord is transplanted on the shores of Liberia and flourishes luxuriantly."[28] Hence, the color question overshadowed other perhaps more critical factors when the final shift of power from mulatto to black Americo-Liberian took place, much as the division of Americo-Liberians and tribesmen obscures more important sources of cohesion and conflict in Liberia today. For, although power shifted from the mulattoes by the end of the nineteenth century, the political importance of the commercial centers, Monrovia and Montser-rado, has endured.

The political strength of the commercial interests depended, of course, upon the economic importance of that sector. A flourishing Liberia—or the coastal portions thereof—had produced a wealthy trading class. By 1870, Monrovia shipyards had built about fifty vessels of between thirty and eighty tons.[29] But the industrial revolution, which so profoundly transformed Europe, served to abort Liberia's modest prosperity. British steamships began to drive the Liberian merchant sailing fleet from the seas in the 1850's. Sugar production declined under pressure from West Indian producers in the 1860's; and the market for palm kernels, palm oil, and ivory also fell sharply by the end of that decade. Liberian coffee was suffering increasing competition from Brazil by the last decade of the century; and synthetic dyes depressed the price of Liberian camwood from $250 per ton to $65 per ton in the 1890's.[30] In short, an economic recession had set in. Flourishing Liberian trading houses had already collapsed in the 1860's, to be replaced by British, Dutch, and German enterprises acting on behalf of mercantile houses and shipping lines in their own nations. A number of former Liberian merchants even went to work for foreign houses.[31]

Government and business leaders, reacting to the declining value of Liberia's foreign trade, began to consider the possibility of pursuing economic development by "opening up the interior to a more profitable and extended commerce."[32] Owing to the country's limited capital resources, the government sought financial assistance from abroad. It negotiated, in 1870, a loan of $500,000 from a British banking firm. The loan, discounted at 30 percent and at 7 percent interest, brought only $350,000 to Liberia. Compounding these unfavorable terms was gross mishandling of the funds; the Treasury may finally have received as little as $100,000 of the original loan.[33] President Edward Roye, who had been elected in 1869 from the True Whig Party, was considered to have been involved in misappropriating these funds. At the same time, it appeared that Roye was seeking to extend by proclamation his tenure in office, which was then coming to a close. He was deposed in 1871, and in 1874 the government temporarily stopped interest payments on the British loan. Thus ended Liberia's first venture into international finance, and what had been intended—roughly speaking—to be state-sponsored economic development.

Liberia's inauspicious entry into the world money market did not, however, deter the Republic from seeking further amelioration of its financial problems by way of foreign loans and advances from local European trading firms. I will not recite the unfortunate circumstances of these and subsequent loans, but this record underscored Liberia's chronic financial difficulties and official mishandling of the funds that came into government coffers after 1870.[34] Not only did Liberia fail to benefit economically, but its sovereignty was embarrassingly impinged upon in the terms of the loans, which included the regulation of repayment by foreign advisers sent to Monrovia.

These fiscal problems, following the general economic recession in the young Republic, coincided with a period of important political change. President Roye, who was born in America, was the first pure-blooded

Negro elected to the presidency. Under the True Whig Party (TWP) banner, his and subsequent regimes (apart from the more-or-less caretaker regimes of former Presidents Roberts and Payne, between 1871 and 1878) represented the displacement of the mulatto-led Republican Party by lower-class Americo-Liberians and Congoes.[35] The Congoes, having played a role in the victory of Benson over Roberts in 1855, increasingly showed their influence as a "swing" group, and in 1878 they were the key factor in election of Anthony William Gardiner—a mulatto of TWP persuasion—to the presidency.[36]

Thus, from 1870 to 1877, the True Whig Party, a party increasingly of lower-class Americo-Liberians, was working its way to power at the expense of the more patrician Monrovian trading class. While the question of skin color played some part in this transformation, at least for the new government leaders, something closer to class membership became the basis of support for the government. A more broadly representative political system, bestowing rewards and patronage, began to hold the loyalties of a larger number of poorer people.

A fundamental and enduring proposition of Liberian political and economic life was established in this period: not only would the holders of political power partake of the lion's share of the economic wealth of the country, but the government itself would become an important, if not the principal, source of income for many of their supporters. The foreign loan proceeds between 1870 and 1926 went largely to pay off previous loans to the government, the principal beneficiaries of which had been members of the ruling class and foreign speculators.[37] By focusing their economic appetites upon the government, the lower-class Americo-Liberians committed themselves to the preservation of the evolving political system and gave it, in a sense, its legitimacy. Such attitudes did not simply spring to the minds of the Americo-Liberians; they translated the values and needs of the politically conscious sector of society.[38] So strong was this commitment that the True Whig Party did not face serious electoral opposition until 1923.

The foregoing discussion should have partly dispelled the notion that the Americo-Liberians represented a cohesive, self-interested force throughout Liberian history. It should also be pointed out that between independence and 1900 one President was denied renomination by his party (Roberts); one was deposed (Roye); and two resigned under pressure (Gardiner in 1883 and Coleman in 1900). Furthermore, there was a major upheaval in political leadership when the True Whig Party first seized power in 1870. As we shall see later, similar internal disputes afflicted the ruling class in the twentieth century, including the period of Tubman's rule.

Yet, the internal divisions in the ruling class were never so compelling as to upset the fragile political system under construction. Implicit in their political behavior was the proposition that all was fair among themselves; but in the face of foreign threats to Liberian sovereignty and conflicts with the tribal peoples, unity was the order of the day.

The Tribal People

Nineteenth-century settler-tribal relations can still be recalled by living Liberians. They still affect contemporary events. But there was a sharp break in these relationships before the turn of the century. This break had to do with: (a) the government's determination, following the 1884 Berlin Conference that accelerated the scramble for Africa, to establish and confirm effective occupation of the territory it claimed was under its administration; (b) a decision to pacify chronically disturbed areas, which had provided excuses to the French and the British to intervene in Liberian affairs, and which impeded the government of and commerce with the hinterland; (c) the relative political peace within the Americo-Liberian community after 1878, which afforded the needed unity to face the hinterland problems; and (d) the need to develop the indigenous economy for business and government revenues, for food for Monrovia's tables, and for manpower for its larger agricultural and commercial enterprises.

Before discussing the two periods of settler-tribal relationships, in the second of which were laid the foundations of tribal integration into the nation, a brief discussion of the tribal peoples is in order.

The majority of the tribal people of Liberia live and have long lived in communities in which chiefs, elders, and priests are the most immediate authority. Their authority has customarily been based upon military, religious, social, cultural, and economic sanctions, in which secret societies play a vital role. Since the advent of nationhood, chiefs have been integrated into the administrative system of the central government, and a number of chieftaincies have been consolidated into paramount chiefdoms. Modern economic activity and social services have penetrated the most remote areas of the hinterland. Nevertheless, the essential societal referents of the majority of tribal Liberians remain the kinship group of the subtribal political community,[39] and the land which they work.

I do not propose to describe in detail the social framework of traditional tribal life, but instead will select those factors which have been significant to national political development.[40] Of utmost importance is the fact that Liberian tribes are not centralized political organizations but in virtually all cases consist of the people of discrete territorial sections organized in a number of largely autonomous petty chiefdoms. Tribes are divided from one another by language and culture.[41] In addition, divisions may exist within tribes on dialectal or cultural grounds—the Kpelle, for example, speak two primary dialects, and several subgroups of these dialects[42]—or between chiefdoms that may be at odds over land. Of the sixteen major tribes officially recognized by the Liberian government (estimates of the number of ethnic groups go as high as twenty-eight), only the Bassa and the Kpelle constitute more than 10 percent of the total population. Six other tribes—the Gio, the Grebo, the Krahn, the Kru, the Loma, and the Mano—number more than 5 percent each. People of no tribal affiliation, of whom some 15,000 are usually defined as Americo-Liberians, constitute a little over 2 percent.[43] There is, therefore, no question of any tribe's numerical superiority (see Table 2).

The status of tribal groups in contemporary Liberia is, however, affected by the way in which each tribe has adapted to modern commerce and politics. For example, the two largest tribes, the Bassa and the Kpelle, constitute a significant proportion of the wage labor force, particularly on rubber plantations and in Monrovia, by virtue of their location—the Bassa on the coast and the Kpelle around the principal road link to the hinterland. But the relatively smaller Kru, Vai, and Grebo, who live on the coast, have more members in the government and commerce than other tribes. Hence, proximity to the Americo-Liberians and greater adaptability to their institutions apparently have provided access to higher contemporary economic and social status.

The Vai have long been known for their independence and advanced culture. They developed their own script in the nineteenth century. They have never been slaves, and often had their own servants working their farms. Some prominent Vais intermarried with the Americo-Liberians and took part in the latter's economic and political life relatively early in Liberian history. The Vai still are an important element in middle and even upper levels of the government.[44]

Few Bassas, despite their location, were assimilated into the coastal culture. As late as 1952, according to one report, the vast majority of Bassas were administered under a system of indirect rule, even those who lived just outside the administrative center at Buchanan. Apart from a small number of their fellow tribesmen working in government or for commercial firms, most coastal Bassas continued to farm and observe traditional religious and social behavior, much as their ancestors had done before the arrival of the American immigrants.[45] Whether this relatively slight association with the modern sector derives from the Bassas' early acceptance of menial labor in the houses and gardens of the early settlers,

TABLE 2
TRIBAL POPULATION OF LIBERIA, 1962

Tribal Affiliation		Number
Bandi		28,599
Bassa		165,856
Dei		5,396
Gio		83,208
Gola		47,295
Grebo		77,007
Kisi		34,914
Kpelle		211,081
Krahn		52,552
Kru		80,813
Kwa		5,465
Loma		53,891
Mandingo		29,750
Mano		72,122
Mende		4,974
Vai		28,898
Other tribes of Liberia		2,299
Other African tribes		8,845
No tribal affiliation		23,478
Lebanese	4,500 [a]	
Americans and Europeans	6,200 [b]	
Americo-Liberians	12,788 [c]	
Total		1,016,433 [d]

SOURCE: Adapted from *Census of Population, 1962*, Summary Report (Bureau of Statistics, Monrovia, 1964), Table 12.
[a] Estimated from Table 6, *Census*, and *Annual Report of Commissioner of Immigration and Naturalization*, 1965.
[b] Estimated from Table 6, *Census*, 1962.
[c] Estimated from Table 6, *Census*, 1962. Elsewhere I use the figure 15,000 for the Americo-Liberian community. The discrepancy may be attributable to some Americo-Liberians assuming a tribal identity.
[d] I have not attempted to project tribal populations on the basis of the 1970 *Population Survey*, which reports Liberia's 1970 population at 1.5 million, but which does not report tribal populations. This table is intended to show only the relative size of tribal populations.

from traditional constraints, or from social discrimination, Bassas appear to be "rare in civilized society."[46]

The Kru illustrate how proximity to Americo-Liberian settlements divided tribal communities into more or less traditional and modern sections. Fraenkel's study of social change among the Kru[47] indicates that a "dual system" of rule obtained on the Kru coast (southeast of Monrovia). Tribesmen who lived a primarily traditional way of life were responsible to tribal authorities, as were tribesmen in the hinterland. Those who had become *kwi* ("civilized"), owing at the outset to the impact of the local Methodist mission and later to their pursuit of commercial occupations in the modern economy, lived apart from the majority of their kinsmen, pursuing a "western way of life in its Liberian form."[48] Even though the two communities were linked by membership in traditional clan organizations, with the important corollary of common land ownership, they lived physically apart, "civilized" Krus residing in the municipality of New York, tribal Krus in neighboring Big Town.

Members of almost all Liberian tribes are also found in neighboring countries. The limited significance of this fact will be discussed in Chapter 10. There are more than one million Mandingoes (Mandingue or Malinke in French-speaking areas) throughout West Africa, principally in Guinea, Mali, and the Ivory Coast.[49] While they number only 30,000 in Liberia, and are generally dispersed in small communities throughout the country, their former political domination of much of West Africa and their later active involvement in trade and diamond mining have afforded them a special prestige. Mandingoes have served as chiefs, in the central legislature, and in the central government administration. Because they are Moslems, however, they have rarely attained high position. (The Liberian constitution does not provide for an official state religion, but the Christian inheritance of the early settlers has made membership in one of its denominations, usually Protestant, a *sine qua non* for political leadership.) Yet, as peripatetic traders, and in their symbiotic relationship in communities close to larger Liberian towns, such as Gbarnga and Voinjama, Mandingoes have played important roles in commerce and as communicators of alien cultures.

While the forces that divided Liberia's tribal people have been greater than those which tended to unite them, intertribal secret societies and ethnic affinities would seem to have had considerable unifying potential.

Liberian tribes fall into three principal ethnic groups, defined on the basis of language: the Mande-speaking peoples, the Mel or West Atlantic–speaking peoples, and the Kru-speaking peoples. There is a high incidence of multilingualism among a number of tribes, in spite of the ethnic separateness suggested by the classification. Multilingualism owes much to the close physical proximity of a number of tribes, and to their long-standing contacts through trade, migration, and shifting political alliances.[50] Vai and Mandingo are widely spoken, as a result of the early political dominance of these ethnic groups. Kpelle is also widely understood, owing to the enslavement of the Kpelle people by other tribes, and currently because of their position on the major communication links to the interior. Among several tribes there is a common content in reference to the past, and evidence of cultural homogeneity.[51] The Kru-speaking peoples of southeastern Liberia, however, have less in common with the other ethnic groups; they share neither linguistic affinities nor the more critical sociocultural binding force of the secret societies.

Secret Societies. The secret societies, Poro (for men) and Sande (for women), are the principal tribal institutions that defend tradition. While the secrecy attending them precludes precise knowledge of their organization and rituals, their basic functions are sufficiently well-known for the purpose of this study.[52] As religious institutions they had to compete at times with secular political claimants to power, such as warrior chiefs. They also served the transcending function of maintaining social stability by appealing to the gerontocratic and hierarchical principles of the ranked-lineage structure of the past.[53] The latter function remains, while the former political competition apparently has been resolved in a synthesis of religious and secular authority. Among the Kpelle, for example, the "authority that chiefs and elders wield as political figures in Kpelle society is supplemented by the ritual authority they hold as highly-placed members of the Poro."[54]

Poro and Sande provide a formal period of instruction for boys and girls whose ages vary, but generally are confined to early puberty. Initiates are secluded in special areas called "bush schools," set aside in the forest, away from the village. In addition to learning basic vocational skills and responsibilities, they are taught social values through instruction in the sacred character and religious sanctions reposing in the societies. Hierarchical authority in Poro is represented by Masonic-like degrees that characterize membership in the society.[55]

Poro and Sande, then, perform both secular and sacred functions in the tribal community. They perform a socializing function through the "bush school"; they reinforce the hierarchical system of tribal authority; and they prepare youth to play specific roles in their communities.[56] In their sacred manifestations, Poro and Sande direct the tribe's relationship with the spirits of the ancestors, which is the foundation of the traditional belief system and ultimately its social-control mechanism.

Poro and Sande are common to most tribes in western and central Liberia, and are vital to the political, social, and cultural life of the tribes in

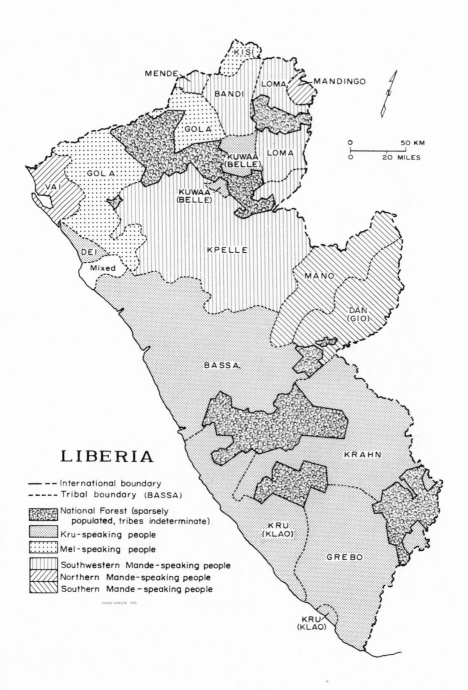

LIBERIA

- – – International boundary
- – – – Tribal boundary (BASSA)

National Forest (sparsely populated, tribes indeterminate)

Kru-speaking people

Mel-speaking people

Southwestern Mande-speaking people

Northern Mande-speaking people

Southern Mande-speaking people

SVEND HOLSOE 1970

which they are active. Poro is strongest among the Mende, Gola, Dei, Kisi, Vai, Bandi, Kpelle, and Loma.[57] These core Poro-linked tribes comprise over 40 percent of Liberia's population. Poro (or a variant thereof) also is loosely practiced among elements of neighboring tribes in east central Liberia.

There are differing opinions about the political potential of a secret society that transcends tribal divisions and, indeed, even links tribes for ritual purposes. Poro probably rarely transcended the village or clan area before the nineteenth century. Yet, like other traditional institutions, it has been transformed not merely by stresses connected with the coming of the Americans, but by the fortunes of the people who practice it. Thus, d'Azevedo, describing changes among the Gola Poro which accompanied the changing military and political fortunes of the tribe in the nineteenth century, writes:

> Of all the changes which took place in Gola society during the period of expansion, none is so dramatic as that which transformed the Gola Poro into a new pan-tribal and inter-tribal institution of diplomacy and solidarity as an adaptive response to the chaotic frontier. It is this institution which may account, more than any other, for the remarkable phenomenon of Gola hegemony and tribal consciousness which survived throughout the period of dispersion and growth of population, and which continues in the present day to exert a powerful influence on political life.[58]

In addition to its political functions, Poro serves to bind different tribes to common rituals and languages. For example, "*Poro* within certain Kpelle areas depends upon Gola and Loma elders to begin ceremonies. In the Bandi tribe, the officials of Poro speak Kpelle instead of their own language."[59] Again according to d'Azevedo, "both the De [Dei] and Vai attribute their own Poro organizations to the influence of the Gola."[60]

Finally, one report speaks of Poro as having become the "organizational and religious focus for anti-government activity" early in the twentieth century.[61] When the Gola called for war against the Americo-Liberians in 1918, Poro appears to have served as an instrument of the tribal political leaders who led the rebellion. D'Azevedo reports, however, that only a few non-Gola chiefdoms joined the Gola.[62]

The brevity of this discussion does not mean that the tribal peoples were unimportant in the past. They still amount to 99 percent of the population of the country, although fewer than 75 percent of them reside permanently in their tribal homelands. Although the tribal communities underwent considerable change owing to the intrusion of coastal traders and administrators in the nineteenth century, and though the impact of these new forces occasioned a partial breakdown of the customary tribal systems, the process of dissolution went on at an uneven pace until the government's penetration into the hinterland during the early years of the twentieth century.

Settler-Tribal Relations

As noted, the early Liberian authorities had only a passing interest in the more remote hinterland. This was partly because the settlers were physically incapable of exercising control beyond (and at times within) the thirty to forty-mile coastal strip. In addition to the obstacles presented by several strong tribal confederations in the northwest, the topography of Liberia deterred easy penetration of the hinterland. In most places, the narrow coastal lowland gives way first to a strip of plateau land and then, somewhat abruptly, to heavy rain forest, which covers about five-sixths of the country. In the east and northwest, there are mountains ranging over 4,000 feet.

These natural obstacles and frequent troubles with hostile tribes near the coast kept the first settlers close to the sea and to supplies from the United States. The importance of trade to the colony, which produced little of its own consumer needs or internal trade goods, eventually brought the immigrants into contact with the indigenous people of the interior.

Long before the arrival of the Americans, competition for control of trade routes between the coast and the interior and the quest for protection against raiding Mandingo and Bambara tribesmen caused the Mande-speaking people of the western forest region to form loose confederacies.[63] In the eighteenth century, with the rich prize of the slave trade at stake, the shifting temporary alliances gave way to one centralized confederacy, called the Condo Confederation, headquartered at Bopulu in western Liberia. Established by Mandingo warlords, it encompassed over its period of power (until the 1830's) sections and chiefdoms from a number of tribes, among them the Mandingo, Loma, Gola, Bandi, Vai, Dei, and Kpelle.[64] This confederacy became the cockpit of settler-tribal alliances, competition, and conflict during the period of early American colonization.

The slave trade began to dwindle in the nineteenth century. But the Golas who had enjoyed the role of coastal middlemen for Bopulu and wished to maintain that position—now for trade with the American settlers—wrested control of the Condo Confederation from the Mandingoes. The new Gola-dominated confederation assumed power by the end of the 1830's after years of conflict, economic pressures, and the influence of a sort of connubial fifth column of Gola wives of leading Mandingoes. Gola-Mandingo marriages served to effect a transfer of power to Gola families through the offspring who were raised as Golas. Although the new confederacy began to fall apart in the 1840's, remnants survived to thwart the extension of Liberian government rule into the western interior until well into the twentieth century.[65]

The same fear of displacement as trading middlemen that impelled the Golas to overthrow the Condo Confederation caused them to seek to keep the colonists from making direct contacts inland. Once their hegemony was complete in the northwestern interior, however, the Golas ceased to harass the settlers. On their part, the colonists appeared to accept the foreclosure of direct trade in the region under Gola control. This arrangement was not simply a truce, but more like a trading partnership in which each respected the rights, territory, and *sovereignty* of the other. Or so it appeared to the Golas.

It is important also to note that none of the key actors in this period acted pan-tribally in its relations with other tribes or the settlers. Indeed, so-called settler-tribal struggles were more often the results of the colonists' coming to the assistance of friendly chiefdoms being warred upon by chiefdoms that were "undeclared" or hostile to the Americans. As a result of their receiving such assistance, elements of the Vai, the Dei, and the Mandingo came to be members of the "Americo-Liberian confederacy" and to secure a place at the base of the young national political system. Insofar as they sought or accepted the protection of the settlers against mutual enemies, and through this association began to acquire "civilized" status, they were held in high regard by the settlers. Important Vai families, in particular, provided wives for the settlers and young men for Christian upbringing in Monrovia (though Islam remained strong among sections of the Vai).

The Mandingoes, who would not give up their Moslem faith and were thus prevented from entering such relationships, were nonetheless regarded by the settlers as a noble race, and were used later to offset Gola claims to power. Today they are well-placed in the Liberian political system. Some of the northern chiefdoms of the Gola tribe, which considered themselves to be sovereign and equal to the newcomers, held themselves aloof and were therefore excluded from the developing Liberian political system until much later. They nursed grievances which erupted from time to time in the twentieth century. The settlers achieved a modus vivendi with the southern Golas, albeit one which denied them access to northwestern Liberia. Other coastal tribes were less accommodating, however.

The Krus and Grebos of southeastern Liberia enjoyed relative freedom from interference by other tribes in their trade with ocean-going vessels. But the Liberian government's anti-slavery activities and its efforts to establish customs agents at the coast came to be viewed by the Krus and the Grebos as a direct threat to their economic lifelines. There was no room for a partnership of sovereign equals here; the government was seen as a threat to their economic existence. Hence, long after the first settlements had won their battles with hostile tribesmen, and the Gola confederacy had broken up from within, tribal "rebellions," perhaps better called a series of skirmishes or disorders, persisted in southeastern Liberia.

In 1856, there was trouble over the settlers' attempt to move some Grebos out of Harper City (in Maryland County) and, the Grebos complained, because the America-Liberians had failed to build some promised schools.[66] In 1875, mission-educated Grebos led fellow tribesmen in attacks not so much against the Liberian government as against the America-Liberian-staffed missions themselves.[67] In 1893, some of the Grebos at Cape Palmas rose in protest against what they considered to be the government's failure to honor certain rights of Grebo chiefs. These Grebos sought, furthermore, to deny outsiders the purchase of tribal lands, and announced that they considered themselves to be under British protection. In this instance, government forces were helped against the dissidents by some of the Grebos who had risen in 1875.[68] In 1910, the Liberian Frontier Force, which had been called in to "oversee" discussions of a land dispute between two sections of the Grebo, provoked fighting by its cruel behavior. Once again, the protracted, but sporadic, hostilities were not necessarily directed against the government of Liberia. Indeed, Grebo chiefs spoke of "the high qualities of the President of Liberia" and his struggle against "the corrupt state of affairs in the country."[69]

The Expansion of the Republic in the Early Twentieth Century

State-tribal conflicts had a considerably more rebellious character in the early twentieth century than in the preceding era. What changes had occurred to alter government-tribal relations? British and French depredations; the exigencies of membership in the international political system, which was entering a period of colonialism, especially in Africa; and the tribal disorders that undermined the national authority, all caused the Liberian government to examine its interior policies around the turn of the century.

The system of administration then adopted, sometimes called one of indirect rule, passed through several stages up to the contemporary one of the nearly complete subordination of tribal administration to the central government.[70] President Arthur Barclay (1904–12) instituted a system of electing tribal chiefs, at least where government fiat prevailed, who served as native authorities and as agents of the central government. Formal procedures were instituted in 1905 by a law for the government of districts inhabited by "aborigines." In this act, Monrovia reconfirmed the tribal people's status, if not their prerogatives, as citizens.[71] This system resembled the indirect rule created by the British in their colonies. A seemingly orderly hierarchy of administrators came into being, from the President of the Republic through appointed provincial and district commissioners to tribal chiefs. The election of chiefs by local people was subject to approval by the President. Councils of chiefs served as the judicial authority for the tribal people, with the right of appeal to the District and Provincial Commissioners, the Department of Interior, and even to the President, if necessary.

The scope of the laws establishing this system was not matched by the capability to administer them, particularly in the regions most remote from Monrovia. In order to extend the authority of the government, the Liberian Frontier Force (LFF) was established in 1908, under British direction. While the LFF could only police a few areas of the country at one time, it did serve to establish Monrovia's seriousness about "effective occupation" of the entire country.

Backed by the LFF, the new hinterland administrative system strengthened supporters of the central government among the contenders for tribal preeminence. D'Azevedo also points out that this system helped pry the southern Golas loose from the northern chiefdoms, for the southern chiefs now had the power of the central government behind them. President Daniel Edward Howard (1912–20) further entrenched "loyal" tribal chiefs by intervening in the election processes and by summarily dismissing apparently disloyal chiefs and appointing others he considered more favorably disposed to the government.[72] The indirect form of rule became increasingly direct under President Howard.

The Kru revolt in 1915 and the Gola war in 1918 represented the last violent efforts of tribal people to throw off the central government, which could no longer be considered the insignificant representative of alien settlements tenuously hugging the Atlantic coast. The tribal people involved were responding to and rebelling against a powerful political system which was successfully assuming more and more control over their affairs. A number of factors triggered the outbreaks. The Liberian government had been weakened by the cutback in trade with its principal partners, Britain and Germany, during World War I. To bolster declining revenues, it had attempted to impose stricter tax regulations upon tribal people who usually had been able to escape taxes theretofore.[73]

Taxes may have been the principal problem for the Golas. But the Krus had been nursing grievances against the government in Monrovia since 1912, owing to policies that diverted trading ships from Sinoe to Monrovia. The Krus, moreover, mistakenly anticipated assistance from the British if they took up arms against the Liberian government, perhaps owing to indiscreet assurances given them by a British diplomat.[74] Fearing British and possibly French intervention, the Liberian government asked for United States help to "save the situation." The Kru rising was viciously put down with the help of American arms, ammunition, and a few officers in 1916.[75] Sporadic outbreaks among the Krus occurred in the 1930's, but they too were contained and eventually suppressed by the government.

The tax issue, and accumulated frustrations over the decline of Gola fortunes and aspirations provoked the "last of the Gola wars" in 1918. The government divided a potentially strong multitribal effort that was supported by the Poro when it managed to hold the loyalty of southern Gola chiefdoms, as well as those of the Dei and the Vai, who also had been summoned to battle by the Poro but did not act. This struggle effectively broke the back of northern Gola resistance to central government rule, [76] though the old ruling families did not lose power until the abolition of slavery in the 1930's.

The administration of President Charles D. B. King (1920–30) further eroded traditional tribal authority. D'Azevedo records one elder's memory of this period:

> We old men were treated no better than small boys in the time of King. He overlooked us, and untrained young men and strangers were made into chiefs over us. Commissioners could place us in stocks before our own people and bad men from Monrovia could take our wealth with the help of such chiefs. We were helpless and our people wept. In the old days when such things happened there would be war, and *Bõn* (Poro) would come among us and set the country in order again. But in these new days we cry and are not heard.[77]

King's intervention in tribal political affairs was to assert the authority of the central government over the hinterland as much as it was to suppress tribal traditions and organization. If King's style was harsh and inflexible, so had tribal risings been troublesome and at times dangerous to the existence of the Republic over the preceding seventy years.

The King era was, however, marked by exploitation and abuse, as is attested to by travelers through the deeper interior in the 1920's and 1930's. King's desire to establish a regular administration in these heretofore ungovernable areas led to the setting up of several levels of commissioners, a number of whom administered their territories like autonomous petty despots.[78] Such officials, including a number of coastal tribal people, were inadequately trained and poorly paid. Using their offices for personal enrichment, they drove away by their oppressive methods many tribal people, often to neighboring countries, with consequent decreases in economic activity in the areas they left. Much concerned about these developments, the government enacted regulations regarding the behavior of its commissioners. They stated: "It shall be the duty of District Commissioners to protect chiefs and people from exploitation or infringements of their rights by traders, travelers, or any other strangers in the Interior."[79] The regulations, however, apparently failed to protect the tribal people against the makers of the laws, or those commissioned to carry them out.

As ambiguous as King's record in hinterland administration appears to be, there has been more moralizing heat than critical light brought to bear on the issue of slavery during the period. Accounts of slavery in Liberia, and the exportation of impressed laborers to Spanish plantations on the island of Fernando Po, date from as early as 1900.[80] But slavery first became a national and international issue during the administration of President King. In 1930 a League of Nations commission inquired into charges of slavery that implicated King (by acquiescence), Vice-President Allen N. Yancy (by involvement), and other Liberian officials in practices of "pawning," i.e., supplying indentured service in return for money or loans in kind, and the use of compulsory unpaid labor. Partly as the result of international pressure, especially from the United States, King and Yancy resigned. Although the government had outlawed slavery and pawning, recruitment of involuntary, paid labor for the Firestone rubber plantations and private Liberian farms continued under policies administered by the Interior Department. One report observed that "one-fourth of the wage-earning labor force was recruited involuntarily" in 1962.[81]

There are varying opinions about the charges against Liberia of protecting and promoting slavery. It seems clear that in spite of constitutional provisions banning slavery (Art. 1, Sec. 4 of the constitution adopted in 1847) and Interior Department regulations outlawing pawning (Art. 19, 1923), practices ranging from the ward system to pawning to outright impressment of workers have existed through much of Liberian history. These practices had long existed among Liberian tribes and in neighboring African colonies, and the leading chiefs had evidently prevented the abolition of both domestic slavery and pawning.[82] Indeed, some of the government-tribal conflicts may have been the consequences of official efforts to suppress these practices. Whatever may be the moral judgment, the ward system, whether abused or not, proved to be an important means of assimilating tribal youth into the Americo-Liberian culture. In exchange for domestic and other services, the ward was treated as a member of the family and often was given the family name. In addition to learning English and attending the schools and churches of the Americo-Liberians, a ward usually received career and other economic assistance and protection from his Americo-Liberian family.

The League of Nations commission of inquiry eventually absolved the Liberian leadership of culpability for the practice of slavery. It did point out the existence of practices of domestic slavery, pawning, and forced labor, carried on by tribal chiefs and some government officials.[83] In proclaiming the immediate abolition of these practices, just before his resignation, President King unleashed far greater disruption among tribal peoples than perhaps even the earlier conflicts had done. D'Azevedo quotes one Gola elder, as follows:

> When President King announced that all slaves must be set free it was a terrible time for all great families who depended on many slaves. . . . Nothing has happened in all the time that the *kwi* [civilized] have ruled over us so terrible as this.

* * *

> If you want to understand the main reason why those old Gola of the interior can no longer make war against the government, you must understand this. When the slaves were freed by President King, those old families and those old ways were destroyed. They became poor and helpless. That is why we now laugh at them and call them poor country men who live in darkness. We did not suffer so much as they did. We had told them that the kwi could not be driven away by war. We must join with them [the kwi] and learn their ways so that we can become great and prosper again.[84]

While recrimination over this issue persisted during the 1930's—and was probably partly responsible for the Kru rising of that period—by the time President Tubman took office in 1944 the ground had been prepared for a more peaceful transformation of tribal social and economic organization. Much of this preparation is owed to President Edwin Barclay (1930–44). Barclay reversed the trend toward political meritocracy among the Gola and other tribes by acknowledging, once again, the hereditary principle and returning to the practice of appointing chiefs. D'Azevedo goes to the root of the success of what he calls "Barclay's diplomacy":

> He is remembered particularly by elder tribal leaders for his support of the traditional ruling aristocracy in each chiefdom, always making appointments or replacements from among the acceptable contenders to office. . . . He made a special point of assuring leaders of the

northern sections that they would not be held accountable for past
resistance to the government, but would be judged by their present
and future actions. As a result, a degree of order and economic
productivity returned to the area, and some of the population that had
fled to Sierra Leone filtered back into their former villages.[85]

The good will engendered by these policies was the principal bequest in
the tribal sector that William Tubman inherited upon his accession to the
presidency.

The Foreign Political and Economic Impact on Liberian Development before 1944

Many writers have contended that the single most profound influence
on Africa has come from outside the continent. Certainly the colonial
period has left an indelible mark in the form of Western (usually European)
technology and cultural influence. Such influence generally came in the
guise of Christian missionary activities, trading companies, colonial
administrative institutions and accompanying variations of Western
political structures, or modern economic and social development (through
"exploitation," investment, technical development, and aid). In its own
way, Liberia has shared some of these experiences.

To take the last first, it appears that the United States took some
proprietary interest in the colony and republic which it spawned. But, it
clearly evinced no great haste to involve itself deeply in the new nation's
fate, or to share—in a colonial or even a neocolonial relationship—in
Liberia's resources or development.

Yet in 1909, the United States convened a commission of inquiry into
Liberia's default on European loans, which the British and French
appeared ready to use as an excuse to take over the country. While refusing
to cover the British debt, the United States government successfully
promoted a plan under which, in 1912, American and European bankers
took over the loan, and the United States provided a General Receiver to
the Liberian government.[86] The Americans again foreclosed possible
British intervention during the Kru uprising in 1915 by providing arms to
the government forces which then crushed the revolt. And in 1930 the U.S.
government associated itself with the League of Nations inquiry into
slavery in Liberia, thus undermining efforts to place Liberia under
international control.[87]

As a condition of its assistance, the United States several times
demanded certain reforms which American advisers would administer.[88]
But in pressing the Liberian Government to accept Harvey Firestone's

terms for a rubber concession and a clearly burdensome loan in 1927, the United States most forcefully intruded into Liberia's domestic affairs. The United States officially supported Harvey Firestone's insistence that Liberia accept a $5 million loan in conjunction with the concession agreement that provided for the company's development of rubber plantations. Three hundred thousand dollars of this loan was to go for the construction of a port at Monrovia. Firestone would have the right to appoint twenty-two officials, paid out of Liberian revenues, to administer the country's financial, military, and native affairs. Members of the Liberian government and legislature strongly objected to these terms as a virtual usurpation of their independence. Liberia finally accepted an agreement limiting foreign advisers to financial matters, and this only as a price for the implied promise of American protection against the French, who were threatening its borders at the time.[89]

Buell's and Chalk's descriptions of the circumstances attending the Firestone negotiations clearly reveal the nature of Liberian fears for the nation's sovereignty.[90] Edwin Barclay, who later became President, complained that United States President Hoover "helped the Firestone Company take Liberia."[91] Four years after Liberia completed payment of the Firestone loan in 1952, the government erected a statue of Tubman to commemorate the event with a plaque reading:

> This Monument erected by the people of Liberia is dedicated to the great relief brought to the Country by the Tubman Administration in the retirement of the (1927) Loan with its humiliating and strangulating effects on the economy of the Nation.[92]

The Firestone Agreement marked the beginning of an increasingly vigorous American private and public role in Liberia. It not only inaugurated an economic reliance upon foreigners unmatched since the American Colonization Society launched the colony and supported it economically for more than twenty years—it involved an enterprise which had the overt blessing of the American government. From that time, the United States did not hesitate to intervene in Liberia's internal affairs, either on Firestone's behalf, or on behalf of later American investors. And it laid the basis for an economic activity that would provide the lion's share of government revenues until iron ore mining—also foreign owned and managed—commenced in the 1950's. Perhaps most important, the Firestone operation was the first Liberian step toward what, under Tubman, eventually became an official Open Door Policy that invited, and afforded a most hospitable climate for, other foreign investors.

In spite of its relatively modest role in the Liberian economy in the 1920's, Firestone played a significant part in domestic politics. A young

Nigerian nationalist, Nnamdi Azikiwe, charged that the company tried first to oust President King in the 1920's (before the slavery scandal) and then to restore him in the 1930's.[93] Nevertheless, the colonial syndrome did not take the same forceful expression in Liberia that it had among her neighbors. Thus, while it survived the first World War politically sovereign, the country remained ill-administered and socially and economically undeveloped until later in the twentieth century.

Rapid change began with World War II. The United States requested and received landing rights at Robertsfield (where Firestone had constructed an airport), built a seaplane base on Lake Piso, and stationed troops in the country. In return for these privileges, the United States agreed to construct military and commercial airports and roads, to assist in the defense of the Republic, and to train and equip the Liberian Army. In 1943, the United States signed a lend-lease agreement with Liberia. During a visit to Washington of President-elect Tubman and President Barclay, President Franklin D. Roosevelt agreed that the American government would construct a deep-water port at Monrovia. Three weeks after Tubman's inauguration, the Liberian legislature declared war against Germany and Japan, thus cementing Liberia's commitment to close relations with the United States and, by implication, announcing its expectation of receiving certain economic rewards for its gesture.[94] At the same time Liberia converted its currency from the British pound sterling to the dollar.

The stationing of American Negro troops on Liberian soil, the inauguration of considerable public works under American auspices, and the eventual arrival of American technical advisers to work in such services as civil engineering, fisheries, and public health, stitched a substantial "loop in the century-old coil of friendship" between the two countries.[95]

The Missionary Factor

The nature of missionary activity in Liberia sets that country apart from most of Africa. For one thing, the North American settlers who came in part to bring Christianity to Africans stayed and became Liberians. But the religion they carried and the proselytizing they conducted first served the immigrant community itself. Christianity in Liberia was the servant and the rock of the early settlers. It reflected their spiritual needs in a harsh frontier environment. It also served to fortify their secular values. Church hierarchies have, for the most part, been "Liberianized," and most denominations have been autonomous about as long as the Republic itself has been.[96]

Eventually, assimilated tribal Liberians were granted admission to the settlers' churches and religious societies. For them they were an important socializing force and a means of attaining education and civilized status. But the different sects also had a divisive influence. For example, the Americo-Liberians were and are largely Baptists, Methodists, and Episcopalians. The Episcopalians, still under strong American influence, have done limited evangelical work among tribal people. But the elite-led denominations largely left the hinterland tribal people to the Lutheran, Roman Catholic, and Pentecostal missionaries. The leaders of the first two are largely foreign and white.[97] The Americo-Liberian churches are open to tribal people, but only the American-Negro-operated African Methodist Episcopal and the American Methodist-Episcopal Zion churches actively seek tribal members, and then principally at the coast.

The missions have provided secular education to settler and native children alike. In spite of the fact that public (government) schools were established as early as 1826, the number of students attending them did not begin to match those educated in mission schools until after World War II. Indeed, up to 1950, 80 percent of all students were attending mission schools.[98] (All missions are required by law to provide secular instruction.) The mission domination of education has been reflected in training of Liberians in the humanities and theology (in such courses as mental and moral philosophy). Mathematics, natural sciences, and languages were available only at Liberia College, Monrovia, in 1911.[99]

While the foreign-supported Christian missions still play an important role in education and philanthropy, they never assumed the critical role in Liberia that they did in many colonial territories in Africa—that is, of introducing the concept of individual rights and its concomitant, political accountability, which were among the foundations of anticolonial movements. Apart from the Lutheran and Roman Catholic churches, Christian institutions in Liberia are, in effect, the ally of the ruling elite.

The nonestablishment churches are in any case reluctant to engage themselves or their communicants in political activities. Not only are they permitted to function only at the sufferance of the ruling elite, but the checkered history of relations between missions and the central government provides some lessons about the perils of such political involvement. The originally very close relationships between the settlers and the American Colonization Society's missionary groups were greatly eroded during the transition to independence. Edward Wilmot Blyden's open break with the Americo-Liberian ruling class was simply one

illustration of the tensions between the missions (chiefly the nonestablishment ones) and the government. These tensions were exacerbated when
mission-educated men led the antigovernment forces in the Grebo War of
1875. Even the Protestant Episcopal mission suffered considerable
government hostility in the late nineteenth century. When the society
prepared to establish a mission at Cape Mount, fears were expressed that
this foreign-administered church might plant prejudices against Americo-
Liberians in the minds of the Vai. In a clearly repressive mood, the
government passed an act in 1881 requiring missions to pay duties on all
goods which they had formerly imported duty free.[100] In his attack in 1912
upon "unscrupulous aliens," who sought "to widen the breach between
the two elements of our citizenship," President Daniel Edward Howard
explicitly included foreign missionaries.[101]

In spite of its early political influence, and its still considerable role in
the field of education, missionary activity provides interesting historical
insights but few clues about how, where, and among whom power is being
developed in Liberia at present. Indeed, however illuminating historical
phenomena are concerning Liberia's political culture and political
development, and however much scholars may find clues to contemporary
events in deep historical roots, the Tubman period launched a decisive
departure from that past.

— 3 —

The Tubman Era

Changing of the Guard

William Vacanarat Shadrach Tubman's accession to power in 1944 occurred at a time of considerable domestic and political uncertainty, international upheaval, and an unprecedented foreign military presence in Liberia. Yet Tubman remained President for nearly twenty-eight years and managed a relatively smooth political transition in a period of great economic and social change. The transfer of power took place "in accordance with the principles and rules of procedure which had governed the selection of Liberian presidents and vice-presidents for more than a century."[1] It is thus perhaps too easy to lose sight of the problems of Tubman's early administration, and the environment in which it was inaugurated.

Tubman's first inaugural address poignantly reflected the problems facing his administration. He announced that the spirit of his government would be one of "No Reprisals; No Pay-Backs; No Get-Even With," and "let the dead past bury its dead."[2] The restlessness and suspicion that existed among various political factions as Tubman took office ranged from recriminations over the slavery issue of the thirties, which had not entirely subsided, to contention over the disappointing returns to Liberia from the Firestone rubber venture, compared to the burden of the loan that accompanied it. Moreover, old geographic rivalries among coastal politicians had surfaced during the contest for the presidency.

Tubman, an Associate Justice of the Supreme Court, had the support of President Edwin Barclay—who, in the view of several observers, wished to manipulate Tubman in order to be able to continue wielding real power. Nevertheless, Tubman's candidacy did not win the day until the Grand Bassa County leader announced his support, observing that it was time that the country had a president from a "leeward" (i.e., eastern coastal) county.[3] Tubman was from Maryland County. His principal opponent, Secretary of State C. L. Simpson, had the support of influential

Montserrado County politicians. Simpson had been, as he recounts it, tempted to raise the issue of his own part-tribal ancestry, but concluded that "this line of argument might arouse emotions which were not desirable from the standpoint of national duty."[4] So vulnerable was Tubman's position that not only did he feel obliged to accept Simpson as his vice-presidential running mate but, after the hotly contested election, he appointed leaders of the opposition parties to posts in his administration.[5] Finally, Tubman's accession to power was accompanied by financial difficulties, shortages of consumer goods, and serious inflation, owing to the war. These problems, however, were somewhat relieved by the considerable American wartime activities in Liberia.

The war produced a great demand for rubber for the Western war machine, which had been cut off from its Southeast Asian sources. By 1943, Liberian rubber exports had risen to 32.1 million pounds, valued at $8.4 million (from some 60,000 pounds in 1932, and 3.3 million pounds in 1936).[6] Wartime demand for rubber was a stimulus for greater production on Firestone's part and attracted Liberians themselves into this relatively simple and inexpensive economic activity. Although substantial economic growth did not occur until well into Tubman's presidency, the first glimmer of Liberia's economic potential, and the promise of increased government revenues and private business opportunities apparently impressed government leaders.

In retrospect, in the first three to four years of Tubman's administration Liberia was at a historical crossroads. The setting may be described as follows: The coastal ruling elite had established their hegemony over the tribal inhabitants of the country. Certain coastal tribesmen, they assimilated. The rest, and the hinterland peoples, they administered through a system of indirect rule. Most tribal people had acquiesced in their subordinate position in this broad and loosely regulated social system. Those who were physically and socially separated from their overrulers retained their traditional communities, within which social, religious, and judicial customs were preserved. The dominant group, while still relatively socially homogeneous, was politically united only in terms of its role as the ruling group within the larger society. Political power within it was not monolithic.

Within the perspective of a promising economic future, two fundamental alternatives faced Liberian leaders at this time. One was to seek to further unify and strengthen the elite, and to contain the tribal people in relative isolation from the modern sector—i.e., more of the same policies most of Tubman's predecessors had followed. From this Liberian-style "Bantustan," labor and taxes could be extracted for the development of the commercial sector. The tribal people had not, in any case, been demanding a greater share of Liberia's economic growth, or greater participation in the political system. The other alternative was to cast the net of the Westernized commercial sector wider and to exploit the hinterland more actively, thus speeding up the economic development of the entire country.

Tubman's enunciation in 1944 of continued support for the Open Door Policy, which had already brought substantial foreign investment to Liberia, tended to cast Liberia's lot with the second of these two alternatives. This transition from Liberia's own domestic "colonial" experience, however, was not accompanied by a desire to transform at a stroke the former political order—as was the stated goal in many new nations of Africa. Liberia's leaders sought instead to maintain the political system which served the interests of their class. Tubman was not out of step with these imperatives. Indeed, his election according to the rules of the elite was followed by his unbending efforts to preserve the system and to enhance the prerogatives of the group which those rules served. To have done otherwise would have been politically hazardous. Tubman's principal task, therefore, was to reconcile the often conflicting interests of the various elements within the ruling class. Over time, however, he had to contend with the demands for a share of power by new claimants from outside that class; and insofar as they were willing to support Tubman in exchange for a greater political role and concomitant economic advantages, he was able to expand his power base outside the old Americo-Liberian elite.

Retrospective determinism would also suggest that the circumstances and the stage of social and political development in Liberia required the type of heroic (or charismatic) leader that Tubman became. But at the time of his first inauguration, Tubman's place in Liberian history was not so well assured. He survived the first years owing to his ability to play the rough-and-tumble game of Liberian politics. He held power for six terms, and had been elected to a seventh just before his death in 1971, because of his skills in harnessing to his increasingly personal leadership the new political opportunities attending Liberia's economic development. Increased revenues from the expanding monetary sector provided financial rewards for political loyalty to the regime and built up bureaucratic, police, and military institutions that supported Tubman's authority. Those who wished to share the fruits of the new economic prosperity had to cast their lot with Tubman. Those who sought to pursue their political fortunes independently risked the application of economic pressures or even political excommunication.

Thus, Tubman strengthened his authority within the ruling class. At the same time he channeled social and political activities into government-

or party-regulated associations, such as ancillary women's and youth organizations. He extended the franchise to Americo-Liberian women in his first administration and to the tribal people in his second term. He paved the way for a peaceful transition into the modern sector by those tribal people who were needed to man the new concessions and to service the new industries. Government-controlled urban tribal communities, greater tribal participation in central government institutions, and the assimilation of tribal leaders into the ruling structure served to bind the tribal people who entered the modern sector to the political institutions of the ruling class. The political system persisted, therefore, even while its institutions and membership changed. This transformation served to strengthen the authority of the Tubman regime. At the same time, it made the President accountable to a broader spectrum of people.

These two aspects of change, economic and political, were interdependent. But if economic growth has been the prerequisite or foundation of political modernization—as I maintain—then it must also be noted that the latter lagged far behind the former. In order to descry the changes in Liberian political life wrought by Liberia's phenomenal economic growth, it is necessary to seek to isolate the political system from the economic environment.

Tubman's presidency might be regarded as falling into three periods. The first was a period of consolidation, from 1944 to 1955, during which time Tubman successfully supplanted certain elements of the old elite with people personally and politically loyal to himself, and centralized power in central government institutions against local foci of power and loyalties. The second, from 1956 to 1966, was a period of modernization of the economy and social institutions. Thanks to foreign investment, the economy developed astronomically, mobilizing great numbers of Liberians for work on plantations, at mines, and in the cities; this in turn produced the need for a more modern institutional framework for the participation of tribal Liberians in economic and political institutions and in the government. The third period, from roughly 1966 to Tubman's death in 1971, was characterized by retrenchment: the "old man," faced by an economic recession, fiscal stringency, and old and new opponents, appeared to wish to slow down political development.

This ordering of history will be difficult. Not only do the events described escape chronological placement and the periods overlap, but Tubman's first term has not been chronicled as extensively as have his subsequent ones. In "One Hundred Achievements of the Tubman Administration," compiled in the *Liberian Yearbook, 1962*, only a handful derive from his first term in office.[7]

Politics among the Elite

The ground rules of political authority that Tubman inherited, and that he adapted to Liberia's rapidly developing society may be stated somewhat crudely as: (1) what is good for the ruling class is good for Liberia; (2) although national leadership may openly be sought by anyone from within the elite, the elected President shall be *primus inter pares*; (3) economic and social change should be managed so as not to threaten the dominant group; (4) those who control the political kingdom shall enjoy the greater part of its economic fruits, either directly from the nation's treasury, or from opportunities concomitant with handling the nation's business; (5) anything which lends itself to these ends, from internal or external sources, is welcome; anything which threatens these basic rules is bad and should be either suppressed or absorbed into the governing system.

If the terms were harsh, so were the settlers' struggles to establish their values and institutions in an alien environment. Moreover, while such ground rules might appear to be no more than a prescription for maintaining the rule of the elite at the expense of the mass of the people, they also served to bind the active polity to a system for making and executing binding decisions.[8] At the same time, this system helped to preserve "the delicate balance required for survival between the maintenance of the traditional pattern of values that serves as the basis of social cohesion and the adaptation to new knowledge that requires a revision of the traditional value system."[9] This is not to suggest that these rules were always rigorously observed or applied, or that unanticipated side-effects were always contained or reversed. Indeed, a growing tolerance of broader sharing in Liberia's development did occur, even while political control mechanisms were expanded to keep pace with the economic and social "opening."

The elite in Liberia were the makers and the principal beneficiaries of these regulations. This elite encompassed a complex array of relationships based upon historical racial, political, geographical, religious, and social groups in the settler community. It consisted, at various times, of remnants of the nineteenth-century freemen of color, the first ruling group in Liberia; ex-slaves, the principal inheritors of power under the True Whig Party; West Indians and Sierra Leone Creoles, who shared power from 1904 to 1944;[10] Congoes, who shared power with all the above groups at different times; and assimilated tribesmen. The elite were divided geographically within and between counties. Montserrado County, in which Monrovia lies, was the most important geographic area. All presidents from 1900 until Tubman's election had come from Montserrado. Members of the elite traditionally held high positions in church hierarchies—though church officials appear to have first become politically and economically prominent rather than to have used the pulpit to build or entrench their positions—and in social organizations whose interests are at least partly political, such as the Masonic Order, the YMCA, and the "crowds," thought to be associations of politicians of similar ages. It is difficult to ascertain the relative political influence of all these divisions and associations. Yet personal relationships were welded within them, and on them political alliances presumably were built.[11]

I may appear to be using the terms "ruling class" and "elite" interchangeably. There is, however, a critical if subtle difference between them. The former refers to those Americo-Liberians (practically all), tribal assimiles, and leading chiefs who share political power, wealth, white-collar occupations, and a distinct style of life that sets them apart from the mass of the people of Liberia. They constitute, and are conscious of membership in, a privileged class. The leading members of that class, Americo-Liberian and tribal officeholders, are usually referred to by the term "Honorable." The elite, on the other hand, possess ascriptive claims to power and privilege based upon their ability, real or at least accepted by others of the elite, to trace their ancestry to the early American settlers. Owing to intermarriage with Congoes and tribal people, the designation elite has become quite broad. Hence, I employ at times the terms "ruling" and "inner" elites to refer to people who control the principal levers of power. Their families enjoy unquestioned claims to historical prominence, possess wealth independent of the government, or have mounted the ladder to political power by attachment to important patrons, usually presidents. This elite category is a changing or at least a circulating one. Some writers would count the inner elite as the leading twenty or twenty-five families of Liberia.[12]

Administration of the Coastal Counties

Administration of the coastal counties as well as the hinterland had always been difficult, owing to poor communications between them and Monrovia. Liberia is divided in numerous places by rivers flowing from northeast to southwest, which widen considerably as they reach the Atlantic coast. Roads did not begin to link the coastal counties until the middle of this century; sea traffic was the major means of communication. And until wireless radio in the 1920's and extensive airplane service in the 1960's (there were sixty airstrips in 1966, in addition to Robertsfield International Airport) expanded and speeded up communications between

Monrovia and the coastal population centers, central government control was sporadic at best. This near isolation had resulted in frequent disregard of Monrovia's authority, for example in the nonpayment of taxes, and the floating of a loan by one county superintendent in the name of the Republic.[13]

America-Liberian settlements also developed a considerable degree of local autonomy within the coastal counties themselves. Royesville, less than thirty miles from Monrovia, practiced a form of local government at the turn of the century. With only 500 inhabitants, the township, under three elected commissioners, assessed and collected its own taxes (there was no national income tax until the 1950's), developed its own budget and public works projects, and provided its own constabulary.[14] In a sense, Royesville resembled the democratic town hall type of local government reminiscent of the New England colonies in the early history of the United States.

As the central government developed, and Monrovia insisted on regulating tax collection and public expenditures, this type of local administration gave way to local boards and commissions appointed by the President. Equally, the tightening of the links between Monrovia and the county seats, through county superintendents appointed by the President, eventually brought the coastal counties under the direct command of the central government. These changes quickened in the Tubman era.

Administration of coastal areas occupied principally by tribal peoples approximately follows that of the hinterland. While physically part of the coastal counties, four "territories" are administered by superintendents appointed by the President. In recognition of the "civilized" status of many of the tribes in these territories, such as the Kru, the Vai, and the Grebo, most of the superintendents have been local tribal people. Each territory elects one representative to the House of Representatives and participates in the election of the two senators representing the county in which the territory is located.

Building a Political Machine

As noted, Tubman's first order of business was to strengthen his position with the elite, and to establish the paramountcy of the central government over local authorities and institutions. Tubman's political base, though it was essentially in the America-Liberian community, had different antecedents from those of most of Liberia's previous presidents. Not only did Tubman, a Marylander, break into the formerly Montserrado-controlled national government, but he did so as a member of a lesser family. In order to avoid becoming a front man for former President Barclay, he built his own power base outside, though not in opposition to, the rather patrician Montserrado families that Simpson, his opponent in 1943, personified. He accomplished this feat by establishing a network of family and geographic alliances early in his incumbency. By giving them high positions in the government, Tubman elevated families, such as the Tolberts, the DeShields, and the Meltons, who had had relatively low social status under Barclay and earlier administrations. He also worked with better-established Maryland families, the Yancys, the Barneses, and the Brewers, and made alliances with some of the older Montserrado families, such as the Grimeses, the Brights, and the Coopers, who had maintained some social and political mobility owing either to independent wealth or to a record of outstanding public service. He sank deeper political roots than had any of his predecessors. He developed support from among lower-class Americo-Liberians and Congoes, principally from upriver (i.e., inland settlements), and from tribal leaders.

Among the notable acts in Tubman's first administration was the expansion of the number of government agencies; for example, Tubman created a Department of Agriculture and Commerce, and upgraded the Public Health Bureau. He also increased the size and salaries of the civil service, enlarging the patronage pie. The Bureau of Public Works became a prime mover in government activities, paving the streets of Monrovia, building 700 miles of roads to the interior, constructing new government buildings, and developing a teachers' college and the University of Liberia. These activities favored Tubman's allies, as he placed them in offices of importance. Hence, Tubman used the still slender governmental resources to build up his own political machinery.

A new array of political associations came to determine who was on top, who was on the rise, and who was on the decline. J. Gus Liebenow has written: "Knowledge of his own ties and the family ties of others is a *sine qua non* for the social and political survival of the individual, for in crucial situations individuals interact not solely as atomized personalities but as representatives of family groupings." A corollary to this is that "divorce and remarriage are as much an instrument of political realignment as they are of social readjustment."[15]

Many members of the new inner elite were related through marriage or extended family relationships. Tubman's natural son, Senator "Shad" Tubman, Jr., for example, is married to the daughter of President William Tolbert; Tubman's Secretary of State Rudolph Grimes is a cousin of Tubman's wife, as was one of Liberia's ambassadors to the United Nations; the former Ambassador to the United States is Mrs. Tubman's brother. Tolbert, in turn, is distantly related to Tubman's Secretary of the

Treasury, Charles Sherman, an important figure in the business community.[16] Monogamy is a legal but not always a social imperative among Liberians; extra-marital liaisons are many. The paramours of the elite enjoy, and pass on to their own mates and relatives, special privileges in the patronage system. Tribal people find this one of the surest ways to rise in the social and political hierarchy.

Integration of the Tribal People

Tubman employed existing institutional machinery to cement his relations with the tribal peoples, but he also sought additional contacts with them. He condemned the exploitation of the hinterland peoples in his first inaugural address in 1944. He urged the improvement of their lives through education and their more direct participation in their own administration. He also implied, however, that their development should continue separate from that of the civilized people. He averred that customary tribal laws, "so far as they are humane and reasonable," would be adhered to in the administration of the hinterland under tribal authorities. At the same time, he expressed concern that the "centers of civilization, placed in the midst of a large semi-civilized population," were in peril of being overrun.[17] To avert that danger he sought to enlarge and strengthen the Americo-Liberian population by the infusion of "new blood of our own race"—namely, through immigration of Negroes from the United States, the West Indies, and the British West African colonies.[18] This, then, was Tubman's first prescription for national unification and the maintenance of Americo-Liberian hegemony over the tribal peoples.

Administration in the Hinterland

Until 1964, when the hinterland was divided into counties, the country consisted of two principal administrative areas: the coastal region, consisting of five counties and several tribal "territories"; and the interior, consisting of the Western, Central, and Eastern Provinces. Each interior province was partitioned into districts (as are the new counties), which were in turn subdivided into paramount chiefdoms, and again into clan and town chiefdoms. The clan division is an administrative, not a kinship, unit.

The administrative division called Paramount Chiefdom evolved over time. It was part of provincial administration in the hinterland and remains in the new counties system. The new counties were created by redrawing of provincial lines; internally they remained virtually the same as before.

Paramount chiefdoms, which exist also on the coast, vary in size, some containing only three or four villages, others up to fifty or sixty. They usually consist of members of a single tribe, but there may be members of several tribes in larger villages under the rule of a paramount chief. There are some fifty paramount chiefs in the hinterland districts, and possibly as many as ninety among the coastal tribes.[19]

The Paramount Chief, the highest administrative official of the tribal population, is elected by the clan and town chiefs (who are themselves popularly elected), subject to the approval of the President. While the process of election may vary, a chief may be removed only by the President "upon proof of mal-, mis-, or non-feasance."[20] Paramount chiefs receive no salary, but are allowed a commission of 10 percent on all taxes collected within the chiefdom, a share of court fees and fines, as well as annual tributes of rice from their constituents. According to the *Liberian Yearbook* for 1962, "chiefs have been known to earn as much as $8,000 in annual commissions, . . . more than the annual salary of most officials of the Central Government."[21]

The political consolidation of territorial units into paramount chiefdoms was essentially for administrative convenience. Most tribes, as noted in Chapter 2, are politically fragmented. Only the smaller tribes such as the Dei, Mende, Bandi, Kisi, and Kwa have now been united administratively.[22] For them and the other tribal people involved, the paramount chieftaincy became the focus of tribal politics.[23]

The ostensibly successful adaptation of traditional leadership to indirect rule from Monrovia depended greatly upon the flexibility of the traditional system in most tribes. While hereditary claims still determine leadership in certain areas, for example among the Gola, status and authority are now usually based upon achievement as well as upon ascriptive criteria. This is well illustrated among the Kpelle, where an "incipient class system" exists, based upon wealth.

> It is the Kpelle man's goal to enlarge his household by plural marriage, and with the wealth produced by his wives (as laborers and as producers of adultery damages) to begin to attract the following of people that make political success possible.[24]

Rich or prominent men are "bearers of prestige and molders of opinion," and it is generally from this class that paramount chiefs are chosen.[25]

The tribal people are further bound to the authority of their chiefs by the system of tribal courts. Customary tribal law applies in adjudication involving tribal people so long as it does not conflict with the national laws and is "humane." As a rule, lower courts are concerned with minor disputes within the villages. The courts of paramount chiefs, however, have authority in more serious civil and criminal cases. As courts of appeal, they handle cases concerning marriage, divorce, and adultery. However far removed the Paramount Chief's role may be from the direct administration of the people, his court of appeal makes him more than the puppet of alien rule.

The dual nature of tribal administration under the Liberian version of indirect rule produced a problem similar to that faced by the British in their African colonies. Chiefs had to combine the exercise of traditional functions with the carrying out of central government orders. The latter usually involved such unpopular tasks as collecting taxes and special levies and recruiting labor. Hence the chiefs' authority came to be viewed ambivalently by many tribesmen.[26] While in the British colonies this anti–native authority sentiment became one of the bases of nationalist movements, Liberia has not witnessed such a phenomenon, perhaps because the Liberians have provided a pressure valve. Liberian presidents of this century, and especially President Tubman, periodically held councils throughout the hinterland, at which grievances against chiefs (and central government officials as well) could be aired. On occasion the President summarily dismissed unpopular chiefs and government officials.[27]

It has been contended in discussions of the British colonial experience that indirect rule, apart from its economies in manpower and expenditures, was employed in order to divide the indigenous peoples and to permit them to be ruled more easily. But tribal life in Liberia before the central government intruded had been one of division and mutual hostility. In fact, the consolidation of chiefdoms and pacification of disturbed areas tended to strengthen indigenous authorities, and served to reduce and reverse the process of fragmentation. The preservation of tribal customs and institutions and hence tribal identities, however, did serve to intensify the cultural division between the coastal rulers and the hinterland.[28] Given the consequences elsewhere in Africa of the curtailment of some tribal customs,[29] and contemporary African efforts to refurbish indigenous cultural values, this preservation of tribal customs in Liberia might now be considered both politic and patriotic.

Taxes. Tribal Liberians are liable to an annual hut tax. Tribesmen also pay health and development taxes, based either upon hut ownership or per capita assessment. In 1911, central government receipts from the collection of these taxes amounted to less than $10,000; in 1925, they reached nearly $180,000; and in 1933, they contributed some 30 percent of all internal revenue collections.[30] By the 1960's, direct taxes upon tribesmen had risen to over $1 million per annum, or $2 million, if the education tax is included. Although tribesmen contribute a decreasing proportion of total national revenues (currently between 2.5 and 3 percent),[31] the gross increase illustrates the growing acceptance by tribal peoples of the paying of taxes, especially during Tubman's incumbency.

More costly to the tribesmen than any of these taxes, however, were the fines, many times the value of legally collectable taxes and cash payments for the redemption of obligatory labor that were, and occasionally still are, collected and pocketed by chiefs and central government officials. Furthermore, the tribal peoples had been the prey of the military forces since the establishment of the Liberian Frontier Force in the early part of this century. The soldiers frequently came as marauders rather than as guardians of the law. Military pillage is a bitter memory for many tribesmen. One government official of tribal background remembers his shame in seeing his father, a village elder, wantonly beaten by such soldiers; and he also recalls how, on another occasion, a drunken soldier relieved him of his school fees. The apparent acquiescence of the tribal people in these arbitrary and harsh practices might be explained by the fact that Liberian peasants, like peasant people almost everywhere, "do not ordinarily defy or resist unless there is some increase beyond customary limits."[32]

It seems clear, and is most important to our understanding of the impact of the Tubman administration in the hinterland, that central government authority was a distant and infrequently represented phenomenon to most tribal people until World War II. District commissioners supervised large areas within which communications were poor. Apart from occasional forays into the forest, the Frontier Force (which numbered only 600 men in 1928)[33] usually confined its activities to the few administrative centers and garrison towns. Buell observed in the mid-twenties that

> the Liberian Government has not been strong enough to impose upon the natives of the hinterland the grinding exactions which an industrialized administration has imposed upon the natives in many other parts of Africa. The native in the hinterland has had a comparatively easy time of it because no economic development has taken place. But this state of affairs is changing.[34]

Thus, whatever guise the central government appeared in, its control of, and influence upon, the hinterland was not pervasive or enduring until Tubman's administration. And if Tubman's administration evoked a favorable response from the tribal peoples, it was because such abuses as there were from government commissioners and the Frontier Force diminished and began to be replaced by a somewhat better regulated and fairer system of tax collection.

National Unification

Tubman had promised during his 1943 election campaign to "strive with all my might to agglutinate and unify our population."[35] The rhetoric of unification began to bear fruit in Tubman's second inaugural address when he announced the government's intention to extend the franchise to the interior population in order to place them on "equal footing" with the rest of the country.[36] At the First National Unification Council in 1954, the President observed that "for more than 80 years since the Founding Fathers settled here, we have tried to destroy each other by internal wars. Both sides have failed." He asked the chiefs to

> destroy all the ideologies that tend to divide us. Americo-Liberian-ism must be forgotten and all of us must register a new era of justice, equality, fair dealing and equal opportunities for every one from every part of the country regardless of tribe, clan, section, element, creed or economic status.[37]

The government also sought to bring Poro if not under its control, at least within its political ambit. Poro was recognized under the law, and a Tribal Affairs Adviser was appointed to the Executive Mansion. Poro and Sande are regulated by the *Laws and Administrative Regulations Governing the Poro and Sande Societies*. These laws recognize Poro as being of assistance in "maintaining law and order and decorum in the hinterland." However, the regulations state that since "no society or social organization should supercede . . . the functions of a central government, the regular routine operations of the Poro shall be under the direct supervision of the Tribal Authority within any and all sectors of the Republic."[38]

The government sponsored the first "national" Poro organization by designating a superior *zo* (priest) who demanded loyalty from all Poro lodges.[39] Moreover, several leading government officials, including President Tubman, who became nominal head of all Poro societies, sought and received initiation into the society (as did Mrs. Tubman into Sande). By these acts the tribal people have used Poro to impress and honor Liberian officials.

At the same time, Tubman began to bring prominent and educated members of hinterland tribes into his administration. Not only did this serve to construct loyal constituencies in the awakening interior, but it provided Tubman with a force that could counterbalance the more advanced, and at times ambitious, members of coastal tribes. For, just as he sought to maintain a balance among the older elites and to dilute their power by recruiting new members into government, he sought to deny to any one tribal group a special position vis-à-vis the others, or a position of great influence within the government. Many Krus, Vais, and Grebos held high office under Tubman, and at times, one or another of these tribes was considered to be in the political ascendancy. But if a tribal leader sought to construct an independent base of power within his tribe, Tubman was quick to thwart him. When the Kru leader of the Reformation Party, Didhwo Twe, sought to oppose Tubman in the election of 1951, Tubman charged him and his associates with treason.[40] Twe fled the country, and the Kru remained out of favor for some time.

Tubman handily won the otherwise uneventful 1951 election. The constitution had been amended so that he could succeed himself for four years after his first eight-year term. Having begun the integration of tribal people into the polity, and their leaders into the Tubman machine, the President further built up his personal power in his second term through a far-flung patronage system. In addition to enlarging the bureaucracy, Tubman instituted a network of Public Relations Officers, whose budget reached $1 million by the late 1960's.[41] These substantial funds bound to Tubman thousands of individuals throughout Liberia. In this and other proliferating security services, Tubman had a virtual private army of informers and potential palace guards. These men and women, and their families, became the bedrock of Tubman's independent power base.

Had Tubman scrapped his plans to build up the elite? Why had he turned to the hinterland for support? Liberia in the early 1950's was on the brink of a period of great economic growth. The Liberian Mining Company had begun iron ore production, and several additional rubber and iron ore concessions were being negotiated. The social consequences of this growth were not difficult to anticipate. The hope—deriving perhaps from the wartime stationing of American Negro troops in Liberia—that large-scale American immigration would bolster the Americo-Liberian community, had not been realized. Hence, neither separate development of the two communities nor the expansion of the civilized population was feasible. How were the handful of Americo-Liberians to absorb or control the tens of thousands of tribesmen who would soon enter the towns, mines, and plantations? The elite directed questions like these to Tubman as the 1955 election approached.[42] Some of them questioned the Open Door Policy, fearing the unmanageable influence of foreigners. To allay their fears, Tubman constructed a policy of carefully managed assimilation. He thereby reassured the elite, who feared encroachment upon their favored place in society, that the entry of tribal people into their ranks would be limited. And at the same time, by bringing tribal authorities into the establishment, he widened the authority of the central government over the hinterland, and broadened his own political base against the eventuality of opposition to his rule from those who had always held political power.

Early Opposition

Opposition did threaten Tubman in the early 1950's. While struggles for power within the elite have characterized much of Liberian history, they had previously reflected the desire of families or regional interests to enter the inner circle more than policy or ideological differences. But, opposition to Tubman reflected resentment of his "liberal" policies toward the tribal people, xenophobic reactions to foreign influence,[43] and suspicion and fear created by Tubman's apparently relentless pursuit of personal power, both in law and in his new tribal constituency.

Tubman requested emergency powers from the legislature in 1955, after warning the country against communist-inspired persons and aliens who would "pollute" the citizenry.[44] At the same time, he reminded the tribal people that they had suffered the denial of basic rights under previous administrations, but that now they were permitted to possess firearms for use against wild animals that destroyed crops, and their taxes, which went to social services, were accompanied by political rights. He spoke of an "opposition" who were angry at him, because "they cannot treat you as they did before."[45]

Open opposition finally appeared during the presidential election of 1955 in the candidacy of former president Edwin Barclay. Barclay, then seventy-three years old, had been pressed into service by leaders of the Independent True Whig and Reformation parties, which from time to time had put up presidential candidates. This opposition represented elite elements which had earlier served in Tubman's administration but had lost their jobs, and dissident True Whigs. One of their number, S. David Coleman, was the son of a former president (W. D. Coleman; 1896–1900) and a former chairman of the True Whig Party. Barclay won only 1,182 votes and Tubman was overwhelmingly reelected. There followed a bizarre assassination attempt, the tracking down and killing of the ringleaders, including Coleman and his son, and the arrest of others (who, including Barclay, were subsequently pardoned) for treason.[46]

Perhaps more significant than the assassination attempt itself was the popular response to it. From all corners of Liberia came protestations of support for the President and gratitude for his survival. Processions of chiefs, coastal dignitaries, the Congo community, youth and professional group leaders, and of course civil servants, paraded through Monrovia during November 1955 in what has become a tradition in Liberian political life. One message was clear, particularly regarding tribal loyalties: were any surviving opposition element to seek to exploit the tension created by the attempt on Tubman's life, it would face the President's growing army of personal supporters from all sections of the country. Tubman took note of this in thanking Marylanders for their offer to come to Monrovia to give him protection.[47] This sequel to the assassination attempt appeared to confirm and consolidate Tubman's singular control of political power. The power of Montserrado politicians had been substantially diminished.

Tubman faced opposition and even alleged assassination plots after these events, but his rule was never again seriously challenged. The political bases of his opposition shrank as he utilized the growing material resources at his disposal to entice recalcitrants into his administration, or employed his growing police, army and security network to keep them cautiously quiet.

The Tubman style of rule that emerged from between 1944 and 1955 followed essentially the lines of his predecessors. But Tubman had accomplished what none of them had ever attempted: he became, in effect, the leader of all Liberians. He was the undisputed leader of the Americo-Liberians. And as the champion of national unification, he came to be considered the great chieftain or father by many tribal people.

— 4 —

The Economic Factor in Modernization

It took Tubman ten years to consolidate his power. He reduced the independent bases of power of contending Americo-Liberians; and his own political constituency included tribal elements, both coastal and hinterland. But despite the resultant one-man domination of government, Tubman was not autonomous, and his direction of government was not only self-serving. He was still essentially the instrument, although now also the arbiter, of the interests of the ruling elite. While Tubman directed or approved virtually all crucial government policies and actions, cabinet secretaries who carried them out were also accountable to the elite and bound by its political ground rules. Thus, the power of government flowed to and from Tubman, but its constraints and legitimacy derived first and foremost from the elite.

To understand the nearly exclusive and more broadly based power that came into Tubman's hands in the late 1950's, one must consider the economic base upon which he constructed it. By 1960, the economy had produced over eight times the still modest revenues of 1950, funds that Tubman could use for patronage, economic opportunities for political friends, and jobs and social mobility for many tribal people.

Liberia's economic growth—which was both rapid and massive— precipitated far-reaching changes in the social system and, ultimately, in the political system as well. Contrary to the idea that new nations should seek first the political kingdom, Liberia's economic transformation created the need for more effective political institutions and for broader participation in them—that is, for political modernization. Economic and political development were, of course, interdependent. Many of the indicators of economic development described in the following pages are both the result of political adjustments and the precipitants of political modernization. This chapter, which describes economic development chiefly from 1955 to 1967, telescopes the crucial period of modernization.

While Tubman successfully harnessed the country's economic growth and political institutions to his own political machine, he also maintained the essential structures and values that he inherited. It is not surprising, therefore, that the Americo-Liberian elite remained politically dominant and thus enjoyed a greater share of the fruits of economic development. But the processes of change also opened the doors to the participation of increasing numbers of Liberians in their country's prosperity and in its political institutions.

Students of the ex-colonial, developing countries sometimes contend that only through state control of the economic life of the country may its citizens resist the perils of neocolonialism. This type of development, moreover, may help a people avoid formation of a class sytem with its inherent conflicts—a condition allegedly alien to traditional African systems.[1] In any case, it is argued, because of the lack of substantial domestic savings, owing to chronic poverty and backwardness, and the consequent absence of a capital-holding and investing class, the state must, by default, become the leading economic actor in the country. It may employ for this task foreign aid, controlled foreign investment, the revenues obtained from taxing the few wealthy citizens and foreigners, and the profits from parastatal commercial institutions, such as development banks, marketing boards, and the like. Such an approach, however, may easily ignore actual economic circumstances. Few good attempts at comparing state-directed development with more laissez faire economic development have been made in the Third World.

Liberia, by virtue of its enormous economic growth in the 1950's and early 1960's, presents a useful case study of the "free enterprise" route to economic development. Instead of prescribing this type of development, I wish simply to consider how it took place and what some of the consequences are. That I agree with Elliot Berg's sensible study of the problems and burdens of implementing any one of the several models of African socialism[2] does not necessarily mean that I dismiss the need for economic initiatives from the public sector. Yet, in the case of Liberia, this conservative approach has thus far produced substantial economic development and a better material life for many people. There is considerable evidence that such development has conferred upon formerly passive Liberians greater appetites for the goods that membership in a modern nation entails.

In the late nineteenth century, following a severe economic recession during which Liberia's commercial class succumbed, trade fell largely into the hands of foreigners. German, Dutch, and British trading companies virtually preempted the field. Up to World War I, Germany was also active in banking and ran Liberia's electric power and telephone systems.[3] Government revenues in 1911 were a mere $483,000, all but $43,000 of which came from customs tariffs. The economy remained weak through World War I. Exports reached $1 million annually in the early 1920's; but although tax revenues had doubled by 1925, they were largely in the form of hut taxes, customs revenues having barely regained their prewar level. Liberia suffered the economic depression of the thirties.[4] Its narrow commercial base had not been greatly improved by the inauguration of rubber production by Firestone. Nevertheless, Liberia had exploitable resources. It simply lacked the technical competence and capital to develop them.

After nearly a century in the economic doldrums, Liberia experienced a boom in the 1950's: "The rate of expansion of the economy of Liberia during the decade preceding 1961 surpassed that of almost any other country in the world."[5] Comprehensive, reliable statistics that would permit a comparison of major economic indicators of the pre- and post-Tubman eras do not exist. The few available are included in Table 3. They reflect the massive increment in the volume of trade, revenues, wage labor, and gross money income over three decades. Of special significance is the $750 million invested in Liberia by foreigners between World War II and 1966, a relatively short span of time.[6]

The figures reveal a profound and impressive economic transformation. Before World War II Liberia had been a country in which over 90 percent of the people were engaged in subsistence farming. Perhaps a hundred farmers became prosperous by growing rubber and coffee, the leading cash earners, and palm products. A few thousand pursued a pseudo-Western life style, based principally on meagre government salaries. Suddenly, by 1966, there were some 100,000 wage earners. Together with their immediate families they numbered perhaps 300,000 to 400,000 Liberians who for the first time were experiencing life in a relatively modern and Western-influenced environment, with schools, shops, hospitals and clinics, and bars and other places of entertainment.

At the same time, the small modern sector was undergoing extensive change. New modern buildings, paved roads, motor vehicles, hotels and cinemas, and an expanding foreign community transformed Monrovia from a provincial to a sprawling, multi-ethnic city of some 134,000 people by 1970.[7] All indications were that the sudden prosperity would continue indefinitely. Indeed, American economic advisers were telling Tubman and other Liberian leaders that their country would be a showcase of free enterprise for Africa.

This confidence was accompanied by a veritable commercial invasion that established American preeminence in the economic development of Liberia. By the end of the 1960's, some fifty United States firms were

TABLE 3
INDICATORS OF ECONOMIC DEVELOPMENT, 1941–1969
(millions of U.S. dollars except where noted)

Indicator	1941	1950	1960	1966	1969
Total exports [a]	$ 5.0	31.0	83.0	151.0	196.0
Rubber	$ 3.6	19.0	39.0	27.0	30.0
Iron ore	$ —	—	35.0	120.0	137.0
Total imports	$ 3.2	17.1	69.2	114.0	114.0
Government revenues [b]	$ 1.2	3.9	32.4	46.3	61.8
Government expenditures (current dollar values)	$n.a.	4.0	33.1	51.2	56.1
Gross domestic product (money economy; current prices)	$n.a.	48.0	191.0	287.0	366.6
Foreign investment	$	cumulative		750.0	—
Foreign aid	$	cumulative		300.0 [c]	40.2 [d]
Wage employment (thousand man years)	n.a.	30	82	100	150 [e]
School enrollment (thousands)	11	25	80	110	147 [f]
Miles of all-weather roads	—	230	750	1,150	1,200 [g]
Motor vehicles	n.a.	650	7,900	14,000	20,000
Electric power consumption (million KWH)	n.a.	n.a.	98	139	214

SOURCES: Robert Clower et al., *Growth Without Development: An Economic Survey of Liberia* (Evanston: Northwestern University Press, 1966), p. 24; U.S. Embassy, Monrovia, and AID, Washington, D.C.; Liberia, Department of Planning and Economic Affairs, *Annual Reports,* 1966 and 1969; and Elliot Berg, "Growth, Development and All That: Thoughts on the Liberian Experience" (University of Michigan, 1969), mimeographed, p. 2. See Louis P. Beleky, "The Development of Liberia," *Journal of Modern African Studies,* vol. 2, no. 2 (March 1973) for more recent data.

NOTE: Blank cells mean nil or negligible; n.a. means figures are not available. All figures are rounded, and should be regarded as estimates. Owing to the use of different sources, there may be discrepancies in some figures and in the bases on which they were determined. For example, most sources put the 1969 GDP at $396.6 million—but that includes an estimated $30 million from the subsistence sector.

[a] No dollar figures for lumber were available to me; however, 18 million board feet were exported in 1967, and 61 million in 1969.

[b] Budgeted (locally raised) revenues only.

[c] Through 1967. U.S. AID contributions for 1967 were $50.3 million.

[d] 1968 and 1969 combined.

[e] The top estimate; the low estimate for 1969 was 110,000 (official Liberian government estimates).

[f] Includes 21,000 preschool and kindergarten students. U.S. AID placed school enrollment at 156,000 in 1972, some 24 percent of the total school age population.

[g] There were about 1,700 miles of secondary roads in 1969.

represented. In addition to rubber and iron ore exploitation, American firms were engaged in banking, oil exploration, engineering and construction activities, and in the supply of petroleum, motor vehicles, construction and agricultural equipment, and parts. American products accounted for about 80 percent of food sales in local, largely Monrovian, markets.[8]

At the same time the United States engaged in a wide spectrum of technical, educational, and financial assistance projects in Liberia under its Point Four, International Cooperation Administration, and AID programs. Together these projects have amounted to some $280 million over the past twenty-five years.[9] The psychological as well as the economic impact of this effort and of the substantial American presence has been significant.

The most salient features of Liberia's economic growth from the mid-1950's to the present are the following:

1. Virtually all investment capital has come from outside Liberia. Most rubber and iron ore production, the mainstays of the economy, as well as trading, construction, and banking, are in foreign hands.

2. Few Liberians joined directly in these enterprises until the late 1960's. Instead, those in positions of power staked their claims to a share of the expected profits by acting as political partners of the foreign concessionaries or by operating satellite commercial activities.

3. Economic growth has been unbalanced: (a) the government has encouraged the production of primary export goods to the neglect of indigenous enterprises or production for domestic consumption; and (b) both private and public investment have tended to produce enclaves of modernity without commensurate economic development of the agricultural sector.

4. Although a substantial proportion of the increased public revenues and foreign aid has been invested in economic and social infrastructure, e.g., roads, schools, and urban development, most public monies have been either spent inefficiently or directed principally to the enhancement of the modern sector. The noncommercial agricultural sector has received only residual benefits from this development.

5. In spite of the hinterland's relatively small direct participation in the economic boom of the fifties, the social and economic lives of many tribal peoples have been altered by their participation in a fulltime labor force, the expansion of the road system, the purchase of well-placed tribal land by coastal dignitaries, and the extension of central government authority.

6. An unexpected deceleration of growth in the early sixties caused the government to attempt to reduce the burden of its external debt. New budgetary arrangements were made and economic regulatory agencies were established, staffed by foreign economists and administrators.

These developments are discussed in the following pages. Their impact upon Liberia was and is crucial to its modernization.

The Foreign Role in Liberia's Economic Growth

Liberia's miraculous economic growth was primarily a result of private rather than public initiative. But the miracle-workers were foreign capitalists and technical managers, not Liberians. Of some $382 million invested in iron ore operations up to 1962, for example, all but $8.5 million was provided by foreign investors.[10] Virtually all technical and managerial skill was provided by foreigners, who directed the transformation of the bush into modern plantations and highly mechanized mines.

The labor, land, and resources that helped to create this industrial edifice were all Liberian, but the role of Liberians in these enterprises has been that of a silent and subordinate partner at best. The government gave foreign investors a virtual carte blanche to exploit the natural resources of the country, and these investors now control economic institutions which produce 50 percent of Liberia's gross national product, 80 percent of government income, and 70 percent of wage employment. If there was opposition to Tubman's prescription for opening Liberia's doors to foreign investment, which was stated in his first inaugural address in 1944 and reaffirmed in his third in 1956, it had faded away by the prosperous early 1960's. Whether for his own political purposes, or to improve the lot of all Liberians, Tubman promoted Liberia's economic transformation through the Open Door Policy and the enabling legislation which afforded such an attractive invitation to foreign investors.

In spite of the economic power of foreign firms, there is little evidence to suggest that Liberia is in the grip of "economic imperialism," a phrase that connotes the subordination of indigenous political authority to foreign influence. Liberia's rulers have kept political power in their own hands. Foreign firms have not, on the whole, intervened in Liberian politics. They have observed existing channels to support the government and the True Whig Party, and to work harmoniously with the nation's leaders. Since elections were uncontested, there was no need to choose between candidates. And since the Tubman government religiously observed already favorable concession agreements, there was no need to press for greater advantage. Where concession officers sometimes sought to circumvent local authorities, they learned, often to their distress, that even the most oblique assumption of political prerogatives that detracted from, or insulted Liberian sovereignty would be dealt with by fines or deportation. Public exposure of foreign racism is not merely blustering. It demonstrates Liberians' jealousy of their abused and often jeopardized sovereignty.[11] Occasional calls, both private and official, for rewriting concession agreements have made foreign investors, if not docile, at least respectful of that sovereignty.

The government has earned greatly increased revenues owing to its partnership with foreign investors. Taxes and profit sharing have provided it with monies for economic and social development. Individual Liberians also have benefited from various forms of commercial and legal association with the concessionaires. But these revenues and private incomes are only a small share of the total fruits of the exploitation of Liberia's natural resources.

Concession agreements have generally been drawn up so that the government receives a certain proportion of the income of the enterprises, either in income tax or in profit sharing as holders of equity, usually at increasing rates over the expected life of the concession. In virtually all cases, however, foreign-owned companies have built up sizable nontaxable reserves for the improvement and expansion of facilities. (One firm went on to depreciate the fixed assets it purchased with this reserve.) Foreign concerns have reported high operating costs on the basis of liberal "annual depletions" (in one case deducting 15 percent of its gross receipts as a depletion allowance before the company became subject to income tax); and, owing to the need, or perhaps the desirability, of resorting to loan financing, have deducted sizable interest payments from their taxable or sharable incomes. These devices for showing small profits may have cost the government some $4.5 million per year in the early 1960's.[12]

Iron ore mining concessions permit parent or foreign participating companies to purchase fixed quantities or percentages of annual production at prices below prevailing world market levels, reducing the net income of the concession registered in Liberia, and hence its taxable or sharable profits. The cost to Liberia of this arrangement in one instance was nearly $1 million per year. Broad allowances for duty free importations, tax exemptions for companies in which the government owns equity, and nonapplication of real estate, per capita, and excise levies also deprive the Treasury of revenues that in more normal business arrangements would accrue to it. In addition to these highly favorable arrangements for foreign investors, there is no restriction on the repatriation of profits.

Given the initially favorable concession terms, the low cost of labor, and the numerous ways in which tax obligations may be avoided, it is not surprising that with an estimated total investment of $28 million up to 1960, Firestone reaped profits in the amount of $13 million in 1961 alone, or a gross annual rate of return of almost 50 percent.[13] The Liberian Mining Company (LMC) in the Bomi Hills, with an original investment of some $37 million, earned annual gross profits of some $19 million up to 1960.[14] The Liberian American-Swedish Mining Company (LAMCO), at Nimba, which did not go into production until 1963, has made the greatest single investment to date in Liberia, some $275 million. This company agreed to pay an income tax of 50 percent of profits after a tax holiday and a depletion allowance of 15 percent. Out of nearly $22 million in profits in 1965, LAMCO deducted $9.5 million as net interest expense, and $5 million as appropriations to reserves, leaving a sharable profit of $7.5 million.[15] LAMCO is one of the firms that sells ore to shareholding companies abroad at relatively low prices.

Foreign businessmen who operate in underdeveloped countries usually consider their investments to be "high risk capital." They therefore seek high profit-to-cost ratios and assurances of the stability of the contracting government and of the inviolability of agreements, especially regarding repatriation of profits. Their costs include, besides taxes and labor, substantial slush funds for meeting frequent requests to contribute to one cause, fête, official function, or another. But why have the Liberian leaders given such generous terms to foreign investors? From the point of view of the educated younger generation, who have been exposed to arguments for national ownership of resources, and perhaps from the point of view of outsiders, the government has permitted unlimited exploitation of valued and finite resources while receiving benefits that cannot by any objective measure be considered fair.

It is easy to speculate that bribes proffered at the time of agreement negotiations moved Liberian leaders to "sell" their country to foreigners. But the history of Liberia is one of care to avoid precisely such an abdication of sovereignty for a handful of gold (as in the Firestone agreement of 1926). Gratuities may have smoothed the way, but the terms foreigners have won can perhaps be explained in part by the Tubman government's incautious haste to attract foreign investment to the country, and in part by the Liberians' own capitalist ethos, which derived from the laissez-faire economics that motivated them in the nineteenth century. They undoubtedly believed that this mode of development—one they certainly could not themselves have launched or sustained, given the dearth of domestic capital or technical skill—would work for them as it had for the United States.

The shared faith in the capitalist system, the requirements and advantages of political stability, and the desire to build a viable, rational, modern economy bound foreign investors and Liberian political leaders together. This partnership produced a capitalist economy in Liberia—but very few Liberian capitalists. It also produced an important Liberian effort to correct some of the inequities of the partnership (see Chapter 8).

The Role of Liberians in Their Booming Economy

In its partnership with foreign investors, the Liberian government assumed the responsibility for constructing a modern infrastructure in the monetized economic sector. It provided basic services to the concessions; and it maintained order and stability. As individuals, many political leaders employed their official positions—as they had in the past, but now on a much greater scale—for personal gain. Some accepted gifts and services from foreign businessmen; others enriched themselves at the public trough. A number of officials joined boards of directors of the new companies, provided legal counsel, operated trucking services, and established satellite enterprises such as rubber farms. With their attention fastened upon the economic prerogatives derived from government positions, at whatever level, few Liberians took advantage of the country's economic expansion to reenter the commercial world they had left nearly a century earlier.

In fact, Liberians did not until relatively recently enter commerce on any significant scale. They may have been prevented from doing so by design. For it seems, in retrospect, that denying aspiring Liberians a base independent of government employment may have been a way of maintaining the rule of the elite. Otherwise, businessmen might have sought to launch political careers from a base of economic power. As one private Liberian study put it in 1959, "the government has not offered Liberian businessmen the incentive which comes from government patronage. As a rule, the government does not do business with Liberian businessmen."[16]

If well-to-do Liberians did not put their newfound fortunes into savings or capital investment, what became of those substantial monies? For one thing, a great splurge of spending on luxury goods took place in the 1950's. Fine houses, large foreign automobiles, and international travel were the more conspicuous symbols of this unprecedented affluence. Foreign bank accounts, less conspicuous and unprovable, also marked this new era. While largely ignoring business and trading, a number of Liberians operated taxi and trucking fleets, purchased land in the towns and cities, and, with cheap credit from banks and foreign construction firms (whose principal business was with the government), built housing for lease to foreign technicians and business representatives and to the government.[17]

Many Liberians also purchased large tracts of land along the growing road system. While considerable speculation obviously took place, it was not an act of false faith on the part of Liberians to place savings in land, especially at the legal rate of only $.50 per acre. The status considerations and historical values attached to land ownership outshone the attractions of investing in unfamiliar and perhaps risky businesses or manufacturing firms.[18] Rubber farming, for which the land was mainly used, had the advantage of combining large land holdings with promising business profits, particularly in the early fifties when the Korean War had caused a substantial rise in the price of rubber. Owing to Firestone's early policy of giving free seedlings and technical advice to any Liberian wishing to start his own farm, and selling plantation equipment at cost, on interest-free credit, a number of leading Liberians (including President King, President Edwin Barclay, and Vice-President Simpson) had already established farms in the thirties.[19]

The attraction of rubber farming remains great: not only do Americo-Liberians enter this occupation, but many "civilized" tribal people who have managed to save sufficient capital for initial investment do so as well. The number of Liberian growers increased eightfold between 1950 and about 1967—to nearly 4,000. They expanded their contribution to Liberia's rubber output from 217 long tons in 1941 to 11,160 in 1965, and 19,880 in 1970, over 25 percent of total production. Private Liberian earnings were $8.7 million in 1966, and Liberian estates then employed some 18,000 workers.[20] Thus, even though rubber has been displaced by iron ore as Liberia's principal export, rubber production still involves the private commercial interest of more Liberians than any other modern occupation.

Apart from its contribution to the nation's economic growth, the business of rubber farming has had other effects. First, the rubber industry has created close ties between the two principal rubber producers and leading Liberian politicians. Since the two concessionaires, Firestone and B. F. Goodrich, and an independent buyer, Allen Grant Company, are the principal sellers of Liberian rubber abroad, Liberian producers are, in a sense, at their mercies. In 1963, when plantation workers struck, Firestone ceased rubber purchases from independent farmers. The government, whose chief officials were unable to sell their rubber, moved quickly to quell the strike. This insidious partnership may benefit the Treasury and the growers, but it is of questionable benefit to Liberian workers.

Second, a list of Liberian owners of large rubber estates would constitute a *Who's Who* of past and present Liberian political leaders: former President Tubman, 1,600 acres; President Tolbert, over 600 acres; William E. Dennis, 1,040 acres; Henry L. Morris, 1,200 acres; and former diplomat R. S. S. Bright, 500 acres; to name only the largest.[21]

Third, tribal farmers have been dislocated often by land speculation, and workers have been employed involuntarily and paid poorly (often at wages below the legal minimum of $.08 per hour).

Fourth, were all such land exploited economically, or even farmed at all, playing politics with the nation's resources or dislocating tribal farmers might not necessarily be considered too high a price to pay for the creation of indigenous producers of a valuable commodity; but as little as half the acreage held by individual Liberian farmers is in production.[22] Of the nearly 4,000 Liberian rubber growers, seventy-five produce half the total private output. Most private estates are producing 500 to 600 pounds of rubber per acre (perhaps ten obtain as much as 800 pounds per acre, far short of Firestone's production of 1,100 to 1,200 pounds per acre).[23] These marginal levels at which most Liberian rubber farmers operate are attributable to the large percentage of low-yielding rubber trees and the inadequacy of planting, tapping, and maintenance procedures.[24]

Few Liberian rubber farmers, therefore, are contributing to the nation's economic development. Moreover, the industry suffered a reversal that assumed serious proportions in 1967, when rubber prices fell below the break-even point for many small Liberian-owned farms. The government established a price support scheme under which it guaranteed loans to growers amounting to the difference between local posted prices and former, more profitable, prices. This scheme, which worked successfully in 1967–68, in that most loans were repaid, permitted marginal farms to survive.[25]

Instead of improving their own production methods and thus sustaining a viable indigenous enterprise (in the sixties, Firestone officials spoke with confidence of another hundred years of profitable production in spite of declining world prices for natural rubber), Liberian leaders fell back on the resources of government, even in a time of financial stringency. Plans for the establishment of a Rubber Institute, whose aim was to improve the quality of the rubber and to provide credit and advisory services in order to modernize the industry, may ultimately relieve the government of the need to bail out Liberian rubber farmers from their chronic problems.

Unbalanced Economic Growth

Liberia's substantial economic growth and attendant increases in money income and revenues would not have occurred had Liberians sought to develop the national economy themselves. This debt to foreign finance, technical skills, and management is manifest. But the major part of the economic benefits of this commercial activity also falls into foreign hands and is remitted abroad to distant stockholders. What have been the consequences to Liberia of its extensive reliance upon foreign investors for the exploitation of its natural resources?

Having, in a sense, virtually abandoned the national economy to foreign domination, Liberia's leaders have also not attempted to direct it toward anything but export production. Because of the small domestic market and the handsome profits derived from the exploitation of primary resources, consumer goods industries have not yet been developed, apart from a few small firms which produce such goods as beer, soft drinks, ice cream, bakery goods, soap, and paints. Most are owned and managed by foreigners, particularly Lebanese. Even the development of a palm product industry, which readily lends itself to small-grower production, has come into the hands of foreign concessionaires. A few Liberian officials have established satellite estates near those of the concessionaires, in response to forecasts of rising world prices for palm products. This pattern resembles that of rubber development. The emphasis on export production, and Liberia's consequent vulnerability to international market factors, show no promise of being checked.

In spite of having one of the most favorable agricultural environments in Africa, Liberia is, therefore, still essentially a two-product country. Government revenues, opportunities for wage labor, and the country's economic health depend almost exclusively upon iron and rubber. These industries, moreover, exist as enclaves in the rural hinterland, whose development is lagging far behind.[26] Only Monrovia, with its central government offices and trading, banking, and shipping businesses, affords an alternative entry into the modern sector. This enclave nature of Liberia's economic development is most important. For the 10,000 Liberian workers who live and work at Liberia's five iron ore mines, for example, there is the experience of modern life, contractual obligations, and reliable cash rewards that by Liberian standards are considerable. Markets, schools, hospitals, churches, and roads have been constructed within these enclaves, making them nearly self-sufficient. Railroad lines to the coast serve principally to carry out iron ore and to bring in machinery and construction materials, as well as a sizable proportion of the consumer goods required by mine personnel, including foreign-grown rice.

This is not to say that the rural agricultural areas have been entirely bypassed by Liberia's economic expansion. For cash crop farming has expanded and subsistence agriculture has declined. But the approximately tenfold increase in cash cropping between 1950 and 1968 must be measured against a very low base. And cash crop farming has by no means kept pace with export industries and commerce, as Table 4 indicates. Indeed, for good or ill, the size of the agricultural sector is shrinking in terms of the numbers of persons who rely for survival exclusively on small-scale agriculture, although it still includes over two-thirds of Liberia's population. And though this number cannot be considered completely apart from the modern commercial economy, since wage earners often remit part of their income to their families, who remain on the land, the traditional tribal sector nevertheless lags far behind. As labor, trade, and additional commercial enterprises move into the already developed enclaves, the inequalities between the poor and the developed sectors have

TABLE 4
Gross Domestic Income by Origin, 1950 and 1960
(millions of current dollars)

Source	1950	1960
Subsistence agriculture	$22.2	$18.1
Cash cropping	1.8	7.3
Other (including plantation rubber production)	21.0	31.4
Total agriculture, forestry and fishing	45.0	56.8
Industry and Commerce	7.4	92.9
Services	2.6	5.0
Government	3.0	16.4
Grand Total	58.0	171.1

SOURCE: Robert Clower et al., *Growth Without Development: An Economic Survey of Liberia* (Evanston, Ill.: Northwestern University Press, 1966), p. 28.

increased.[27] Most small farmers are not sharing in their country's wealth.

Nor are they supplying the modern economic sector with the food the urban or concession populations require. The modern sector of Liberia has come increasingly to depend on imports from abroad for food, as for almost all manufactured goods, with a concomitant diminution of reliance upon domestic production. Government exhortations to produce more have had little, if any, effect. Imports of rice (the staple food for most Liberians), for example, continue to grow each year. Given Liberia's continuing concentration and dependence upon production for export, the production of food is likely to further dwindle. The government's recognition of the burdensome costs of importing food has produced, so far, many words and plans but few concrete policies and actions.

The Role of Government

Before asking what the government might have done to ameliorate the consequences of unbalanced economic growth and the disparity in the economic conditions between the modern and traditional sectors of the country, it is well to recall the nature of the government's commitment when it inaugurated the Open Door Policy, which unleashed this type of development in the first place.

In order to attract foreign investment, the government needed to be able to preserve political stability and to ensure the safety of private property. It also provided the administration with basic public utilities and services, communications, and the regulation of labor necessary to safeguard those areas in which investors were interested. Thus, the investment in and benefits of development flowed to the modern sector, as did additional private and public investment and foreign aid.[28]

But is it not the task of the government to attempt to provide goods and services to develop the backward sections of the country? In most developing nations, public sector investment has been and probably will remain the principal means of reaching the mass of people who are engaged in low-return economic activities. Liberia, however, has not employed its revenues in this way. The lion's share of government expenditures remains in the developed, largely urban, sector, as salaries for government employees, public buildings, and other urban-oriented projects. Not only does the active polity reside in this sector, but it also is the sector that can be most easily developed, and thus offers the quickest returns on investment. And as it is enriched, so is the ruling elite.

The Liberian government's role, therefore, has been limited to: (1) providing basic infrastructure, such as roads, public buildings, communications, harbors, power facilities, and urban services, usually with foreign aid financing; (2) linking the modern enclaves, both physically and administratively, with Monrovia, the port and the marketing and political core of the modern sector; (3) creating central control of heretofore semiautonomous administrative units; (4) displaying the central government's effectiveness both domestically and to the outside world, by fulfilling basic governmental responsibilities, that is, by providing public education, health care, and other social services.

A fifth goal might be added: the government also tried to assume a greater role in guiding economic development. But its capacity to act as an instrument of economic change has been limited by deficiencies in organization and in trained manpower. Moreover, even such mild reforms as instituting a progressive income tax or protecting wage laborers might have strained the political unity of the regime, since its leaders have a vested interest in the somewhat regressive tax system and the availability of cheap and unorganized labor.[29]

Government's Role in Agricultural Development. What of the one million people who are engaged principally in subsistence agriculture? They work one-third of Liberia's land, but produce less than one-tenth of the national income, reflecting the slight commercialization and inferior technology in this sector.[30] Any attempt to transform their economic and social environment and behavior would be a heavy burden to the most rational, efficient, and honest administration. Indeed, the subsistence sector might even be said to have absorbed resources in excess of its visible contribution to the economy. Hence, even the small investment in this sector may have retarded other lines of development.[31] It might be argued, as some economists have, that indigenous, small-scale commercial agriculture would be the most fruitful and equitable kind of national development in Africa over the long run.[32] But in Liberia, at least, the short-term prospects and rewards of investment in the modern sector have been irresistible. More important, political imperatives rule that economic and social change should not upset the favored position of the elite or endanger their political control, which is based in the modern sector. Hence, their sector must receive the greatest share of both private *and* public investment.

Notwithstanding these factors favoring the modern sector, from time to time official Liberian statements emphasize the importance of agriculture in Liberia's development. President Tubman often said during the austere 1960's: "Nothing is more important than that we should become self-sufficient particularly in our food requirements and export more than we import."[33] But government initiatives in agricultural development have been almost totally ineffective, where they have been made at all.

Agriculture has been the least favored of the major public sectors classified in the Liberian budget. Annual appropriations amounted to only 2 percent of total government expenditures in the 1960's. Over 70 percent of department expenditures have been for general administration and services. In such a potentially important field as agricultural extension services, only $20,000 was appropriated for purchases of materials and machinery in 1965, while $166,000 was expended for employee compensation.[34]

Where givers of foreign aid have sought to improve agricultural production methods and to establish alternative sources of food, the government has not participated directly, or, if it has, officials have turned the projects to their own profit. An American-sponsored fish-pond-stocking project came to naught as Liberian officials fished out the pond for their own consumption or for quick sale in nearby markets.[35] Similarly, piped water and local roads were made to serve resident dignitaries or tribal leaders before the needs of the local population were considered.

Liberia's version of agricultural "self-help," a device to mobilize farmers for greater production, which is popular elsewhere in Africa, is simply another source of patronage. Called "Operation Production, Priority Number One," this program was promulgated in 1964 to increase agricultural production by 100 percent "or more."[36] Operation Production was administered by a two-man staff for the entire country, and there were no public appropriations for its coordinating activities, at least until 1970. The President simply made on-the-spot grants to honorary county chairmen. In one area, $5,000 of a $14,000 subvention went for the purchase of an automobile for the local chairman.

The government's small budget devoted to small-scale agriculture and its minimal efforts to increase production indicate a great gap between rhetoric and action in this field. In its proposed development plan for 1967–70, the Department of Agriculture defined its responsibility as one of stimulating private investment in medium and large-scale commercial and modern agriculture:

> To the extent that private investment does not come forward fast enough and in sufficient amounts to exploit opportunities which appear to be commercially viable on the basis of properly elaborated feasibility studies, the Government in cooperation with international organizations, should establish such commercial enterprises as public corporations.[37]

The various agencies established to provide technical and financial assistance to these farmers, however, show little promise. The Agricultural Credit Corporation, which the government established in 1962, could make no unsecured loans and could not accept crops as collateral.[38] Other parastatal development agencies, such as the Liberian Development Corporation (whose aim is to find industrial opportunities and capital investment) and the Liberian Produce Marketing Corporation (LPMC is a joint venture of the Liberian government and the Danish-run East Asiatic Trading Company), were constrained from developing owing to their inability to secure sufficient capitalization during Liberia's financial austerity in the 1960's.[39] LPMC has monopoly export rights on coffee, cocoa, and palm kernel. And it has a monopoly on the importation of certain foodstuffs, most notably rice. Given the ineffectiveness of these agencies, the failure of the government to pursue a public economic role more assiduously may be counted a blessing to the country.

The preoccupation of the government with a hydroelectric dam at Mt. Coffee, near Monrovia, a new sewerage system and industrial park for Monrovia, and a network of primary roads connecting Monrovia to the farthest reaches of the country more accurately reflects its development priorities. Nevertheless, even when the principal objective of such projects is to assist in the development of modern economic activities, the residual consequences in the precommercial sector may be far-reaching. Such is the case with the road-building program, which has profoundly affected the economic as well as the social existence of many hinterland peoples, sometimes adversely. But the roads which lead from Monrovia to the borders of Sierra Leone, Guinea, and the Ivory Coast have accomplished more than any official policy in making physical unification a near reality, and in establishing the bases for economic and political integration of the entire country.

The Impact of Roads on the Hinterland

In 1945, Liberia had no paved or hard-surfaced roads, and only 206 miles of "unimproved" roads, mostly in poor condition.[40] By 1962, paved and surfaced roads totaled nearly 800 miles; and by 1969, there were 1,200 miles of hard-surfaced roads, bringing the total road mileage to nearly 3,000. Foreign concessions had constructed some 300 miles of these all-weather roads, many sections of which were open to public traffic, such as Firestone's paved roads which give access to Robertsfield International Airport. All the iron mines have constructed rail lines to the coast which are sometimes used to carry passengers and goods other than for the mines.

A critical feature of these new communications is their direction inland, that is, to the tribal hinterland. The coastal counties have been later and only secondary beneficiaries of this substantial construction program. As a consequence, the three principal hinterland counties had 46 percent of the existing road mileage in 1964; Montserrado County had the largest part of the balance, some 21 percent. Furthermore, the road-building program tended to favor the hinterland areas in terms of land area served (that is, land within one mile of primary roads) and brought them nearly to parity with the coastal counties in terms of population per mile of road (600 to 960 people per mile, excepting Cape Mount and Grand Gedeh counties, which had fewer).[41]

This is not to suggest that road construction was undertaken for the purpose of serving one part of the country over another. It seems clear that practical economic considerations were important, particularly since foreign donors contributed the greatest share of funds for the primary road program. The roads could not, in any case, so easily have been constructed directly to all coastal counties, owing to the physical configurations of Liberia's coastal strip, with its swamps, wide river mouths, and sandy soils. But in the twenty-five years since the program began, the consequences to the hinterland of these new communication links have been most profound, in terms of access to Monrovia, the rubber plantation, and mines, the opening up of internal market centers, and facilitating personal travel. Physical mobility is crucial to modernization and integration in Liberia, for it permits the horizontal movement of people into the modern sector, which is the nation's political arena.

In addition to the benefits the new roads provided to the hinterland, they also brought with them "more unofficial tax gatherers (including soldiers and agricultural extension workers), more labour recruitment, more petty corruption and graft, and more official tax levies for the building of offices and homes for resident government officials."[42] But even with attendant drawbacks of corruption and inefficiency, the central government was able to substantially penetrate the hinterland for the first time.

As the hinterland began to experience more direct government control, the tribal people in turn obtained greater access to national institutions, such as county administrations, public schools, the True Whig Party, the central legislature, central government departments, and the President himself. Whereas the two communities, coastal and hinterland, had been nearly separate, now they began to share some of the same institutions and to function as one society, albeit in a dominant-subordinate relationship. This stratified society, whether "good" or "bad," is more nearly integrated than one in which the members share basic, compulsory institutions, but practice different ones.[43] While the "civilized" and tribal communities maintain certain relatively exclusive institutions, their more crucial growing economic and political interdependence is moving Liberia from a socially and culturally heterogeneous system to a more integrated one.

Although political change occurred slowly as a consequence of extending the roads, a sharp economic transformation took place in many rural areas. As discussed above, private rubber farming expanded greatly in the early 1950's, principally in response to the new demand created by the Korean War. Most of these new farms were along the new paved motor road from Monrovia. For example, of some 500 independent Liberian rubber farms operating in 1951, only thirty-five were outside Montserrado County and the then Central Province (now divided between Montserrado and Bong counties). In fact, 60 percent of all Liberian rubber farms were within an average of thirty-four miles from the Firestone plantation at Harbel, many on poor roads. The nearness of a purchaser for the rubber, however, compensated for the poor conditions of most roads in that period.

While the number of rubber farms has increased between three and four times in the area around Harbel since 1951, they have multiplied fifteen times elsewhere in the country. Moreover, the newer farms along the main motor road are, on the average, twice as large as older farms in Montserrado County and have more acres planted in mature rubber trees.[44] This expansion of rubber farming has created a new, if small, economically independent class of Liberians. But the purchase of land in the hinterland by coastal residents, whether for rubber farms or for speculation, has also uprooted small farmers who had the misfortune to occupy the coveted land along the new road. As one government report stated in 1962, "Speculative purchases of land along proposed highways, together with the planting of rubber farms along new roads, have dispossessed tribal occupants of land, . . . with consequent disruption of economic activities."[45] The attraction of wage labor and the recruitment of workers for the new rubber farms also upset traditional economic patterns for people of the hinterland. Given the choice of entering employment of the new estates or moving back into the bush to start new farms, a good many of the dispossessed farmers accepted the former course.

Who Owns the Land?

According to customary land tenure, tribes "owned" land insofar as they exploited it. The constitution of Liberia prohibits the purchase of land "by any citizen or citizens from the aborigines" for private use.[46]

While "aborigines" are now citizens in law and fact, this statute remains law. The impulse behind the original declaration is still partly recognized, and hence affords *some* protection to tribally held land. Land is held collectively by tribal people, usually in the name of their chiefs or headmen, who determine which member or family may use which tract of land. Tribal land is considered public land that is reserved for tribal use; but it may be occupied by government establishments or leased to concessionaires; unoccupied or unimproved land generally is considered forest reserve or "residual" (i.e., public) land. Privately deeded land (in fee simple) may be owner-occupied or leased, for example to Lebanese traders, but non-Liberians may not own land.[47]

It is clear that the law is flexible, for tribal lands have been sold to Americo-Liberians from the coast and even to tribesmen themselves.[48] According to one observer,

> in practice, these [constitutional] safeguards are essentially nominal and are largely ignored. . . . Individual tribal farmers have been dispossessed from lands on which they have planted coffee, cocoa, and rubber trees, entire communities have occasionally been swallowed up in government grants to foreign concessions, and large tracts of public land along newly constructed roads have been sold to nontribal individuals for business, farming, or speculative purposes.[49]

This system of protecting tribal land, therefore, is obviously open to abuse. Bribes paid to chiefs, presidential favors for political purposes, and land disputes are commonplace. But the manner in which land is obtained secures some respect for tribal prerogatives. Applicants require certification from the relevant chief that the parcel of land is not occupied; and payment must be made to the tribal authorities "as a token of good intention of living peacefully with the tribesmen."[50] Ultimately, every application for a land deed requires the approval of the President of the Republic. Some tribal leaders have resisted extensive intrusions into their areas by coastal land-seekers by refusing certification or by appealing directly to the President. On the other hand, a new phenomenon is the acquisition of private land holdings by chiefs themselves.

Some tribesmen have been disturbed by the sale of tribally occupied land to people not of their own blood, particularly along the major roads now running through much of the country. These sales have probably occurred where the political influence of the purchaser was irresistible. There have also been complaints about the consequences of the presence of a political notable in the hinterland, such as compulsory free labor, or labor at poor wages, fêtes for visiting dignitaries, requiring "donations" of rice, chickens, palm oil, and the like.

The consequences of land shortages in areas where land has been alienated to outsiders are unclear—if there are in fact serious shortages. But the displacement of tribal farmers may have played a part in the decision by some of them to undertake work on concessions or private rubber estates. For, while concessionaires could not obtain enough workers except by compulsory "recruitment" as late as 1960, that no longer appears to be the case.[51] A growing number of Liberians serve some part of the year for wages on the Firestone plantations, including those who have not been forced off their land. The improved roads, which carry heavy taxi and bus traffic, facilitate their travel to and from the plantations in time for the rice farming cycle in their home areas. The rubber plantations tend to attract workers from neighboring tribes, whereas the iron ore mines generally show a more even distribution of tribal membership in their work forces.[52] Whether the latter case would have obtained without the improved road system cannot be stated on the basis of present information. Almost certainly the far higher wages at the iron mines are their prime attraction, but it may be assumed that mobility is a factor in the multitribal nature of the mines' work forces.

Cash Cropping

The new roads also have provided better marketing and transportation facilities for cash crop farmers, as is evident in the proliferation of rural market centers throughout the hinterland, and the increase in cash and export crop production. In 1964, for example, I visited Johnny Town, a small village near the Sierra Leone border in western Liberia, on its weekly market day. "Iron money," ten- to twelve-inch sticks of beaten and twisted iron, served as the principal currency for tribal people, as it had in the past in much of Liberia. On my return in 1967—then some five years after the main road from Monrovia had reached the area—only hard currency (U.S. dollars and Liberian coins) was in evidence at the market.

Although increases in agricultural production for domestic consumption are nearly impossible to ascertain, export figures provide basic indicators of such growth. Cocoa and coffee exports, for example, increased fourfold and ninefold, respectively, between 1953 and 1964 (although some of this increase may be attributed to growing smuggling from Guinea and the Ivory Coast, whose export sales were limited by international agreements); piassava production doubled in the same period. These usually are small-farm crops. Estimates of rice production, on the other hand, show a 20 percent reduction between 1952 and 1960.[53] Rice imports increased from 19 million pounds in 1955 to 100 million pounds in 1968, and reached the highest volume ever experienced in 1970.[54]

Given the new access to export markets, Liberian farmers are acting quite rationally when they put their land and labor to production for export. For one thing, in the past at least, rice prices often were manipulated by importers and merchants, so that they fell at harvest time (sometimes to as low as $3.00 to $4.00 per 100 lbs., rather than the normal $8.50).[55] More important, one economist has estimated that a farmer growing three acres of rice would, at 1963 prices, have an annual loss of income of $400, assuming the value of his labor to be $.64 per day (the basic daily wage at Firestone).[56] Finally, farmers often were, in a sense, penalized for additional production, since local or central government officials expropriated rice that appeared to be in excess of a family's needs.[57]

It cannot be presumed, on the basis of this scant information, that subsistence farmers will be quick to respond to new opportunities to market their crops solely on the basis of economic criteria. The question of the varying importance to peasants of economic and noneconomic stimuli has hardly been resolved by social scientists. This is not the place to seek to answer this question. But some hinterland farmers in Liberia have increased their output during the last fifteen years, apparently because they had better access to market.

Wolota – A Case Study of Modernization in the Hinterland

The farmers of Wolota are an example of Liberians who grasped the opportunitity to enter cash crop production once roads and markets became available to them.[58] The clan area of Wolota is some thirty miles from the important communication and marketing link of Gbarnga, on the old Gbarnga-Tapita Road. The "pacification" of the Mano people by the Liberian Frontier Force around 1923 brought, among other things, an increase of trade with the coast. Money (British coins) began to circulate. In another twenty-five years the motor road from Monrovia came within twelve miles of Wolota. David Blanchard states that "the nearness of a market at which to sell rice and to buy imported goods stimulated a marked increase in agricultural production. . . . By the end of the fifties rubber, coffee and cocoa were being planted."[59] Famines, which frequently afflicted this area, were eliminated for the first time. By 1961 the Wolota clan area was crisscrossed with almost twenty miles of roads, and tribal people who had moved out to be closer to the old highway returned to farm.[60] Lebanese shopkeepers, Mandingo traders, and rubber farmers moved into the area, opening up the possibility of local markets for agricultural products: rice, cane juice, vegetables, and fruit.[61]

Blanchard concludes that under the impact of roads and new wage opportunities, "the old economic system was destroyed and a new economic base and structure were introduced"—though they were still based on agriculture.[62] The new economic system also provided to tribesmen the opportunity to attain "civilized" status through acquiring wealth, "some understanding of Western civilization and spoken English," which permitted intertribal communication, and knowledge of "one's legal rights and duties" in the modern sector.[63] Registered landholdings began to replace customary land tenure.[64]

There were other important economic and social developments in this period. The *kuu* (a Kpelle word for a sort of traditional labor cooperative), the members of which would work in rotation on farms of other members, began to change to a more modern type of cooperative. The concept of the *kuu* was broadened to include not only the pooling of labor and money but also investment and marketing.[65] That this type of enterprise is not confined to the Mano area is illustrated in at least one other case. A Gola labor cooperative, which had been working together for some time clearing sugar cane farms for its members, joined together to purchase a $1,400 sugar mill in 1968.[66]

Perhaps the most unexpected finding in Blanchard's study was that "of all the influences of government the strongest factor pushing the tribal man to increased production has been the tax structure." Blanchard points out that since the tax structure is regressive, the annual hut tax and the education tax are applied uniformly to every house and individual regardless of income. "For the individual farmer the tax burden becomes proportionately less as his income increases." Moreover, if a farmer can establish *kwi* status, he will be relieved of the obligation to contribute cash and rice to the tribal government for public expenditures of the clan. And "he will also be relieved of the burdens of public labor and militia training. There is thus a strong incentive not only to increase production, but to shift to cash crops and try to become *kwi*."[67]

The experience of Wolota suggests some of the potential modernizing and integrating effects of the expanded road system in Liberia, as well as the commercial opportunities that have been seized by Liberian farmers in the hinterland. Traditional rule and customary economic and social behavior are gradually giving way to the imperatives of the marketplace and contract labor. Perhaps above all it shows that given the opportunity and sufficient incentives to enter the cash economy (without excessive penalties for producing surplus crops), many tribal Liberians will do so. It also is interesting, and possibly important, that they do so while remaining in the rural area of the country. Finally, the general rise in the standard of living throughout the area appears to have convinced the people of Wolota that "the average man is a good deal better off today than even the rich were forty years ago."[68]

Conclusions

There have been varied responses to the new roads in the hinterland. Some tribal chiefs have resisted the blandishments and no doubt material rewards from coastal notables who have sought land in their chiefdoms. In Lofa County, in particular, relatively little land has been sold to outsiders. Moreover, one of the more progressive chiefs in this area has exploited the new opportunities afforded by the primary road link to Monrovia. Paramount Chief Tomba Taylor claimed in 1967 that he had built over a hundred miles of feeder roads since the main Monrovia road reached Kolahun, and beyond to Sierra Leone in 1962.

Such voluntary public works, the establishment of marketing and investment cooperatives, and a shifting of labor from relatively uneconomic production, such as that of rice, to more economically rewarding work, are the more impressive in that they took place not at the behest of government, but rather in response to a fortuitous confluence of opportunities.

The roads have brought not only the *means* to market crops, but the flow of ideas and "modern" economic and social behavior from the cities, either in the persons of new settlers or in returning migrant workers. These ideas, reinforced by the advantages accruing to those who assume "civilized" behavior, have lent themselves to a transformation of the more progressive tribal farmers, without material or technical assistance from the government.

We have seen that the new roads helped to develop large agricultural estates. Tribal farmers who held land along the roads often were dispossessed and as a consequence spent part of their time in wage labor. For some, it brought the possibility to engage in rubber farming; for many others, the development of large towns provided the chance to market crops for shipment to the coast for export. The roads came to serve a growing two-way traffic of workers and traders migrating to plantations, mines, or towns on the coast, and returning to their villages as witnesses and communicators of "civilized" standards of behavior. Some of these semiurbanized tribesmen enjoy prestige and respect at home. *Kwi* tribesmen often advise chiefs in matters that go beyond local traditional affairs. This beginning of the transformation of the social and economic system of the hinterland was accompanied and hastened by the existence, for the first time, of central government administration, social services (especially schools), and a new array of communication links with the coast.

In spite of mixed results and a most uncertain future, Liberian economic development appears not to have placed the fate of its people in foreign hands, or to have irrevocably locked them into a rigid class structure in which one class enriches itself at the expense of the "masses." At the same time, Liberia appears to be no worse off than most Third World nations in its reliance on one or several export products, with the concomitant vulnerability to fluctuations in world market prices. As far as the public sector is concerned, while it is no less wasteful than those of other African states, the Liberian government's smaller and less costly efforts in the economic sector have taken a lesser toll on its citizens.

Thus, in spite of the unfair deal Liberia has received at the hands of foreign investors and marketers of their goods, and in spite of the government's concentration on production for export, Liberians have had opportunities and *choices* to undertake wage employment or cash farming in increasingly advantageous ways and with limited government restriction. In sum, for all its inequities, in that one class has gained relative advantages over the mass of Liberia's people, economic development has made all Liberians materially better off than they were before. How long the question of the distribution of Liberia's growing wealth remains inadequately answered or unresolved must be sought in the political system, including the developing or refurbishing of institutions through which people express their demands.

— 5 —

Labor and Society

The modern sector, as I have employed the term, refers to the centers of commerce—the port and semiindustrial city of Monrovia, a handful of trading towns, and the rubber and iron ore concessions. This sector is also the locus of the ruling class, which holds economic, military, and political power. As soon as the writer leaves the realm of abstraction, however, and tries to describe living people, he encounters many difficulties. For the modern sector embraces, in addition to the nation's political leaders, businessmen, and foreign managers and technicians, a great variety of Liberians of different tribes, cultures, and aspirations. Their physical, social, and psychic mobility represents "the primary process whereby modernization is activated."[1] The major features of this modernization are urbanization and industrialization.

As tribal Liberians entered the towns, the plantations, and the mines, they became civil servants, small businessmen, mine and plantation workers, construction laborers, seamen, domestic servants, and unskilled laborers of various sorts. Many of them moved about a good deal, from one part of the country to another; and they frequently changed their employment. Many mine, plantation, and urban workers returned to their farms for a time and then left again to take up jobs for wages once more.

Movement into the Modern Sector

In the 1950's opportunities for wage employment brought great numbers of tribal Liberians out of their tribal habitats into the Western, commercial sector for the first time. Population figures for Monrovia show that the greatest rate of growth in this century occurred after World War II.

1900	4,000	1956	42,000
1926	5,000	1959	53,000
1934	10,000	1962	82,000
1940	12,000	1970	134,000[2]

There has not been comparable urban growth elsewhere in Liberia. While precise data are not available, Buchanan, the capital of Bassa County, with its iron ore pelletizing plant (LAMCO) and port, is probably the only town, apart from Monrovia, with a population greater than 5,000 persons. Gbarnga, Bong County seat, at the "V" of the major road to the northeastern and eastern hinterland, and Zorzor, an important historical and contemporary market center in Lofa County, may each have 3,000 to 4,000 inhabitants. The remaining six county capitals, as far as I can tell, have 2,000 to 3,000 inhabitants each. The larger concession sites, Firestone at Harbel, LMC at Bomi Hills, and LAMCO at Nimba, comprise substantial population concentrations, which are discussed below.

There are no published data on the ethnic distribution of Monrovia's population. Fraenkel estimates that members of the neighboring coastal tribes, such as the Kru, Bassa, Dei, Vai, and Gola, and smaller numbers of the more distant Grebo from the southeast and Mende from the northwest, constituted 60 percent of Monrovia's population in 1959; persons identified as Americo-Liberians then accounted for about 16 percent of the population.[3] More recent data indicate that about 33 percent of the population of Montserrado County had been born in the Central and Western provinces, as against the 17 percent this group accounted for in Fraenkel's data on Monrovia.[4] These data suggest that increasing numbers of the more distant tribes have been migrating to Monrovia and near-by Harbel since the mid-fifties.

The proximity of various tribes to wage-employment opportunities apparently determines where their migrant members go. In 1964 the Kpelle, in whose tribal area Firestone's largest plantation is located, was the largest single tribal group among Firestone's 18,000 to 20,000 Harbel employees (some 7,100), followed by the Kisi, the Bassa, the Loma, and the Gio.[5] Firestone's smaller plantation at Cavalla, in Maryland County, employed neighboring Krus and Grebos almost exclusively. The 2,400 employees of the Liberian Mining Company (LMC) at Bomi Hills, north of Monrovia, were fairly evenly distributed by tribe in 1964, with only the Gola, who occupy the Bomi Hills area, and the Loma, their northern neighbors, each accounting for more than 10 percent of the total, followed by the Kpelle, the Kisi, the Kru, the Bassa, and the Bandi. (LMC also employs a number of Ghanaians and Sierra Leoneans in clerical jobs.)[6] The preponderance of the 2,000 employees at the Liberian Swedish-American Mining Company (LAMCO) mine in the Nimba Range were principally from among the neighboring Mano in 1961, when the mine was under construction.[7] LAMCO claimed it did not have information on tribal distribution for its more stable work force after it began full-scale operations in 1963. The Mano still appear to predominate, but several informants observed that there were also many Bassa and Loma working at the mine.

It appears that it is principally the young who tend to move into the modern sector. The fifteen to twenty-nine year olds in the populations of virtually every county or former province, except Montserrado and Maryland, is around 25 percent of the total. In Montserrado County, this age group constitutes over 30 percent of the total population; in Monrovia it is about 36 percent.[8] Thus, these young people appear to come to Monrovia and Montserrado County in roughly equal proportions from all regions of the country.

Economic and social opportunities apparently attract most migrants from their tribal homes, particularly young people. Few have been forced off the land in spite of extensive alienation of choice locations by coastal dignitaries. Liberia does not share with many other underdeveloped countries the problems of land shortages. And few have moved because of economic hardship. Other forms of social and economic pressures in the traditional milieu are sometimes considered to have contributed to the exodus of many people from their home areas. For some migrants, the move to the modern sector means emancipation: for women, emancipation from heavy domestic work and, in places, near chattel status; for children, from field work, herding and onerous social obligations that preclude attending school; and for farmers, from the tyranny of the land as well as from the incessant taxes or obligatory labor, and even kinship obligations, that beset them.[9] These pressures have always existed, but in the 1950's the general atmosphere of social change tended to generate mobility. "Western contacts having created needs and aspirations impossible to satisfy in the countryside,"[10] Liberians by the thousands fled the land in search of a better life.

Possibly the most important inducement to young people to leave their homes has been the expanding system of secular education, which is concentrated in urban and semi-urban areas. This assumption is supported by a comparison of the proportion of the population at various levels of education in the country as a whole and in Monrovia. Nation-wide, a little more than 10 percent of Liberians five years and older had completed at least one grade of schooling in 1962; 3 percent had attended at least the eighth grade. In Monrovia, over 40 percent of the same age group had completed at least one grade in 1962, and almost 17 percent had completed eighth grade or higher.[11]

The numbers, dissimilar origins, and differing motives of the new entrants into the modern sector are clues to the level of social change that has occurred. The behavior and organized activities of these people in the evolving urban social structure may provide some measure of the impact of modernization on Liberia and the degree of national integration that has been attained. Furthermore, the migrants communicate some aspects of change and modernization from the urban and other modern centers to the tribal areas, to which they carry some of the trappings of the modern world, such as money, radios, Western clothing, and the language and habits of the Westernized man. They are admired, emulated, and looked to for answers to the mysteries of modern life. The "urbanized" tribesman who resettles permanently in his tribal area is not only a fashion setter, but an opinion leader and, often, an unofficial adviser to local chiefs.

Levels of Social Change

Although deeply ingrained social norms and customs persist among the new townsmen, they are incessantly undergoing change. There is not in the town or city the same cycle of work, the same face-to-face relations, and the same criteria of social status that obtain in the village. Traditional values are constantly being impinged upon by modern ones: status according to occupation, Western-style dress, Western standards of social behavior, strict work schedules, and unfamiliar consumer habits. The need to speak English in order to coexist with fellow workers of other tribes or with Americo-Liberians, and also to "get ahead" in a job; the use of money for every economic transaction and many social ones; and the recognition of personal property—all are part of the new life in the town.[12]

Patterns of traditional behavior are less disrupted on the plantation than in the town. There the worker or his wife may do some gardening; families usually live in areas reserved for members of their own tribe, often physically distant from workers of other tribes. A form of chiefly authority and customary social relationships, which were a critical part of village life in the traditional setting, have been transposed to the plantation. But a chief's authority on a plantation is vastly different from that in the village. Not only is he obliged to help maintain peace and order and to adjudicate matters concerning marriage and divorce and personal property (but not land); he must help to ensure the daily appearance of workers at their posts, tapping trees or clearing brush and weeds. However much plantation work may resemble obligatory communal work in the village, the service is rendered not for the corporate benefit of the specific community but for the "company"—white, foreign owners and managers. And one works to earn a cash wage rather than to fulfill a customary obligation.

The environment at the mines stands somewhere between urban and plantation life. Like the rubber plantations, the mines are relatively isolated modern enclaves. But the relatively high wages and the skills needed to operate a highly mechanized industry require a more technologically advanced performance from the mine worker than is required of his unskilled countryman on a rubber plantation.

All three—townsman, miner, and rubber worker—stand apart from traditional village life, and the distance increases both with the number of people moving into the new environment and with the length of time they spend there. Yet tribal migrants "are at once tribal and urban in their orientation and operate selectively both sets of values and the appropriate social relationship."[13]

Tribal Society in Monrovia

The majority of tribesmen who have entered the modern sector have moved to the capital, which, like urban centers elsewhere in Africa, is "the seat of government, the source of news and innovation and the point of contact with the outside world."[14] Tribal migration to Monrovia dates from the earliest American settlements. As Americo-Liberians set up houses and farms, they employed gardeners and house servants from among the neighboring tribes, especially the Bassa.[15] As ocean commerce developed, the seafaring Kru took to manning ships and working as longshoremen in Monrovia's port. The Vai, who have long been noted for their independence and advanced culture (they developed their own script in the nineteenth century, had never been slaves, and often had their own servants working their farms), were quickest to adopt Western ways and reached higher levels of modern occupations relatively early in the Republic's history. The Vai, with the Kru, are probably still the leading, though not dominant, tribal component in middle and even upper levels of the government.[16]

In the past, the tribal population of Monrovia resided principally in tribal communities in the city, such as Vai Town, Kru Town, Bassa Town, and the like. The correspondence of occupation and tribe—and, to some extent, of church congregation—served to reinforce this tribal identity. Fraenkel observed that in 1959 even second- and third-generation Monrovians still identified themselves first and foremost as members of particular tribes.[17] At the present time, however, as many Monrovians live outside the tribal communities as within them. As educated and semiprofessional persons moved outside the tribal communities, there developed a correlation between neighborhood and social status. Areas in which either the Westernized or non-Westernized tribal people predominate are easily recognizable by the type and quality of housing and by the dress of the inhabitants—especially the women, since "civilized" women rarely wear the *lappa*, a distinctly African costume.[18]

Monrovia, then, manifests those characteristics which Aidan Southall describes as the "old towns" and the "new towns" of sub-Saharan Africa.[19] Working townsmen are engaged predominantly in clerical or commercial, rather than industrial occupations (there is little urban industry); there are numerous independent entrepreneurs, largely street vendors and market women; residential patterns are uncontrolled, and housing policies are loosely administered. Monrovia retains many of these characteristics even today. And the tribal communities persist. Thus neighborhoods consisting of ramshackle buildings spring up without regard to health and safety or access to water, electricity, and sewerage.

When the townsman leaves the urban tribal enclave, he moves, in fact and in effect, into the new, modern town. He does so as a civilized man whose legal problems are dealt with in civil as opposed to tribal courts; he lives with his nuclear family if he is married, or he shares lodgings with other "civilized" tribesmen, not necessarily of his own tribe.[20] The new resident of the modern section of Monrovia, however, enters it at the lower rungs of the social ladder, in terms of job status, wages, material possessions, and church congregation.[21]

What becomes of those "members of tribal communities who live in towns but are not townsmen? Who seek industrial employment but, being unskilled, find it only intermittently? Who are "insecure, unstable, surviving by expedients"—a class that Leo Kuper calls the *sous proletariat*?[22] The secularization of their social life necessarily erodes their attachments to tradition and the ability of traditional social organizations to meet their new needs. For example, judicial recourse is circumscribed insofar as the urban tribal chief's authority is limited to cases arising from tribal customary law.[23] Where wage earning and cash commerce involve the majority of people, therefore, the relevance of traditional tribal authority is questionable. Where occupation, income, and educational qualifications determine social status, traditional criteria become even less important.

Tribal affinities may be reinforced, however, even while traditional norms are breaking down.

> The result of social change may be a reincarnation and expansion of communal solidarity rather than an integration of diverse groups. Increased consciousness of group antagonisms and cultural differences [in the multitribal environment]—not increased sentiments of national unity—can be the initial result of modernization.[24]

This statement suggests that urbanization and the loosening of traditional controls will not immediately or even necessarily lead to the subordination of tribal identities to a national one. But a critical point here is that traditionalism, not so-called tribalism, is the primary obstacle to national integration. Indeed, in Liberia's case, the reinforcement of tribal consciousness and loyalty in a modernizing environment may be an unavoidable step, and even a vital contributing step, on the road to political integration. The confluence of tribal identification and modern norms in the urban setting may be witnessed in voluntary tribal associations.[25] These voluntary associations may be viewed as important adaptive and integrative mechanisms in the process of modernization.[26]

Voluntary Associations

As the tribal townsman gives up his responsibility to and reliance upon the authority and support of the tribe in the rural milieu, so he gives up, temporarily at least, the social and economic insurance and security that residence in rural areas bestows. Liberian national institutions are designed to serve broad systems of administration and the modern economy, not the needs of unskilled laborers, petty traders, and small craftsmen.[27] Hence, these institutions afford tribal immigrants few if any intermediate forms of association to replace the traditional community. The new townsman must, therefore, seek on his own to revive or replicate traditional principles of cooperation. The most familiar form of this cooperation is the voluntary tribal association.

Observing that there were over 200 such organizations in Monrovia in 1959, Merran Fraenkel describes the reasons for this plethora of associations, and for membership within them. In the first place, associations are

> another reflection of the general insecurity of life in the capital: mem-
> bership [in] associations is used, as tribal and kinship bonds are, to
> provide a measure of social security. A great number and variety of
> associations include mutual aid—especially burial insurance—among
> their aims. Secondly, Monrovia lacks a formal social structure
> through which [groups of] its citizens might participate in the
> management of their [internal] affairs, and through which they can
> exercise leadership. Many of the associations provide such
> opportunities, and some have, indeed, almost as many office-holders
> as members. The same individuals often hold offices in a number of
> different associations. Thirdly, the multiplicity of associations arises
> from the correspondence of their membership not only with class, but
> also with tribal cleavages in the overall population. Certain types of
> association are formed among the civilized, and membership [in] them
> is a mark of civilized status. Membership [in] organizations of this
> kind usually, but not invariably, cuts across tribal groups. On the
> other hand, associations formed among the less-educated section of

the population are almost always tribally homogeneous in their membership, aligning people of like interests within each of the urban tribal populations.[28]

The *Liberian Yearbook, 1962* acknowledged tribal clubs and associations as "important elements in the social and educational life of the country."[29] In the list of Monrovia associations which followed, both tribal and geographic names were employed. Fraenkel found among their members many with secondary and some college education (none was illiterate). These were "young men who had moved out of the tribal milieu but were not yet members of civilized society."[30] Fraenkel also points out that such associations, unlike the associations of the "civilized," do not as a rule cut across tribal divisions to unify young intelligentsia from different tribes, partly owing to the fragmentary nature of Monrovia's occupational structure and segregated residence patterns.

Tribal associations have largely limited their activities to mutual assistance—e.g., financial help for education or in times of trouble and assistance in finding jobs and housing—social events, and entertainment. A number of them, however, supported candidates in the 1967 election. Such political involvement appears to be limited to election periods. Indeed, some tribal associations seem to have been organized specifically for this purpose. In every case that I have observed, they restricted their interest and support to candidates in their home tribal areas. An exception is the Grand Gedeh Association, which in 1966 demanded that the government establish a teacher-training college in Monrovia. Its members asserted that the Grand Gedeh Association was a political as well as a mutual aid society, observing that the injection of politics was not improper: it would serve to help the government know its needs.[31]

It is difficult to determine how far "politics" of this nature may be allowed to go by the government. There are few residents of Monrovia who are not aware of the tacit limits to tribal-based political activity. That is why urban tribal associations generally restrict their political interests to their tribal home areas. In any case their concern for their erstwhile rural co-tribesmen may well be generated by their members' intentions eventually to return "home." Whatever the motivation or expression, and whatever adaptive, modernizing functions they may serve, most tribal associations in Monrovia primarily direct the feelings of solidarity of urban tribesmen toward tribal, as opposed to urban or national, interests.[32]

Among tribal communities indigenous to the coastal or urban areas are more tightly knit associations, not entirely voluntary in nature. Such a body is the Kru Corporation of Monrovia. It obtained recognition under Liberian law as a "property-owning body" in 1916.[33] Apart from its judicial function of settling disputes among the Kru before they reach the Kru Governor's court, and the usual welfare functions, the Corporation plays its most important role in connection with dock work, the occupational interest of most Krus in Monrovia. For example, the shipping companies place a share of job assignments through the Corporation. In 1958, the Corporation acted as a trade union in a dispute with the shipping companies over wages and working conditions. This long-standing urban association, which has more Kru members than any other association, and is the largest one in Monrovia, is an important force in the Republic, and it apparently is treated as such by the government.[34] In turn, the Kru are often called upon to demonstrate their loyalty to the President, which they invariably do on public occasions.

Another form of tribal association is urban financial savings groups, sometimes called *susu*. The *susu* arrange periodic sharing of the joint savings of their members. The *neklondi*, developed by the Kru, has advanced the *susu* arrangement. It lends its joint savings at interest, often to non-Kru, and then divides up principal and interest at the end of the year.[35] We have seen how the same principle has produced a cooperative enterprise among some rural *kuu* members.

The political potential of urban tribal or savings associations is limited by their narrow social welfare functions and their tendency to divide the urban immigrants according to tribe, rather than to unite them according to their shared lower-class status. Tribal organizations that identify themselves with their rural homelands may act as deterrents to class formation in the urban milieu, since they focus identity on noneconomic relations and blur perceptions of inequality.[36] The government appears to prefer to deal with the relatively apolitical urban tribal entities rather than with groups based on occupation or class.

The ephemeral nature of most tribal associations and their constantly changing membership suggest that such associations do not long remain relevant to most younger town dwellers. Fraenkel writes that when students "finish their studies, establish themselves in 'civilized' occupations, and become more confident of their new status, they are more likely to form friendships in which tribal membership is a minor factor."[37]

Occupational and Elite Associations. Examples of non-tribal associations are the Junior Chamber of Commerce, the Bar Association (dominated by Americo-Liberians, but lately including tribal lawyers), and the National Teachers Association (which is not a trade union, but has expressed itself as an interest group).[38] There also are urban voluntary associations that are reserved almost exclusively to the socially dominant and culturally separate ruling elite. Although the YMCA and the Masons, among others, permit tribal members, few if any tribesmen ever become office-holders. I have never uncovered one tribal name in reports about the elitist social clubs such as the "crowds" and the Hungry Club, which bring together income, age, or civil service rank peers. If there is resentment over exclusion from these social groups, however, the tribal townsmen have not yet manifested it.

Church Congregations. Even when they are members of the same religious denomination, the "civilized" and "uncivilized" do not meet in the same congregations. According to Fraenkel, "the division of the Christian population among the many congregations thus coincides with the dichotomy of the population into 'tribal' and 'civilized' elements, and helps to maintain this dichotomy rather than break it down."[39] She believes that Christianity has created little real unity in the capital, firstly "because of the plethora of denominations operating, secondly because of the correspondence in some of the more important denominations between social status and specific church congregations, and thirdly because the siting of missions has produced a strong correlation between denomination and tribe."[40]

Secret Societies. Poro and Sande persist in Monrovia and, it must be assumed, provide spiritual comfort and social cohesion to those tribal people who practice it. Only the Christian churches have more tribal members. We might ask whether the persistence of these traditional societies would not fortify the tribal population's awareness of cultural apartness from the civilized community; and if so, whether it would not also inhibit the urbanization and integration of young, town dwellers? To the extent that the societies are influential, they probably would. Fraenkel points out, however, that "it is obvious that neither Poro nor Sande can fill their traditional roles in the modern urban social system." It is unlikely, therefore, that they have significant social or political influence there.[41] The stronger social and economic demands of the city, and involvement in modern occupations and activities, have simply made Poro and Sande membership less relevant than it had been in rural Liberia. As secular education reaches more children for longer periods, the relevance of secret societies will probably continue to subside. Such a conclusion, however, must remain most tentative.

To summarize, tribal associations in Monrovia, both secular and religious, owe their existence to the persistent desire for links between urban and rural tribal centers and, above all, to the new townsmen's need of some form of social security and camaraderie in the alien urban milieu. But tribal customs and tradition are not the specific interests of these associations. They have been formed to contend with the new urban environment, the strains it imposes upon the migrant, and the place within its social structure in which the migrants find themselves.

Wage Labor

Wage labor binds more Liberians together into a common reference
group than any other modern activity. It produces highly focused
occupational and class interests which cross tribal, social, and religious
boundaries. I will discuss wage labor in order to answer the questions (1)
Have occupational or class referrents become essential? (2) Do new
attachments preempt traditional group membership? (3) What are the
implications of the answers to these problems for the formation, survival,
and strength of labor unions? To this end I will examine the size, character,
and stability of the wage labor force; the question whether tribal or secret
society membership preempts or inhibits membership in more modern
associations; and the educational levels of wage workers.

Apart from Firestone's work force, which did not reach full strength
until the company began producing in earnest during World War II, the
employment of full-time wage workers on a large scale is a relatively recent
phenomenon in Liberia. There were only 30,000 wage earners in the
country in 1950, of whom 20,000 worked for Firestone.[42] LMC did not
begin production until 1951, LAMCO in 1963. Thus we are, in the main,
examining a period of ten to twenty-five years.

In the earlier stage of Liberia's economic growth, "target-labor" was
dominant among the new wage earners. That is, peasants migrated to
places where they might trade or earn wages, but remained only long
enough to accumulate a predetermined amount of savings for purchasing
land or materials for building a house, for paying taxes, school fees, or bride
price, and the like. If and when wages increased, the worker would reduce
the period of time spent in wage employment. Economists describe this
phenomenon as a "backward-bending supply curve for labor; i.e., the
supply of labor called forth by a higher price at a certain point, instead of
increasing with an increase in wages, bends backward and decreases."[43]

Monrovia's ever-growing population suggests, however, that there is
now a permanent, or at least a semipermanent, work force, as do
Firestone's recent reports that they are troubled less by labor shortages
than they were in the early 1960's. The iron ore mines, which pay the
highest wages for both skilled and unskilled hands, have never suffered
serious shortages; indeed, there is a constant reservoir of manpower
outside the principal mines. It may be surmised, therefore, that in Liberia,
as elsewhere in present-day Africa, a sufficiently attractive or rising
"wage-rate stimulates many more men to emigrate to paid jobs and leads
far fewer to reduce their time in paid employment."[44] Firestone, however,
still reports labor shortages at rice-planting and harvesting seasons, when
many of its workers return home to work their farms. But reemployment
exceeded new hirings in recent years, according to Firestone spokesmen.

The Liberian Department of Planning and Economic Affairs conducted a manpower resource survey in 1965. It characterized the work force as follows: some 41 percent of the population, or 431,000 Liberians (according to the 1962 census), were "economically active," that is, earning wages or self-employed in agriculture or commerce. Of this work force 330,000 members (80 percent) were engaged in agriculture, forestry, hunting, and fishing.[45]

By considering agricultural wage workers as part of the modern economic labor force, we get the picture shown in Table 5. We might add to the total the 30,000 to 35,000 persons without regular or visible employment who reside in Monrovia and near the mines. In spite of poor prospects of obtaining employment in these areas,

the 9,000 workers made jobless by the completion of construction at the Mount Nimba mine and Buchanan harbor in 1963 refused to accept jobs offered them at the Firestone and Goodrich plantations principally because most of them . . . could not [or were unwilling to] live on the lower agricultural wages.[46]

They stayed on near the mines, waiting and hoping to be reemployed. Satellite settlements at Bomi Hills in 1964 and at Nimba in 1967 each had populations of between 5,000 and 10,000. Few of these people then had any visible means of support. Many of them now do business with the miners.

If we assume that workers at the mines and on plantations bring with them families which average three members, including themselves (Firestone reported 60,000 people living on or near the Harbel plantation, including their work force of 18,000 in 1967; LAMCO indicated the same ratio), and include the total population of Monrovia and the major coastal towns, we find in the modern economic sector between 300,000 and 400,000 people. In other words, nearly 30 percent of Liberia's population engage in or depend entirely upon wage labor.

How can we determine the extent of these peoples' commitment to life in the modern economic sector? Part of the answer may be found in data on labor turnover. While published figures do not exist for Monrovia, information is available for the Firestone plantations and several mines.

The rubber plantations have the highest labor turnover rates. Firestone showed an annual rate of about 50 percent in the early 1960's. That is, about half the total labor force had to be replaced every year.[47] Since the introduction of high-yield trees in the late sixties, fewer workers have been required than in the past, and, as noted, the concession was not greatly concerned about labor shortages in 1967. Goodrich also has introduced high-yield trees.

The rubber concessions, therefore, are tending to consolidate and stabilize their work forces. While tappers will probably remain the least

TABLE 5
LIBERIAN WAGE LABOR FORCE, 1967 AND 1969

	1967	1969^e
Agriculture	42,000^a	60,000
Mining	10,000^b	21,000
Manufacturing	9,900^c	12,000
Commerce	13,200	20,000
Construction	9,000	15,000^f
Transportation and communications	4,500^d	8,000
Government (includes public utilities, army, police, and teachers)	16,300	20,000
Total	104,900	156,000

SOURCES: Department of Planning and Economic Affairs, manpower study cited in *Economic Survey, 1969;* U.S. Agency for International Development, "Summary of Basic Data (Liberia)," July 1967; U.S. Embassy reports, 1966–67; Office of National Planning, *Industry in Liberia: Structure and Planning Implications,* Monrovia, August 1965; Rubber Planters Association, interview, 1967.

a A figure of 24,000 workers in rubber concessions, provided by the RPAL, appears high. RPAL also reports 18,000 workers on Liberian-owned plantations. The 42,000 total for agricultural workers may include other agricultural employment, such as forestry, for which figures are not available.

b Probably includes related workers, such as transportation and processing workers at Buchanan.

c This figure also appears to be high, and may overlap with processing industries and transportation associated with rubber, iron, and forest products.

d See b above.

e These official figures are probably high, in view of the depressed economy of the mid-1960's. There was, for example, a cutback in construction. An ILO Mission reported 1970 permanent wage and salary employment as 125,000, broken down as follows: Agriculture, 46,000; Industry, 34,500; Service, 44,500.

f Listed as "Services" by the *Economic Survey, 1969.*

stable element, the 2,300 semiskilled and supervisory personnel at Firestone's Harbel plantation have established impressive records of job tenure: in 1967 over 1,400 had served for more than five years, and 900 had worked ten years or more.[48] These workers are more highly paid than tappers, and escape the drudgery of tapping, carrying latex, and weeding, in which most workers are engaged. Thus, higher wages and status produce a greater willingness to remain in the wage economy.

Firestone may have more steady workers in the near future. Because of falling prices and growing competition from synthetic rubber, the rubber industry throughout the world is seeking to increase productivity and reduce costs by mechanizing and by planting high-yield trees. Both processes demand greater skill from the workers. Rubber producers are reducing the total number of workers needed for a given number of trees, and compensating for the reduction by incentive systems. These facts suggest, therefore, that over the next twenty years, Firestone (and Goodrich) will probably have fewer but more highly skilled and better-paid workers.

Iron ore mines have relatively low rates of labor turnover. LAMCO reported 373 terminations of employment in 1965 and 309 in 1966, of which only 104 and 108, respectively, were voluntary—less than 5 percent of its labor force at the mine.[49] (Data for LAMCO's 1200 employees at the port of Buchanan were not available.) LMC, the only mine with a long enough history to permit a census of its employees' tenure, reported that of 2,200 Liberian employees in 1964, 1,400 had more than five years of service at the mine; of this number, half had ten or more years of service.[50] The miners' low rate of turnover reflects the higher wages they receive as well as their prospect for advancement. LAMCO workers' earnings started at $.17 or $.18 per hour, and ranged as high as $.77 in 1967. About 52 percent of the work force then earned over $.30 per hour.[51] (LMC has roughly similar wage rates.) Miners have the opportunity to work overtime, and many do so at higher hourly rates. Until 1973 Firestone paid most of its wokers only $.08 to $.10 per hour, or an average of $.64 to $.80 per day, plus bonuses for additional work. (Rubber tappers worked on a "task" system until the new incentive system was introduced in 1966; they could complete their work in less than eight hours and still receive a full day's wage. Few of them chose to work more than one task per day.)

Concessions provide most of their workers with free housing and subsidized consumer goods, medical care, and, as required by law, schooling. LAMCO calculates that these benefits double the effective earnings of their employees, which average $118 per month.[52]

Secret Societies Among the Workers. It was noted above that traditional institutions have proved to be of less and less relevance to tribal inhabitants of Monrovia. Where Poro or Sande are practiced, almost unrecognizable variants of the rituals which take place in the tribal areas are produced. This is not the case in modern enclaves outside Monrovia, however. Initiation into the secret societies among the children of employees persists at Firestone and LAMCO. This, no doubt, is made possible by their proximity to the home villages as well as the socially less disruptive modes of life in these enclaves, particularly on the plantations. Both managers and workers at Firestone informed me that most workers still send their children to "bush school," either in their home areas or in specially designated areas bounding the plantation. Although the Swedish management at LAMCO believed that this was not the case with their workers ("otherwise we would notice a decline in school attendance"), I was assured by several workers and Liberian management personnel that Poro training does take place. Generally, the workers wait until secular schools adjourn for vacation before sending their children home for brief Poro or Sande training. Hence, traditional institutions and practices coexist with modern ones. But the former yield to the latter in such mundane matters as the timing and period of indoctrination in bush schools and initiation into the secret societies. They would appear, therefore, not to be a countervailing force to modern forms of association which identify a person according to occupation or class.

   Education Levels of Workers. The largest element in the labor force, the 85,000 to 95,000 unskilled workers on rubber estates, in iron mines, in construction work, and in domestic service, is also the section of the population with the lowest educational or technical qualifications. For example, of 319,000 farmers and lumbermen in 1962—which would include the 42,000 rubber workers—311,600 had had no schooling; and of the remaining 7,400, only 600 had had more than primary schooling.[53] Of nearly 7,000 miners and quarrymen, only 851 had completed any grade of education; and of this number, only 140 had gone beyond primary school. An exception to these low educational attainments is the category "production process and related workers" employed, for example, in processing latex at rubber plantations; as skilled and semiskilled workers at the iron ore mines; in light industry in Monrovia; and at LAMCO's pelletizing and port facilities in Buchanan. Some 15,000 workers of this group had no education, but 5,000 had a primary education, and over 1,000 had some high school education—the highest proportion in any nonprofessional category.[54] These generally low levels of education have limited the prospects of wage laborers to advance in their employment to skilled or even semiskilled levels.

   On the basis of education levels, therefore, urban workers employed in small manufacturing, dock work, transportation, distribution, and other services would appear to be the most amenable to labor organization, followed by the miners and last, again, the rubber workers. But uneducated and illiterate workers have demonstrated their ability to recognize their poor economic conditions often as sharply as do the educated. In Liberia, as elsewhere, they have sustained work-stoppages while their demands for better wages and working conditions were being pressed. But they cannot be expected easily to comprehend the need at times to subordinate their immediate requirements to possibly better *future* conditions. They may only vaguely understand the delays and intricacies of collective bargaining for a few pennies per day which are being worked out at some remote place by representatives in whose election they may not have actively participated. Moreover, the mining and rubber workers are physically cut off from their better-educated, urban fellow workers, who may not fully comprehend the complexities of wage and benefit disputes themselves.

Jobs and the Labor Supply. Their low educational qualifications, and hence their lack of skills, also make Liberian laborers easily replaceable. Given the recent static labor market,[55] their bargaining position must be considered further reduced. For example, in addition to the thousands of apparently unemployed workers living near LAMCO and LMC, there is a reservoir of under- or unemployed workers (perhaps as many as 20,000) in Monrovia. This situation must be attributed at least in part to the contraction in public and private construction which beset Liberia in the last decade. Construction employed nearly 16,000 workers in the early 1960's; in 1967, this activity employed only 9,000. (Later reliable figures are unavailable.) Yet new, unskilled aspirants for employment continue to come to Monrovia at the rate of five to ten thousand per annum.

Rubber and iron ore production appear likely to remain Liberia's economic mainstays for the foreseeable future. Earlier hopes for diversification, in palm products and timber for example, have been disappointed by unstable world prices for these products. And in spite of increased production and export receipts earned from small-grower crops, such as coffee, cocoa, piassava, and palm kernels, they remain less than 3.6 percent of total exports.[56] Plans for the expansion of timber exploitation tend to be linked with another potential iron ore producing area in the Wologisi Range in northwestern Liberia. Offshore oil exploration, which has produced tentative predictions of rich deposits off Liberia's continental shelf, also figure in projections of future sources of exports, government revenues, and employment.[57]

It is not yet certain whether Liberia's economic potential will produce an industrial or a rural proletariat. What does seem likely, however, is that these trends and the government's orientation to large-scale, export-related economic activities will continue to expand wage employment, so that the subsistence sector may virtually disappear over the next thirty to forty years.[58]

Labor Unions

Based on the information presented above, the prospects for labor unions should be quite good. As we have seen, the wage-labor force now consists of some 125,000 to 150,000 people in eighteen major locations (Monrovia: Buchanan: four rubber concessions: five iron ore firms: six timber concessions; and one major oil palm plantation).[59] But in view of the small proportion of Liberians who work full time in the modern economic sector; the low educational and skill levels of the largest component, the agricultural workers (who are difficult to organize even in developed countries); the legal exclusion of civil servants and teachers from forming unions; and the tacit restriction on unionizing rubber workers (by the legal proscription of "industrial" and "agricultural" unions from joining the same national organization), the more or less "organizable" labor force in Liberia must be counted in the region of only 30,000 to 40,000 workers.

Further limiting the potential size and effectiveness of labor unions in Liberia are the paucity of experienced union leaders and of funds to finance the training or even to pay the salaries of such leaders. Liberians also lack experience in democratically operated voluntary associations, and they have not had, until recently, much managerial advice or financial assistance from a metropolitan labor center (which the African movements in the British and French colonies usually enjoyed from the outset). Neither is there a Liberian political movement with which trade unions could join in opposition to an employer-government alliance, as they could in many parts of colonial Africa. A government-employer alliance does exist in Liberia, but is supported by the only political party. Government leaders themselves are employers, on rubber farms and in service industries. Thus, they join the business community in search of plentiful and cheap labor.[60]

It is hardly surprising that labor unions should be weak and fragile in Liberia. Yet, labor unions have existed since 1949, at times with tacit or open government sponsorship. The Labor Union of Liberia was founded in the late 1940's; the Labor Congress of Liberia (LCL) in 1953; and the Congress of Industrial Organizations (CIO) in 1959, arising from a split within the LCL. (The non-CIO faction became largely moribund.) Most of the officers of these organizations have been government officials. The president of the LCL, for example, was President Tubman's social secretary. "Shad" Tubman, Jr., the President's son, was president of the CIO when it finally emerged as the strongest, and apparently a bona fide, labor organization in 1962. The CIO (not related to the American CIO), which is the only viable survivor of these early organizations, claimed in 1967 that its total membership in affiliated unions stood at 16,000.[61] If true, it is an impressive accomplishment.

Membership figures, however, are of limited importance in this study. There is no published information on what would be more interesting, namely the nature of union membership: whether semiskilled or unskilled workers join in greater numbers; whether long-term employees become unions members, or whether, fearing the loss of jobs and tenure, they abstain from union activities because they may no longer have recourse to tribal farms. More significant than numbers are the strikes that have occurred in every industry over the past fifteen years, and the pattern of wage gains won by organized workers during that period. Labor organization is a vital area of social change in Liberia, involving modern kinds of association (i.e., the integration of people of different tribes in associations established for a common cause), and the aggregation and expression of shared economic interests.[62]

Strikes

A labor strike occurred in Liberia as early as 1949, led by Ghanaian garage mechanics. Over the years 1949 to 1961, there were twelve to fifteen strikes, mostly of minor significance.[63] A strike of Kru stevedores in 1958, in which the Kru Corporation played an important role, is one example of how workers may unite without a union. In this case the strikers displayed tribal as well as worker solidarity.[64]

The first major labor trouble occurred in 1961, when some 800 workers at the LAMCO construction project at the Nimba Range organized a wildcat strike. Another strike of some 100 workers at the new Ducor Palace Hotel in Monrovia took place the same year. The strikers demanded higher wages and complained of racial discrimination. While the government quickly rejected workers' demands for higher wages and ended the LAMCO strike, the Monrovia strike was joined by dock workers and others, which led to public demonstrations and some violence. The strike finally ended when President Tubman personally confronted several thousand workers at a public meeting and ordered the arrest of several CIO leaders who were said to have been inciting trouble. Soon afterward there were several small strikes elsewhere in the country, one of which occurred on a Liberian-owned farm, the first against a wholly Liberian-owned enterprise. The government blamed the Monrovia strike and subsequent demonstrations on foreign intervention, and expelled several Ghanaian and Egyptian diplomats.[65]

The Monrovia strike by workers in several kinds of jobs is important as an example of how urban unrest can be welded into mass action. It also revealed that the government regarded organized labor's potential as principally political rather than economic. The government broke the Monrovia strike by the carrot-and-stick technique: Tubman promised the strikers consideration of their grievances and ultimately appointed an ad hoc commission to investigate ways and means of solving labor problems; at the same time, the Legislature provided the President with emergency powers, and troops were at the ready to put down the strike forcibly. But the strike and demonstrations were also noteworthy for the apparent ease with which workers had mobilized mass action, even though it was not only illegal but daringly defiant of the government and of President Tubman personally.

Liberia's largest strike took place from July 2 to 14, 1963, at Firestone's Harbel plantation. Initially involving some 9,500 rubber-tree tappers, and later swelling to 20,000 employees, the strike spread over all forty-five divisions of the plantation. This strike demonstrated, above all, that large numbers of workers of different tribes could be organized secretly and efficiently to strike against Liberia's largest employer. And they did so without any sort of formal organization: rubber workers did not have a union. It has never been revealed, if it was ever known, who the strike leaders were. CIO leaders were seen on the plantation only *after* the strike began; yet the government blamed them for its occurrence. The strike closed down operations at Harbel and resulted in the suspension of purchases of latex from independent growers. Government leaders were understandably concerned by the consequences of this strike, including the loss of revenues from its then principal source. Not until the government put down the strike did Vice-President William Tolbert's intercession with Firestone produce an agreement with the workers and the resumption by Firestone of rubber purchases from private producers.[66]

The government's earlier mild interest in the activities of labor unions quickened at these events, apparently aiming to head off the formation of an independent labor movement. President Tubman had appointed his son, "Shad," Jr., as President of the CIO in 1960, and the government, aided by a $5,000 donation from LAMCO, had provided the CIO with a building for its headquarters.[67] But only in 1963 did legislation provide for the establishment and regulation of labor unions and for collective bargaining between employers and employees. The new laws also provided for government mediation of labor disputes: strikes were to be considered legal only after a government commission had determined that workers' demands were valid, and then only if management still refused to submit to the demands. The Labor Commission met for the first time in 1966. Thus, all strikes between 1963 and 1966 were technically illegal.

These labor laws were employed not only as an economic regulatory instrument of the government. In conjunction with the emergency powers which the Legislature accorded the President during the 1961 Monrovia strike, they were a political response to what the government apparently regarded as political disloyalty and foreign subversion, rather than as evidence of economic discontent.[68]

Yet, the government's attitude regarding labor unions was ambivalent. On the one hand, it did not wish to see too strong an interest group develop outside its control. On the other hand, Liberian leaders wished at least to appear to place the welfare of indigenous workers above that of foreigners, particularly when they came to realize how much concession agreements had benefited foreign interests at Liberia's expense. During CIO-LMC wage negotiations in 1964, LMC managers claimed that the government was supporting the union in order to put pressure upon the LMC to renegotiate its concession agreement. (This accusation was made during the first round of renegotiations with most foreign concessions that took place in 1964 under International Monetary Fund auspices and that were aimed at mitigating Liberia's fiscal difficulties.) Furthermore, international pressures and adverse publicity had made the government quite sensitive about past labor practices and its official tolerance of recruitment of non-voluntary labor. Partly in response to such pressures and publicity, the government passed amendments to the Labor Practices Law in 1966 which so restricted involuntary labor recruitment that it was virtually outlawed, and sought to protect workers by regulating employment contracts.[69]

The government's belated efforts to rectify certain employment malpractices also led to the establishment of a National Labor Affairs Agency, first under the Department of Commerce, and later, in May 1967, as a separate executive agency. (The Secretary of Commerce, Romeo Horton, was notoriously unsympathetic to organized labor.) The last few years have witnessed a renewal of independent trade union activity and a new rash of strikes. The strains imposed by these activities have clearly revealed that the government has changed but little in its suspicion of independent trade union activity and its fear of the political power that organized labor might wield. ("Shad" Tubman, Jr., had left the CIO in 1964. CIO leadership came thereafter from within the union, though the government probably had influence with the figure-head president of the CIO, Susan Berry, the Social Secretary of the Montserrado County True Whig Party.)

There were five major labor disputes in 1966. On February 1, 1966, without prior warning, the entire tapping force at the Firestone plantation at Harbel went on strike. Five strike leaders, calling themselves the Negotiating Committee of the Liberian Workers Association, summed up the strikers' demands for a minimum daily wage of $1.25 (they were getting $.64) in a letter to the Secretary of Commerce and Industry.[70] They contended that, in addition to normal tapping, workers were in fact performing 5,500 hours of unpaid labor each year. During the strike, destruction of latex and trees, and some personal violence, occurred at Firestone. Even after President Tubman assured the workers' representatives that there would be no punishment for the strikers and that the government would consider their demands, the strike continued. In fact, the striking workers set upon the five leaders when the latter returned with a letter from the President; the workers claimed that the letter was not on presidential stationery. A second letter delivered by the President's aide-de-camp and a visit by Shad Tubman, Jr., failed to stem the disorder. The strike was finally put down by riot police and army units.

Rubber workers at the African Fruit Company (AFC) plantation in Sinoe County also struck a few days after the Firestone strike. A presidential letter promising arbitration convinced the workers to return to their jobs. In both these strikes, which were technically illegal, since the workers had not requested government arbitration, the government acted with restraint where it might legally have sought to end the stoppages immediately by force. Moreover, no punitive action was taken against strike leaders at either plantation. The strikers' petitions to the government clearly expressed the *economic* grievances of workers, who considered themselves to be inadequately remunerated for their labor; and in the case of the African Fruit Company workers, they included complaints about inadequate transportation to and from work, having to pay for their own tools, and insufficient fringe benefits.[71]

I have seen no evidence of Firestone's or AFC's response to the workers' demands. Instead, a "Memorandum Submitted to the Secretary of Commerce and Industry by the Rubber Planters Association of Liberia" seems to have placed the case of the entire industry before the government.[72] The Memorandum neither answered nor denied the Firestone workers' claims. It baldly asked that "the recent illegal strike," a result of "unknown influences," be put in the perspective of the possible "industry-wide" impact of any decision to increase the basic wage. Employing cost-productivity figures of private Liberian farms—not Firestone—the Memorandum concluded that "any increase in labor costs unrelated to increased productivity will spell ruin for an appreciable number of Liberian owned farms."

The Labor Practices Review Board decided to allow a daily wage increase from $.64 to $.68 for AFC tappers. This became the standard wage throughout the industry. The Board argued that the workers' wage demands were "neither practical nor justified . . . considering the overall cost of rubber production and the constant shrinking of rubber prices in the world market."[73] In Firestone's case the Board recommended that an incentive system (which had been started in several divisions) be extended to all divisions of the plantation within ninety days. Certain fringe services and benefits demanded at AFC were also accepted by the LPRB.

It would appear that these strikes finally persuaded Firestone and the government of the desirability of organizing an agricultural trade union. The Liberian Rubber Tappers Association had all the earmarks of a "company union," that is, it was as much an instrument of management as of the workers.

In July 1966, LAMCO workers launched a wildcat strike in spite of having agreed to a wage contract earlier that year. The mine was almost completely shut down for one week. The President once again appealed for a return to work and the submission of grievances to the government. A number of strikers refused to return to work and were expelled from the mine compound. Government troops eventually put down the strike, and three leaders of the National Mine Workers Association were jailed. The strike itself had little apparent basis in employee grievances—it was called suddenly and without consultations within the union membership or with management.[74] A Swedish television crew, which happened to be on hand, filmed the intervention by government troops. The final TV version highlighted the cooperation of the government and Swedish management in suppressing the strike and jailing strike leaders. In Sweden, where the film was exploited by the governing party's left wing, trade unions, and the more radical press, the incident was a source of great embarrassment to the Grängesberg Corporation, which manages and holds a share in LAMCO. Criticism of Grängesberg's part in putting down a strike by force persisted through 1967. (Elections were due in Sweden in 1968; and in 1967 the Riksdag was debating an investment guarantee act which the Left opposed.) There appears to have been a clear connection between the uproar in Sweden and a subsequent peaceful settlement of wage negotiations between the CIO and LAMCO in June 1967 in which the union won most of its wage demands. The 1967 agreement also served to enhance the CIO's hold on the Mine Workers Association at LAMCO.

Two other strikes occurred in 1966: at the National Iron Ore Company (NIOC) mine at Mano River, and on the Goodrich rubber plantation between Monrovia and Bomi Hills. The latter strike completely shut down the Goodrich operation for several days, and required police intervention.[75] There were also during 1966–67 a number of collective bargaining settlements between CIO-affiliated unions and several oil companies, six

garages and the Ducor Palace Hotel, as well as the LAMCO agreement.
And in December 1966 the Labor Bureau helped to produce a wage
agreement between the LMC and the CIO for mine workers at Bomi Hills.

The CIO also began to enter actively into the internal affairs of certain
of its affiliates, where local officers appeared to be misusing union funds or
violating the rights of its members. While it was successful in replacing
officers of the United Mineworker Association at LMC, similar efforts to
control the Transport Workers Union in Monrovia caused that union to
break with the CIO.

The CIO had, in 1967, union affiliates at the two principal iron ore
mines, including 1,200 LAMCO workers at Buchanan, and at a third, the
Bong mine (opened in 1965) operated by the German-Liberian Mining
Company (DELIMCO). The CIO also claimed to have affiliated unions at
all petroleum terminals in Monrovia, except the Italian AGIP, and among
construction, garage, airline, and a handful of restaurant and domestic
workers. The CIO claimed in mid-1967 to have 5,000 members in the latter
category and 7,000 to 8,000 at the mines.

Conclusions

In barely twenty years, from 1950 to 1970, the face of Liberia's social
map changed dramatically. Over one-fourth of a largely rural population
became urban or semiurban (if plantations and mines as well as trading
towns and county capitals may be so considered). For these 300,000 to
400,000 people, indirect rule had given way to central government
administration; they had become directly involved in the modern economy
and had achieved access to modern social services. Tribal horizons had
been expanded to permit social, occupational, and residential mixing with
peoples of other tribes and even with Americo-Liberians and foreigners.
While tribal associations persisted, they had become oriented not to the
preservation of tribal identities and structures, but to contending with
urban problems and, in some cases, to representing members' interests in
the national political arena.

The cultural context also changed as one moved from the tribal
community to the tribal association or labor union. One worked for cash;
one's land or property was personal, not communal; and one's associations
with others were based increasingly upon occupational and class identities,
not merely ethnic ones. Even church attendance distinguished groups
socially and religiously, as well as culturally, from those of their urban and
rural tribal brethren who continued to practice traditional beliefs and
rituals.

Much has been written of the alienation of the new African townsmen or *sous proletariat*. In the quest for a new identity, for new sources of security and authority, many such people turn their attention to their employers and to intermediary social and economic institutions. Ultimately, their quest is in the political sphere. Insofar as political institutions develop to meet these needs, even if only to contain or constrain them—the working out of new sets of rules, conditions of wage employment, social services, law and order, and eventually participation in associations supporting or opposing the rules—the fate of the socially mobilized Liberian is ultimately determined in the political system.

— 6 —

Political Modernization

As the population became more urban and the economy expanded in the fifties and sixties, the business of governing the country became more complex. The regime had to manage the revenues which had enriched the Treasury beyond anyone's dreams; to treat with the interior, now linked to the coast economically as well as by all-weather roads; to contain the power of foreign investors upon whom the country's economy, including most public revenues and wage labor, depended; and to handle popular demands, increasingly political in consequence, for a greater share in the nation's material wealth.

As noted in the Introduction, a regime that wishes to survive the social mobilization of its citizenry and the formation of class perceptions and interests must modernize. Political modernization is, therefore, as likely to be a response to economic and social changes as it is a blueprint for change. That was the case in Liberia.

The following chapters suggest that although the Tubman regime may have begun to modernize only for "defensive" reasons, modernization, once launched, transformed the traditional rules of the game. Chapters 6 and 7 examine Tubman's fourth and fifth terms (1960–68) and the transformation of the institutions and underlying norms that had supported Americo-Liberian dominance in the past. Chapters 8 and 9 focus on the consequent changes in the bureaucracy, and the expansion of the educational and communications systems. Chapter 10 describes the transition of Liberia's foreign policy from an orientation toward the United States and Europe to an orientation toward Liberia's place in an independent Africa, as well as in the wider international community. Chapter 11 discusses the countervailing forces which came first from the Americo-Liberian elite, then from dissident elements outside it, and finally, in Tubman's last term (1968–71), from his own efforts to contain the forces unleashed by modernization—what I call "retrenchment."

Institutions of Government

A visitor to Liberia is likely to be impressed by the many government buildings constructed in the Tubman era, which stand amidst the jerry-built slums of Monrovia. The lavish Florida-hotel-style Executive Mansion is a symbol of national pride as well as a testimonial to its occupant's grandeur. The Supreme Court building, and the Capitol, which houses the Senate and the House of Representatives, might seem to testify to a nation's dedication to the rule of law and to representative institutions; but the institutions they house are merely the instruments, not the foundations, of that system.

Liberia's national emblem bears the words inscribed over 100 years ago: "The Love of Liberty Brought Us Here." This motto has been of questionable relevance to the indigenous tribal people whose liberty was hardly enhanced by the arrival of the settlers. The constitution adopted in 1847, and other statutes, had long principally expressed the will and served the interests of the descendants of the settlers and a few assimilated tribesmen. Moreover, where the law and the interests of the ruling elite were in conflict, the law tended to be disregarded, loosely interpreted, or amended, thanks to the pliable nature of the legislative and judicial branches of government. But it is precisely against this background that Liberia's development can best be understood. For if any group enjoyed an "evolution of privilege,"[1] it was the formerly excluded tribal people, who under Tubman began to play a more important role in and to receive more equitable treatment from the formal structures of government.

The Presidency under Tubman

The centralization of political power, and its personalization in Tubman, were the most crucial political developments of Tubman's first ten years in office. He tried, quite successfully, to restrain all independent sources of power. For one thing, he undertook at first to write *all* official checks over $25 (later $100). His personal "green letter" appointing or dismissing civil servants became the single most important source of patronage. His personal signature on *every* transaction involving the sale of land was the passport to wealth and local power for those who wished to acquire land along the primary roads and near the larger concessions. His surveillance of the educational system and particularly of students going abroad on government and foreign scholarships made clear to the young where their lot was being decided. (Students returning from abroad were almost always summoned to an audience.) Through his appointments and favors Tubman manipulated the functioning of departments throughout the government. He maintained at least indirect control of the tribal people by appointing chiefs or, at a minimum, endorsing candidates in tribal elections, and by overseeing the regulation of Poro. In short, his politics were aimed first at enhancing his personal power and limiting opposition to it. If this were the sum of Tubman's record, however, then it would not be especially noteworthy. But the forces his economic and social policies unleashed, and his political responses to them, distinguish his administration from the more repressive variety of authoritarian rule.

Though the power concentrated in Tubman's hands was great, it was not unlimited. Power struggles in the past, and the ousting of previous presidents, sometimes violently, show that disaffected groups within the elite were not powerless. Thus, the absence of effective opposition to Tubman indicates that he was a master at sensing and manipulating political relationships.

Tubman's Cabinet

It would be illuminating if one could determine by the membership of Tubman's cabinet at a given time which element was preeminent, if any, and which individuals constituted his inner circle of advisers. It is difficult, however, to identify any dominant group or independent political orientation, owing to Tubman's frequent reshuffling of the cabinet, which grew from eight members in 1947 to thirteen in 1969. Few members lasted more than one term. In 1971 only Postmaster McKinley DeShield remained from Tubman's first administration. It was never even reasonable to speculate that any of the members of the cabinet enjoyed Tubman's special confidence or approval, or his tacit preference for the heir-apparent. William Tolbert, Tubman's Vice-President for five terms, and now President, enjoyed seniority but few of the political perquisites attending it. In spite of the positions of his brothers—Frank, a senior Senator from Montserrado County, and Stephen, the Secretary of Agriculture in the mid-1960's—William Tolbert was regarded by most observers as having modest political potential. From his fourth term on, Tubman invariably designated Secretary of State Rudolph Grimes as acting Chief Executive during his frequent absences from Liberia, rather than Vice-President Tolbert. The reason probably was that Grimes, unlike the Tolberts, had not sought to construct an independent base of power and was clearly loyal to the President, and not that Tubman was grooming Grimes for the presidency.

Tubman's cabinets usually contained representatives of the principal regional and family groupings within the elite, who sometimes appeared to share common political outlooks. Yet mutual sympathies did not create blocs or alliances, perhaps because cabinet members and their families owed their ascendancy more to Tubman's sponsorship than to their status as established Americo-Liberians. There were, however, what may be loosely described as an older, conservative element, and a younger, more progressive element. The former clearly recognized that their political power was the source of the well-being of their class as well as themselves and generally were unprepared to see it whittled away. Their attitude was shared by such establishment leaders as House Speaker Richard Henries, Senator Frank Tolbert, and Supreme Court Justice A. Dashward Wilson.

Members of the conservative group, who were of Tubman's generation and were sometimes considered to have been his cronies, held the majority of high offices in the government. But their numerical majority was overshadowed by the fact that key ministries, such as Economic Planning, the Treasury, and Education, were from 1964 on in the hands of relatively young and highly educated men such as Cyril Bright, James M. Weeks, Charles D. Sherman, John Payne Mitchell, and Augustus F. Caine, who held cabinet posts at various time. Grimes, though somewhat older, had more in common with these younger officials than with the old members of the cabinet since he, like them, had been educated abroad. These "new men" were generally better able to influence Tubman in cabinet meetings owing to their competence.

The more progressive cabinet officers, and perhaps the majority of subcabinet officials by the late sixties, were those with "modern" qualifications, such as Western education and technical competence in their jobs. These accomplishments often superseded, or at least supplemented, family influence. While members of such prestigious families as DeShield, Bright, Morgan, Wilson, Parker, and others were often found as department heads within the government, so were the less well connected.

At the middle levels in several departments there was an important "workhorse" group of young civil servants who kept the government's wheels turning. Their official rank does not suggest the important responsibilities they bore. They were, on the average, thirty-five years of age (when the average age of the cabinet was about forty-eight); they had been educated overseas; and they were competent and progressive.

Within the cabinet, tribal origin, unlike education, was not necessarily a measure of representative or modernizing tendencies. Tribal people had held cabinet and other high governmental positions in the past, both before and under Tubman. For example, two vice-presidents and two chief justices of the Supreme Court had tribal backgrounds; former Secretary of State Momolu Dukuly, an adviser to President Tubman, was a Mandingo; the late Nathaniel Massequoi, former Secretary of Public Instruction (now

Education) was a Vai, to name only the most prominent. Several cabinet officials in 1968 had tribal antecedents, for example Grimes, whose mother was a Vai, but only Augustus Caine and Secretary of Public Works Alexander Ketter were "pure" tribesmen. This tribal infiltration into high office did not signify a shift of power, for these so-called tribesmen had in fact become members of the coastal elite, and were so considered by both tribal people and Americo-Liberians. Neither his Vai heritage, his youth, nor his relatively modern and liberal orientation protected Caine from accusations by a group of students of having "gone over" to the ruling establishment.

By balancing geographical, family, ethnic, and age groups within his cabinet, Tubman managed to keep power in his own hands. The one common denominator in the cabinet was loyalty to Tubman, the man and the President. Members whose loyalty came under suspicion were promptly removed. Christian A. Cassell, a self-styled liberal, a True Whig Party leader, a prominent Mason, and a friend of Tubman, served as Attorney General from 1944 to 1957. However, when he criticized Tubman's acceptance of a fourth term in 1959, he fell out of favor. He later regained Tubman's confidence, became his advisor on African affairs, and served at numerous international conferences. But after he criticized the Liberian judicial system at a conference of African jurists he was dismissed from his post and was disbarred by the Supreme Court.[2]

Tubman not only did not welcome criticism, he was extremely wary lest members of his official family construct their own power bases. For example, Secretary of Defense Harrison Grigsby, an Americo-Liberian, had fashioned an informal following of members of the Kru tribe in his home county, Sinoe, and in Monrovia, and had become a popular figure among the new generation of Western-educated Liberians during the early 1960's.[3] Tubman dismissed him in 1963 for having failed to uncover a purported army plot against the President. Grigsby was subsequently cleared of this charge, and reentered the political arena as the newly elected Senator from Sinoe County in 1967. His vindication and political reinstatement appear to have occurred because of the disquiet aroused among the Kru in Monrovia and Sinoe County, not because Tubman desired to redress an injustice.[4]

In spite of the limitations upon the political activities of cabinet members, cabinet posts carried prestige and status owing to the officeholder's proximity to the President and to the patronage and commercial opportunities that derived from an official position. Moreover, cabinet officers could win some measure of prominence by managing their departments well. The administration of departments with a thousand or more employees, such as the Treasury and Public Works, or budgetary expenditures of over $7 million in education and $4 million in health (in 1966), conferred substantial responsibility, hence power, upon these cabinet heads. Finally, as the increasingly complex business of governing a country in the throes of economic change eventually prevented Tubman from maintaining his former day-to-day surveillance, the importance of the cabinet gradually increased.

Representative Institutions

In 1946 suffrage was extended to women and to tribal people who held property, i.e., real estate, including a hut on which they paid a tax. The division of the hinterland into counties in 1964 and the assignment of a certain number of representatives from each county increased tribal representation in the legislature. Prior to that time the hinterland provinces held six of the thirty-nine seats in the House of Representatives and none in the Senate. The four hinterland counties now have two senators each, that is, eight out of a total of eighteen; and four representatives each in the House, that is, sixteen out of a total of fifty-two. There also are four tribal representatives from the coastal "territories." Although the 1964 rearrangement gave the hinterland counties 30 percent of the House seats, their inhabitants comprised 47 percent of the population. The constitutional prescription for one representative for each 10,000 people is not yet being met, but the basis for just representation has been established.

The House of Representatives and the Senate were virtual rubber stamps of President Tubman, and all of its incumbents were members of the True Whig Party. There has not been in recent history any serious opposition from either chamber to the President, particularly on important issues; and no major law has been passed owing to parliamentary initiative. Nonetheless, the legislature became under Tubman a body of politicians who were prominent in their counties and regions, and included a number of chiefs and high-ranking Poro officials. Legislators held office at least partly in recognition of their local leadership; they could keep it as a reward for their loyalty to the ruling establishment or specifically to the President. A 1952 account described the lawmakers as follows: "Senators and Representatives are not actually the electees of the people but friends of the President; their favor is sought after, their enmity is dreaded."[5] A number among them hold considerable power at the local level. Their official positions have afforded them great prestige, commercial opportunities, and influence in their home counties through patronage and other forms of largesse at their disposal.

House Speaker Richard Henries, President Pro-Tempore of the

Senate James N. Anderson, and Senator Frank Tolbert were core members of the ruling establishment. They even had considerable influence over President Tubman. In 1964, for example, it became known that Tubman was preparing to make extensive changes in his cabinet, apparently at the expense of the conservative "old guard." Henries, Anderson, and Tolbert, along with Chief Justice Wilson and Postmaster General and TWP General Secretary DeShield, in a heated confrontation with Tubman, dissuaded him.[6]

Legislators, particularly senators, often exercise power in their home counties in an executive style, notwithstanding the paramount official position of the County Superintendent, who is a direct appointee and personal representative of the President. There are frequent conflicts between these officials. For example, in Bong County, four county officials were suspended and temporarily jailed in 1967 for "stirring up the chiefs against the constituted authorities of Bong County."[7] In fact, these county officials had been acting on behalf of the local Senator—a long-time resident, but not a native of Bong County—to discredit the recently appointed Kpelle Superintendent, in what can only be considered a struggle for political supremacy. The decision made by the Department of Interior to side with the County Superintendent against a well-known establishment figure was not lost upon the tribal people of Bong County, nor, it may be assumed, on the old guard.[8]

Elections

Election frauds and inadequate enforcement of electoral laws were commonplace early in this century. For example, in the 1927 election, in which the qualified electorate was only 15,000, the opposition People's Party presidential candidate won 9,000 votes, and incumbent President Charles King, the True Whig Party candiate, claimed a return of 243,000 votes.[9] This bizarre result was not without precedent. After some 6,000 persons had been qualified, as property-owners, to vote in the 1923 election, King won with 45,000 votes.[10] Manipulation of the legal and electoral processes are evident in Tubman's victories as well: in 1951, when the opposition candidate (a Kru) was forced to flee the country; in 1955, when the legislature outlawed the major opposition parties "because of their dangerous, unpatriotic, unconstitutional, illegal, and conscience-less acts"; and in 1959, when Tubman obtained 530,472 votes against his opponent's 55.[11]

In the presidential election of 1967, in which he was unopposed, Tubman won an unprecedented 567,000 votes.[12] There were 600,000 people of voting age according to the 1962 population census.[13] Observers in hinterland towns reported numerous cases of multiple voting. Election day was one of great pageantry, and the opportunity to vote time and again for President Tubman was obviously one way of expressing high spirits as well as support for a revered leader. One Liberian official put it in a somewhat different way:

> There will be no need for "any feverish last-minute rechecking of the votes; no demand for a recount; no sour expression of surprise or vexation on the part of the opposition when the name of the winner is announced." Liberians prefer leaving this experience to other peoples and countries, not because they do not believe in the democratic process, "but we are sensible enough to realize that when we are blessed with a type of leadership in quality unsurpassed in our continent we should hang on [to] it."[14]

Vice-President Tolbert unaccountably received some 3,800 fewer votes than Tubman.

Although participation in electoral processes was a sharp break from the past for thousands of Liberians, I do not wish to make too much of its socializing effects. Whether political cynicism or political trust is the product of such electoral experience is moot. It may, however, be the beginning of a process of politicization which, when accompanied by economic and social changes, will have great impact on representative institutions and ultimately the entire system of government.

The Judiciary

Even more than the legislative branch, the judiciary has historically been subordinate to the executive; constitutionally, it is subordinate to the legislature as well. The Constitution provides that the legislature may impeach judges and, by a two-thirds vote, authorize the President to remove them from the bench (Art. LV, Sec. 1). A Supreme Court Justice who had protested publicly against this form of political control and the attendant abuse of judicial powers was removed from the Court in 1914 under this proviso.[15] Two other justices were removed in 1957 by the same means.[16] Raymond Buell's description of the judicial system in 1928 appears to apply to the Tubman era as well: "In cases involving the government, it is difficult for a Liberian to get justice from any court because of the interference of the executive. No lawyer in Monrovia . . . would dare to apply for an injunction against a prominent government official."[17] Except for some local magistrates in the hinterland and a few lawyers of tribal background, the law and the judiciary appear to be the last stronghold of traditional Americo-Liberian social and legal authority over tribal people in the modern sector. Where the tribal systems of justice, which apply only in the hinterland, conflict with "civilized" law, they give way to the latter.

Local Government

Just as the central government is an instrument of the ruling elite, the county and district administrations are instruments of the central government (and the True Whig Party). The following description of the administration of Bassa County in the early 1950's probably represents quite fairly the style of administration in most coastal counties throughout much of Liberia's history.

> The true representative of the President in Bassa County is the Superintendent. He resides at Bassa [Buchanan?] and bestirs himself only to visit his *farms* or to go to Monrovia (to attend patriotic celebrations, to make the necessary obeisances to an all-powerful and willful master, and to give his account of malpractices before his personal enemies transform them into public scandals). This tactic is indispensable, since the Superintendent is chosen by the President, and is assigned, paid (the insignificant sum of $80 per month), and removable by him at will.[18]

Since tax collection and revenue disbursement have always been the responsibility of the central government, the county administration has no statutory source of income apart from central government subventions and such ad hoc levies as the "development tax" (introduced in 1964) for local self-help projects, or special collections for presidential visits or birthdays and the like. Under Tubman, these local taxes were levied by the county or district councils, nonstatutory bodies of chiefs, notables, and county and central government officials. Collections of local levies were haphazard and expenditures not well-regulated or audited. During a visit to Bong County in 1967, for example, I learned that there had been no development levy collection since 1965. When I asked why, the County Superintendent stated that "the people do not like it." Several local residents subsequently informed me that after the first levy was collected by the newly appointed Superintendent, rumors spread that he had "eaten" the monies. He allegedly had purchased a farm and constructed several buildings in Gbarnga, the county seat, in that year. A similar episode occurred in Nimba County. This time the Superintendent apparently retained a portion of the money collected for the President's birthday celebration. He was subsequently suspended.

As is the case elsewhere in Africa, the chief regional official stands above local officials, including the many local representatives of central government departments, e.g., Public Works, Education, and Agriculture. But the latter are directly responsible to their own departments and receive their appropriations and salaries from them. While the County Superintendent may seek to influence such expenditures, he cannot control them. Deprived, therefore, of power of the purse, the County Superintendent's political power is limited. Yet, because he is a personal representative of the President and may communicate directly with him; and because he oversees tax collections and is the chief legal officer in the county, commanding the local police and holding court, his wishes may not be lightly dismissed by a central government official without the backing of the department secretary.

There are no elected county officials. There are two appointed advisory bodies that are supposed to work with the County Superintendent. The Executive Council meets annually to consider broad administrative questions. Its membership includes the Superintendent, his deputies (called county commissioners) and their assistants, revenue agents, Frontier Force commanders, and leading local personages, usually specially invited tribal dignitaries. A larger body, the Consultative Board, which meets monthly, coordinates county services. Its members are the Executive Council and the county representatives of central government departments. Both of these bodies are subordinate to the County Superintendent and, depending upon his character, he may dominate them completely.[19] While the various local councils might be considered to have some representative function, they more often serve appointed officials by giving information or instructions to the people and by announcing new levies, for example, for militia uniforms, or the construction of a school or a medical clinic.

Political disputes between local officials were usually referred directly to President Tubman. If many people were involved or if the case was very serious, a special meeting of the Executive Council, at which the President presided, was held in the county capital. In his last term Tubman delegated much of this judicial authority to senior government officials. The Vice-President, the Speaker of the House, and the Chief Justice often visited the hinterland to deal with local grievances.

In spite of the increasing presence of central government officials in the hinterland, chiefs retained their positions as tribal judicial authorities with responsibility for land, marriage, divorce, and the like. The central and county governments did not greatly impinge upon their legal and moral authority. Several chiefs informed me that they welcomed the county system. Owing to the greater proximity of the county administration they were required to travel to Monrovia less frequently for the adjudication of serious disputes.

The counties, however, had little political autonomy. They fed on the central government in a vast patronage network that provided, for example, a traffic court judge in a township with fewer than forty automobiles. Three years after the counties were established a new array of officials, including court officers, clerks and constables, revenue officers, four classes of traffic judges and recorders, and magistrates and associate magistrates had already inundated the small offices that were formerly those of the provincial commissioners. The mountain of government checks at county headquarters at the end of each month (for teachers as well as other functionaries) was evidence of the central government's grip on the county administration and its officials.

The very limited form of local government was also not democratic. The only elected local officials were chiefs. But it may become more representative over time. There have recently been suggestions that local governments should be elected.[20] Thus far, government by tribal chiefs has been augmented by party and bureaucratic cadres. Most rural-based civil servants were native to their areas. A number of chiefs were also TWP officers. Together these groups were the local surrogates of the central government. But they were also increasingly representative of and responsive to people who perceive political life as a local, regional, or tribal affair. This development, moreover, gave scope at the local level to those whose eyes and appetites formerly would have fastened on Monrovia. Their advancement, however, depended upon adherence to the rules of the national political system and their loyalty to the President, the party, and the government. The new counties system, therefore, has brought national politics to the local level; political favors, party selection of representatives to the legislature, presidential justice, and dispensation of patronage have a new locus in the county capitals, and the national political community has been enlarged through the addition of diverse ethnic and regional interests.

Security—Internal and External

Scholars still debate the question raised in the 1960's: does the military play a progressive or conservative role in modernization in the developing countries?[21] Neither a single answer nor much comfort can be had from the activities of the military in a number of African countries in the past ten years. Samuel P. Huntington, correctly I believe, looks for the answer in the way that political institutions work in the society.[22] Like most political institutions in Liberia, the military and other security forces reflect the society and the system that they serve. They are at once conservative and modernizing.

Noted in the past for their crude and often cruel use of force, the security forces under Tubman became more restrained and professional (owing in part to United States assistance and training beginning in 1961). Although they are hardly well-disciplined or efficient, they have fulfilled the security functions required of them. Because Liberia has enjoyed peaceful relations with her neighbors the external defense requirements of the Liberian National Guard (LNG—the successor to the Liberian Frontier Force) have been small. Hence, the LNG, rather than the weaker and smaller national police force, has become Liberia's principal constabulary force.

The LNG, several secret or semi-secret security services developed by Tubman during his presidency, and the regular police have maintained law and order—there are few major crimes—and have kept the Liberian population politically cautious, if not cowed, and potential opposition disorganized. Moreover, during the Tubman era Liberia's prisons were reputed to be harshly punitive. Prisoners supposedly left Belle Yella prison only after they died. There is evidence that this was not true, but the rumor entered into folklore, and it has never been publicly repudiated. It may be that the hint of terror was intended to deter unlawful civil and political activities.

Tubman employed a vast network of Public Relations Officers (PRO's) and other secret informers who, together with the array of public officials responsible to him, identified for him his potential enemies, real or imagined. Yet Liberia was not a police state under Tubman. In fact, expression of dissent was permitted if it did not directly attack the President or other government leaders.[23] There appears to have been a tacit understanding of the limits of such dissent; and from time to time real or contrived cases of sedition were reported in the press, perhaps as a reminder.

The 1,100 member national police force, which was first organized in 1924, has been the least effective defender of internal security. In addition to the larger force in Monrovia, there were small contingents of county police throughout the country, under the jurisdiction of the Monrovia headquarters. They were usually subject to direction from the County Superintendent, at least in respect to minor breaches of the peace.

The National Bureau of Investigation (NBI), the Special Security Service (SSS), and the National Intelligence and Security Service (NISS)—the three principal internal security services—were directly responsible to President Tubman who founded them; their operating budgets came under Executive Mansion allocations. The NBI, whose chief function was to protect the President and other government luminaries, had offices in several county capitals, and its officers traveled to the interior when investigations of major crimes were required. In 1970, the Bureau had a strength of 111 men.[24] Its budget was smaller than that of the SSS, which had the largest budget of the three in 1970—$459,000. Its precise functions were not made public. The NISS, evidently smaller, had a budget of $329,000 in 1971. The most secret of the services, it alone among government agencies did not publicly list its officers apart from its Director and Deputy Director.

The armed forces consist of the National Guard, a small Coast Guard, and a militia. The militia is not a regular standing force, but meets periodically for rather casual training and drills; it is a ramshackle organization of 20,000 men. The Liberian National Guard, a force estimated in 1971 to have 3,000 to 4,000 men, is the country's principal defense and security force.[25] Apart from its brief and not very creditable performance with the United Nations in the Congo in 1961, the LNG has been called to action only to put down domestic disturbances, such as the Monrovia strike in 1961, and the Firestone, Goodrich, and LAMCO workers' strikes in 1966.

The officer corps, formerly the preserve of Americo-Liberians, like everything else, began to open its ranks to tribal members in the early 1960's. Among the younger officer class, both Americo-Liberian and tribal, a more professional and career-minded leadership has been evolving. Many of these junior officers received training in the United States under the auspices of the American Military Mission attached to the Liberian Department of Defense. All officers were appointed by President Tubman, but increasingly by the end of the 1960's he deferred to the recommendations of American advisers, whose nominations were based on merit. The remainder of the officer class were recipients of patronage, representing the elite's guardianship of the military establishment. Their guardianship and Tubman's frequent shifting of top officers were apparently aimed at preventing plots against Tubman. Nevertheless, one such plot was alleged to have been discovered in 1963, and the Commander of the LNG was jailed. Another in 1966 resulted in the dismissal of the Commander, and his "rustication."[26]

Since the inception of the LNG the enlisted ranks have been composed almost entirely of tribal Liberians, many of them Lomas. Pay at the enlisted level is low, but the prestige of the uniform, and even the small income, have afforded sufficient inducement to make an army career attractive.

There has been little friction between ranks up to the present, perhaps because discipline is not imposed. There does not appear to have developed a cult of heroism in Liberia's military history. The LNG's record of respecting civil authority may be expected to continue in the near future, or at least as long as the ranks of the ruling elite are not broken.

The conservative role of Liberia's security forces is evident, and Tubman's concern for security was manifested in the monies allocated to them. The budget of all the security services was estimated at $1.15 million for 1971. Combining this figure with available figures on the 1970 costs for police ($969,000), armed forces ($3.2 million), and "special intelligence" ($175,000), it appears that Liberia was spending approximately $5.5 million annually for what was essentially internal security, although this represented less than 10 percent of budget expenditures.[27] The modernizing functions of the military and police services are even more modest. But soldiers and police do receive literacy and technical education; both services admit tribal people at all ranks, increasingly on the basis of merit; and all are experiencing some of the rigors of discipline and modern management.

Conclusions

Alone, the security services can perform neither a conservative nor a modernizing function. In supporting and complementing other national institutions and the growing ethos of Liberian citizenship, they support the existing political system, just as security forces in modern states do. But insofar as these services and other institutions are changing, they reflect and reinforce the processes of modernization.

Like the security services, the cabinet, the bureaucracy, the legislature, and local government all came by the mid-1960's to include persons who had hitherto not participated in any national political activity other than voting, and began to perform broader functions than they ever had before. Younger, technically trained men served in the cabinet as the heads of Treasury, Economic Planning, and Education—the most important departments. The legislative and judicial branches of government were the least flexible and responsive institutions. But they were never the critical instruments either of elite maintenance or of political development in Liberia. Indeed, they have rarely played a creative role in any of the developing nations. Yet they, too, partly adapted to political change: the legislature in representing a broader electorate, now including the tribal hinterland, and the judiciary in applying "civilized" law universally and in admitting lawyers of tribal origins to the bar.

Positions within nascent local governments, which had been the goal of local aspirants to wealth and power, also became the route to influence within the national political system. The bureaucracy, which had been little more than an extensive patronage system that bound legions of Liberian civil servants—most of them ill-equipped for their jobs—to Tubman's regime, began to experience an influx of better educated and skilled people in Tubman's fourth and fifth terms, as did the military and police.

In every area of government, the trend was toward increasing political rationality, specialization, and participation, described by Samuel P. Huntington as the most crucial aspects of modernization.[28] But by keeping the key to modernization in his own hands, Tubman sought to regulate the institutions which reflected and reinforced modernization. The True Whig Party illustrates this effort.

7

The True Whig Party

Some scholars contend that the developing nations can achieve national unity and enjoy political stability only if they create a political party system—or more specifically, a single party. Liberia has been ruled by one party since 1884. As the True Whig Party (TWP) candidate, William V. S. Tubman faced little serious opposition after his first election; he was unopposed in 1963, 1967, and 1971. But to attribute Liberia's survival and stability, or Tubman's political longevity, to the existence of a single party would be inaccurate. Liberia has but one party because opposition has thus far been ineffectual or hazardous to those who tried to organize it. The Attorney General pointed out in 1966 that there was "no law prohibiting the formation of other political parties"; the election law provides that "a political party may be formed by any group of eligible voters composed of not less than 300 persons organized, probated and registered in the Probate Court of any county."[1] He further observed that opposition parties had existed in Liberia, but had "gradually faded away"; others, such as the Independent True Whig Party, had been outlawed.[2]

After nearly a hundred years the True Whig Party remains one of the principal instruments of Americo-Liberian power and prestige. It has proved to be acceptable to most members of the polity. Moreover, a tough security and police system, sometimes repressive laws, a politicized judicial system, economic pressures, patronage, and social control mechanisms have cleared the field of all challengers. One party historian noted that the party's goals and values resided in its constancy and consistency, and then, perhaps inadvertently, stated its implicit policy when she said that its constancy "lies in the fact that it seeks to preserve a state in which the descendants of the Alien Founders of Liberia remain in control of the system."[3]

The party was slow to react to growing tribal participation in Liberia's economic life. And though there may be more form than substance in its response thus far,[4] its new members and the representativeness of its leaders, particularly in rural areas, suggest that some integration has occurred within the party. Thus the party must be seen as serving a modernizing as well as a conservative political function. But its conservative bias would seem to set Liberia apart from other single-party states in Africa.

Liberia also differs from single-party states in Africa in that the only party does not pretend to formulate or represent an expression of national consensus on any issue. It did not grow up in opposition to a European-imposed government. It is not the natural successor of a populist-inspired mass movement aimed at mobilizing the population for national liberation or for economic development. It has not sought to serve the government as a two-way means of communication between the masses and the national leadership. And it has not attempted to run all the nation's diverse interest groups, such as tribal organizations, trade unions, cooperative societies, and elders', women's, and youth groups.

What then is the TWP? And how did it change under Tubman? According to a semiofficial history of the party from 1869 to 1967, it is "an organization whose members are sufficiently homogeneous to band together for the overt purpose of winning elections, which entitles them to exercise governmental power, in order to enjoy the influences, prerequisites [sic] and advantages of authority."[5] Since Tubman expanded suffrage and opened representation to the hinterland, the TWP has provided more and broader channels through which local branches of the party could nominate candidates for national office, and served as a dispenser of patronage to the people of the hinterland. It has a staff of paid officers, regulations, and a "platform." But unlike Maurice Duverger's definition of modern parties the True Whig Party is distinguished not by the nature of its organization but by its program and the class of its members.[6]

Its official program, or platform, has usually been a carbon copy of existing government policy; the implicit program was most candidly revealed above. The membership of the TWP would identify it in the narrowest sense as a "cadre party," that is, as "a grouping of notabilities" brought together "for the preparation of elections, conducting campaigns and maintaining contact with the candidates."[7] The TWP is not a closed party. But its *General Rules and Regulations* do not establish the qualifications or the mechanism for becoming a "member,"[8] and the party does not publish membership figures.[8] If, however, we consider that all civil servants were required to contribute one month's salary each year during Tubman's rule, then the party may be said to have included all 14,000 government civil employees. Tubman announced in 1960 "without such loyalty, political patronage might be withdrawn."[9] While the genuine loyalty of party members so taxed may be doubtful, their reliance upon employment in the government has bound many of them to the party.

The party controls patronage. And the President, as standard-bearer, is the ultimate dispenser of it: for example, jobs in the government, commercial licenses, contracts with the government, cash subventions, and approval of land purchases. The party's *General Rules and Regulations* state that the President shall appoint "on his own initiative" (i.e., without party consultation or approval) the members of the cabinet, county and territory superintendents, judges, collectors of customs, district officials, and heads of executive departments and bureaus. All other county officials "may be recommended by the Senators of their County and ought thereupon to be appointed, unless for good reasons given by the President, it is found impossible to make the desired appointment."

The party did not report its income or expenditures during the Tubman era, though they must have been substantial.[10] For example, one-twelfth of the annual salaries of the 14,000 civil servants alone would yield $1.4 million per annum, if all such levies were regularly collected. And it may be assumed that foreign concessionaires and Lebanese businessmen "contributed" generously to the party. Candidate subscriptions of $200 each, plus the annual payments of 2 percent of their salaries by members of the party executive would, if paid, have further fattened the party purse. Additional income for special party purposes has been exacted from civil servants. In 1967 they were taxed 50 percent of their May and September salaries at the start of three years of fund raising to conclude the financing of the $3 million TWP headquarters, the first such physical structure for the party.[11]

It is difficult to know how these apparently vast monies of the TWP were spent. Party conclaves were not so frequent as to require great expenditures; nor did the party need to spend vast sums on advertising, travel, or vote-buying during elections, since there was no serious threat from the opposition. Three party officials were paid salaries (totaling $2,600 per annum), and county TWP chairmen, among others, received party subventions for "expenses." A young Liberian official suggested to me that the TWP slush fund was often used, much as if it were a pension, to mollify older, less important members of the ruling class who had lost some of their authority to the young men who were assuming more important positions in the party and the government owing to their greater competence. "The younger men," he said, "don't need to play that game." The funds paid out for this purpose were not audited. Had the recipient used the funds to build up a political organization in his own locality, however, it might have been construed in Monrovia as a suspicious undertaking, so the funds were perhaps more often used for personal rather than political gratifications.

Patronage was but one political instrument used by the ruling class. There were also institutional devices for directing the politics of the population of both Monrovia and the hinterland. In the absence of a unified system of urban administration—since "a great deal of the direction and coordination of the city's affairs" was "undertaken personally by the President"[12]—the social and political organization of the several tribal communities in Monrovia was particularly important. Most of them were relatively homogeneous, although their cohesion was weakened as a result of increased numbers. Tubman appointed the Governor or Paramount Chief of each unit or subunit, after consultation with tribal dignitaries.[13] Their relationship to the President was similar to that of ward leaders to city bosses in American urban politics. While these chiefs were not necessarily party officials, they participated in the political system, had the responsibilities and enjoyed some of the perquisites of other government and party leaders, and were often summoned to the Executive Mansion along with TWP leaders (by special radio broadcasts, among other means) when political matters that concerned them were under discussion. In this way, urban tribal people had a form of political representation within the party and government.

Ancillary bodies of the True Whig Party, like the numerous tribal associations found in Monrovia, served a primarily social function; they had no independent political role. The Liberian Women's Social and Political Movement, for example, served chiefly as a social organization in Monrovia. In the counties, it offered a public arena in which wives of aspiring politicians could praise the President, apparently hoping to outdo others in manifestations of love and loyalty for him, and thereby win favor for the family.[14] The Young People's Political Association apparently played an even less significant role in national, county, or family politics.

Notwithstanding the relatively limited functions of its auxiliary groups, the TWP was an important vehicle of the ruling class in maintaining its control. It held local political disputes in check at least until the central organization, or the President, personally, could resolve the more serious differences. As a channel for political ambitions—through it the county political caucuses manifested their preferences to the executive—and as a framework for local politics in the absence of any other modern forms of local government, the TWP was a vital means of access to the national political arena.

Party Organization

The True Whig Party has two basic units: the national party, which meets every eight or four years to nominate presidential and vice-presidential candidates; and the county party.[15] The national organization is represented by the Executive Committee, which includes the President, all senators and representatives, other officials elected on the party's ticket, and cabinet members and other officials appointed by the President. The President obviously dominates this unwieldy body, which makes party policy and ratifies county and district nominations for public office. County and district party organizations, aptly called "caucuses,"[16] consist of national leaders (who usually include visiting officials from Monrovia, as well as the county's representatives in the national legislature); county officials (who may include education supervisors and local postmasters as well as superintendents); paramount, clan, and town chiefs; and leading personages. In 1967, one hinterland district caucus included a large land-owner, an electrical contractor, a Lebanese merchant, a *zo*, and a representative of the ex-servicemen's association. The county organizations meet at least every two years in convention to nominate candidates for the legislature. This is their most important function.

Party Politics

The struggle for sectional influence within counties and the consequent family or regional influence in national politics form the warp and woof of county convention politics. In the 1967 election, 61 seats in the legislature were contested (9 Senate seats and all 52 House seats).[17] In that election, as in others, President Tubman arbitrated and ultimately chose the various party candidates in a number of contested races. The President could also veto a county convention slate, as Tubman did a senatorial candidate unanimously chosen by the Grand Bassa County convention in 1959.[18] The numerous political consultations that took place at the Executive Mansion before the 1967 True Whig National Convention, at which President Tubman was asked to decide or confirm county nominations, illustrate not only the intensity of competition but Tubman's great powers in the selection of legislators. The press reported that Tubman "decided" upon nominations for Sinoe, Lofa, Grand Gedeh, and Nimba Counties, the last three being new hinterland counties. He overturned a Sasstown Territory convention decision by naming a candidate—the incumbent—whom the convention had rejected on the grounds that "he does not care for them in time of trouble."[19] This was a case, moreover, in which the national party was not required to support the incumbent, for he had already served two terms, the limit to which the party by tradition is committed.[20] In another contest, the President presided over a meeting of Maryland County party officials and reversed their 51–24 vote against nominating the incumbent, Yancey, for a third term.[21] (Yancey was from an old and distinguished Americo-Liberian family which was especially close to President Tubman.) Further, Tubman apparently used his appointive powers to buy off incumbents. James N. Anderson, incumbent

Senator from Maryland County and long-time President Pro-Tempore of the Senate, was persuaded not to run in order that "Shad" Tubman, Jr., could take the seat. After the election Anderson's own son was appointed as Superintendent of Maryland County.

There were other ways in which the President could control the outcome of county nominating conventions, and hence the electoral process. Rather than make final selections or overrule nominations, he could make his preferences known before or at the county convention. In 1964, he intervened in a county convention contest between two men, one of whom was a chief, by observing that the House of Representatives would be improved by the presence of a few more "chiefly robes." In another case, when a local TWP chairman sought to circumvent Tubman's preselection of a party nominee, the President suspended him for having failed to adhere to a decision that "the National Standard Bearer" —himself—had made the previous year in favor of a candidate from the majority tribe in the constituency.[22] Tubman apparently never hesitated to interfere in the nomination of TWP candidates for office in order to balance or conciliate contending factions. But by the 1960's he appeared to be acknowledging the demands for greater representation of previously excluded elements of the population, particularly in the new hinterland counties. At all times, however, Tubman sought to ensure his own supremacy and popularity.

The New Politics in the Hinterland

Although these cases illustrate the way TWP politics have traditionally been conducted, they tend to obscure the very real significance of county convention nominations, especially once the hinterland counties began to participate in the process. For the new counties, too, sought geographic and ethnic balance in their legislative representation. The party provided for the equitable distribution of local political influence and seats in the legislature among various population centers and chiefdoms. In Lofa County, for example, one Paramount Chief was made TWP Chairman in order to balance the establishment of the County Headquarters in another Paramount Chiefdom. Also in Lofa, Tubman appointed a Mandingo as Circuit Court Judge as a gesture to this small but influential community. "Upper" and "lower" Bong County each held seats in the legislature. And in Nimba County there were considered to be tribal, subtribal, and sectional constituencies. In the special election in 1964 for the new county seats in the House of Representatives, and again in 1967, the TWP nominating contests hinged on local issues and personalities.

A significant power struggle occurred in Bong County in 1964, where a group of relatively well-educated young clan chiefs managed to engineer the nomination to the House of an old and authoritarian Paramount Chief. They then filled his chieftainship with one of their own group.[23] In Nimba County, in 1967, a young American-educated schoolteacher, supported by an important Paramount Chief, won the nomination over a rich but illiterate candidate who had the support of the County Superintendent. The victor had also been the protégé of a Cabinet Secretary, however, and had enjoyed his support for the nomination to the House seat.

Neither the structure of the TWP, nor the tactics employed to win party nomination, changed much under Tubman. But new and more broadly based representation was at stake in the electoral process, as is suggested by the above two cases and the use by the press of such expressions as "young, educated" and "the most popular" candidates. There was also a semblance of a democratic choice among national candidates at the county level. County nominating conventions were open to the public. Candidates solicited support from local notables and opinion leaders, such as chiefs, officeholders, wealthy landowners, and businessmen before such conventions.

The new counties system, therefore, brought a new political experience to the hinterland. But neither political power nor the central political arena has shifted from the coast to the hinterland. It is unlikely that the hinterland counties will soon—if ever—acquire the political importance or strength of the coastal section, especially of Montserrado County. By 1971 these county governments and party organizations still had only derivative power and had virtually no local finances with which to expand it. Moreover, they were subject to the influence of members of the elite who held land and often lived on the hinterland counties.

There was little, if any, evidence of tendencies toward autonomy among the various TWP county organizations during Tubman's administrations; winning factions did not take control of the county political organization. But it is unlikely that Tubman could have won the support and loyalty he enjoyed had he disregarded too often the preferences of local opinion leaders and strong ethnic or geographic groups. By acceding to their wishes, Tubman increased communications between hinterland peoples and Monrovia and fortified his own authority and popularity.

In the process of assimilating leading hinterland individuals into the party, the entire ruling elite gradually opened its ranks to new elements. Not only the new legislators from the hinterland, but tribal county officials and the progressive chiefs partook of the rewards of this policy of political assimilation. Even if such assimilation strengthened the elite and the existing political system, it also altered the composition of party membership. And if hinterland leaders assumed the character and habits, the external values, of the old elite, they did so as representatives of a wider spectrum of people than heretofore. Some scholars have suggested that these are potentially a class of "political entrepreneurs"—that class which may bridge the gulf between the elite and the mass.[24] Through such people the TWP has developed as a political machine that links the regime, the party, and the bureaucracy to traditional authorities and local leaders and has served to expand the political community.

The True Whig Party, therefore, played an important integrative role in the hinterland in the Tubman era. It was not, however, the only national institution playing such a role. Education, roads, and the bureaucracy in general also penetrated the hinterland during this time. But the party, whose leadership was one with the government, best expressed the political direction and control desired by Tubman and other political leaders. For, as we will see in Chapters 8 and 9, the other institutions produced some unintended political consequences.

8

The Bureaucracy

The bureaucracy perhaps best illustrates the character of political development in Liberia: it has, to a large extent, maintained the position of the ruling elite; but it is also the most promising vehicle of rational, as against politically expedient, government and of economic, social, and political modernization. Notwithstanding the drag of tradition, the bureaucracy is becoming a problem-solving agency increasingly able to tackle complex issues such as budgeting, regulating foreign-owned industry, and negotiating foreign aid and foreign investment agreements.

The High Cost of Government

In Liberia, as in many other developing nations, government employment is the principal source of income for the elite. The costs of running the government impose heavy financial burdens on the rest of the country. A Special Commission on Government Operations (SCOGO), appointed by President Tubman in 1961, with its Chairman having cabinet status, reported in 1964 that most government departments were overstaffed, that civil servants' salaries depended on criteria other than merit and seniority, and that many government employees were either inadequately paid or overpaid.[1] Few changes followed from the SCOGO report, and the salary system remained inequitable. In spite of the establishment of a Civil Service Commission in the early 1960's, the inflated civil service grew at about 10 percent per annum. Government rolls carried about 14,000 employees in 1967 (or 20,000, if the police and regular armed services are included), and 18,000 in 1969, figures I have been unable to corroborate or refute.[2]

The heavy cost to Liberia of its patronage system is reflected in the high proportion of the budget that goes for employees as opposed to supplies and materials. Below are examples of this imbalance in ministries that might have been expected to have a high non-personnel component.

Department of Agriculture[3]
   Expenditures $738,589
   Personnel Services   527,000
Department of Public Works[4]
   Appropriation $298,404
   Personnel services   247,724

From 1964 to 1970, the proportion of the total budget spent for compensation of employees was about 50 percent,[5] considerably higher than that of other African countries, such as the Ivory Coast (42 percent) and Ghana (33 percent). Given the fact that debt servicing takes about 20 to 25 percent of Liberia's annual budget, the personnel component of the operating budget in 1967 was over 60 percent.[6] Government is thus an important business.

Government servants benefit from the unofficial use of public supplies and properties, such as official vehicles, and from the sale of such items as school furniture and books.[7] These constitute an important aspect of the rewards of government employment. Before 1964, as much as 40 percent of total government expenditures was disbursed outside budget channels.[8] In addition, gratuities, called "dash," for the rendering of official services, such as registering a deed, were a source of supplementary income for civil servants. Yet another was the President's Contingency Fund (about $1 million in 1964)—a slush fund with no perceivable budgetary controls.[9] From it the President, much like a Tammany boss, dispensed monetary rewards to chiefs, party members, civil servants, and "needy" causes. Official foreign travel and conference funds, which amounted to $700,000 in 1962 and $400,000 in 1967, were important supplements to official salaries.[10]

There are fewer opportunities for substantially supplementing public salaries in the hinterland than in Monrovia; but the field is wider in terms of the various forms of taxes, levies, and fines which pass through administrators' hands. Requisitions of crops and livestock are a standard part of rural life.[11] The beneficiaries range from chiefs to visitors from Monrovia, county and district officials, revenue agents, agricultural agents, and soldiers.

Obviously not the salaries alone attract people into the civil service. Most salaries are barely adequate for a comfortable urban existence. The cost of living in Monrovia is among the highest in the world. Moreover, civil servants have to pay a plethora of "taxes," for example, "voluntary" donations to the True Whig Party, equivalent to one month's salary; an "austerity tax" of 4 percent on gross salaries over $600 per annum, imposed in 1967; an education tax; and a "donation" of one month's salary per annum for the construction of a TWP headquarters. Even a cabinet member's salary of $6,000 (the average for senior secretaries in 1967), or a County Superintendent's salary of $3,000, or the $1,500 to $2,500 annual income of upper-level bureaucrats[12] was not sufficient to afford a family the trappings which the Liberian elite's standards of affluence require, such as a farm, a large imported automobile, and annual trips to the United States or Europe. In 1971 nearly 11,000 civil servants earned $1,000 or less per year. The high absenteeism in government offices throughout the country attests not merely to the idleness of public servants but also to other employment. Many government officials spend a great deal of time on private business, law practices, and the like. Teachers too have poor attendance records, and often supplement their earnings by selling school property. The reason is obvious: in 1964, teachers who had had two to four years of college education received average gross incomes of only $60 to $100 per month.[13]

Thus, the business that is government serves neither good government nor a rational allocation of scarce material or manpower resources. The civil service system practically encourages diffident work habits, as well as corruption and graft. Although civil service regulations with respect to hiring, firing, examinations, and promotions have been on the books since 1935, they have not been effective. It is even questionable whether they were supposed to be. Foreign advisers to Liberia and aid donors as well often insisted that retrenchment in the civil service was essential for rational budgetary management and an end to chronic deficits. Tubman's rejection of the advice must be seen in political terms. He could not (nor can his successor) reduce the civil service without seriously undermining his own political base.

It should surprise no one, therefore, that the bureaucracy, which for the last one hundred years has been little more than a patronage device, has not played a creative role in economic and political development. In the fifties and sixties the country grew to genuinely need a functioning civil service, for budgeting, coping with the consequences of an economic recession, and drawing up and revising concession agreements; thus bureaucrats are now expected to do more than draw their salaries. This is a new and almost revolutionary departure from the past. Furthermore, the centralization of economic planning under a Department of Planning and Economic Affairs in 1966 requires all departments of the government to improve their own organizations and budgeting procedures in order to defend their requests for appropriations. This type of nascent intra-bureaucratic competition may yet have a healthy impact upon public administration.

It appears that Liberia's leaders recognized that continued modernization required the development of institutions and people capable of handling continually changing problems and demands. The need for innovation produced an obvious contradiction, however: How could the bureaucracy serve its traditional function as the means of commanding the loyalties of the most politically relevant segment of the population and at the same time become the rational, efficient instrument that was needed if Liberia were to maintain the advantages of the modernization taking place in other sectors of national life? Further, how could the old ruling elite retain its power when the need for effective public administration required more technically competent administrators and other professionals?

To answer these questions, we must consider what happened to the economy, especially in the 1960's. Effective administration is considered to be a precondition for economic development;[14] in Liberia, the recession of the sixties intensified the need for it.

Budget Reform

The economic boom that enriched the Liberian treasury and fostered an expansion of the public sector produced a patchwork of overlapping and competing government agencies that, according to the SCOGO report, were "lacking order or logic."[15] It also served to inflate the public payroll. Development economists, both foreign and Liberian, found their ethos of administrative rationality and efficiency in conflict with the older civil servants' haphazard management of government affairs. The stringency that forced Liberia to seek loans from the International Monetary Fund (IMF) and other foreign sources finally inaugurated an era of more rigorous budgetary procedures. Under pressure from the IMF and other foreign donors, Liberia agreed to rectify some administrative shortcomings. Unfortunately, there is no device for measuring the extent and effectiveness of administrative reform. One can, however, look at certain experiences during the first years of austerity which illustrate the contradictions mentioned earlier.

A 1964 report on Liberia's performance under its stand-by agreement with the IMF, whereby Liberia's public debt and fiscal programming would be rearranged with the help of IMF credits, noted that the budget had been trimmed to a minimum and that transfers of funds were to be allowed "only in exceptional circumstances and then only by authority of the President." Other specific budgetary measures recommended in 1963 included "reduced Liberian representation at international conferences, reduction in travel and entertainment allowances, reductions in gasoline allowances for public officials, discharging surplus personnel, etc."[16] Few of these measures were fully implemented, for they struck at the heart of the patronage and political reward system—at precisely the ways in which Liberian officials were able to better their standard of living. As one economist put it in 1965:

"Austerity" has so far prevailed in only one main sense: restrictions have been placed on Government borrowing, and hence on aggregate Government expenditures. Within that aggregate, dubious spending undoubtedly still takes place. In 1964 almost a million dollars was spent on foreign scholarships, and over $1.25 million on foreign conferences. At the end of the year and amidst a growing budgetary pinch, one million dollars for additional military expenditures in the 1965 budget were proposed.[17]

On the basis of the new budgeting system and the priorities established by the Planning Department (see below), the old remedy of across-the-board reductions of appropriations gave way to eliminating low-priority projects. Moreover, the President's Contingency Fund was reduced, by Tubman himself, from $1 million to $800,000 in 1965, and budgetary reductions *were* effected for overseas conferences, scholarships, and government-paid house rentals.[18] Nevertheless, in 1967, chronic budgetary problems were still being reported, this time by the American Embassy: "A decisive cut in the Government's operating costs would be necessary if the Government were to fund these payments [IMF and other foreign debts, which were about $255 million in mid-1966]; *this is not to be expected.*"[19]

The government's current expenditures, that is, new annual obligations, increased by $3 million from 1964 to 1965, $6 million in 1966, and another $2 million in 1967.[20] The year 1969 marked the first time in Liberian history that government revenues covered expenditures, leaving a surplus of $5.7 million, owing to a higher rate of income than of spending. In that year, too, a "development budget" was created, entirely distinct from the recurring budget, and in 1970 a Development Fund was established to ensure the implementation of development projects and to avoid having to carry over unspent development funds to succeeding years. Revenues increased by $10.1 million from 1968 to $61.9 in 1969, whereas expenditures rose by only $2.5 million.[21] A part of these gains is attributable to the establishment of a Tax Commission in 1968. The government had engaged a team of foreign experts to review the existing system and to advise on reforms, particularly in tax administration. These moves—particularly the establishment of the Tax Commission—helped broaden the tax base.

Administrative Reorganization

SCOGO, whose task it had been to strengthen the organization and management of government departments, achieved its greatest success in such areas as automobile licensing, tax collecting, and limiting travel allowances. The transfer of the motor vehicle licensing bureau from the Justice Department to the Revenue Service, for example, had good results. Almost all vehicles are now properly licensed, and licenses paid for. Until this was done, licensing was a haphazard affair, depriving the government of revenues and leaving motorists vulnerable to arbitrary penalties (usually paid on the spot to whatever police or security officers were on the scene).

Without the ability to enforce compliance with its directives, however, SCOGO could do little more than point out deficiencies and recommend reorganization. That it did so ceaselessly reflected, perhaps, Tubman's determination to carry out administrative reforms, even if they were ephemeral or only superficial. In 1962, nineteen draft acts involving reorganization of the executive branch of government were written and passed by the legislature. Many more reforms have occurred since that time, often by executive order.[22]

Perhaps the most notable changes took place in the Treasury Department, where the Bureau of Audits was relieved of normal accounting and expenditure control, leaving it with only the post-audit function. A British firm of chartered accountants was engaged in 1966 to perform selected audits and to introduce procedures which, it was hoped, would survive the termination of the firm's contract. A Bureau of General Auditing was created. Its foreign adviser claimed that he had established procedures which succeeded in reducing to a few days the period elapsing between the presentation of a voucher and its payment—a procedure that formerly took several weeks. A central government purchasing agency is now also in operation.[23]

Another important change in government administration occurred with the formation in 1963 of the National Planning Agency. This body has operated since 1966 as a cabinet-level department called the Department of Planning and Economic Affairs. In this now quite powerful agency, first managed by resident advisers of the United Nations–financed Harvard Advisory Project, but now all-Liberian, one may find some of the senior civil servants who hold the greatest promise for the government. Of the fifteen-man Liberian professional staff in 1966, all held degrees (and several, advanced degrees) in economics or statistics from reputable universities in the United States and England. Another twelve to fifteen were being trained abroad, largely in economics and statistics.[24] Not only did this represent the best-trained senior staff in any Liberian department, but the work of the Planning Department has been conducted under two able Liberian directors, both holding higher degrees in economics.

Perhaps the most important accomplishment of the Planning Department to date, and one that betokens possible pressure on foreign concessionaires, was its work in preparing for the renegotiation of several concession agreements in 1964 in order to increase the contributions of the concessions to public revenues. Armed with data on income earned by the companies and that earned by Liberia, the government was able to persuade the mining companies to redress some of the past inequities in tax payments and profit sharing. Improved arrangements were also made with the rubber producers and foreign-owned banks. A new corporate income tax structure was introduced which yielded an additional $1 million each from Firestone, the Liberian Mining Company, and the International Trust Company of Liberia (in which an American bank held an 80 percent interest) in 1965.[25]

Personal income taxes remained relatively unprogressive, however, and the inequity was compounded by a universally applied per capita levy of $10 for educational development and by a regressive "austerity tax." That minor improvements in the collection of customs, real estate, and personal income taxes were made, however, was evident in the almost weekly reports of litigation undertaken by the tax prosecutor. A banner headline in the *Liberian Star* of May 8, 1967, announced: "100 Tax Summonses to be Served Today." On May 11 the *Star* asked, "Are Some Payroll Clerks Padding Govt. Payrolls?," and reported: "New Method Begins at Bureau of Supply." Such public gestures toward greater efficiency and order in tax administration were common.[26]

Few other government agencies were as effective as the Planning Department, perhaps because that agency was newer than the others and remained small. The Treasury had a thin cadre of able and dedicated senior officials, but was plagued with an overlarge and poorly trained staff, numbering over a thousand in 1971.

The Department of Public Works, which administered and carried out the greatest part of Liberia's public sector activities during Tubman's administration, was also the most overstaffed and improperly run of all agencies of government. Estimates of the number of employees ranged from 1,000 to 1,700 in 1964, most of whom had little or no technical competence; wages for persons holding the same job title varied as much as five hundred percent.[27] Apart from the misuse of public vehicles, machinery, and building materials—which apparently was widely practiced—the gross mishandling of public funds and maladministration of contracting procedures, revealed in an audit in 1963, caused the summary dismissal of the Secretary of Public Works. (The cost of the new Executive Mansion, for example, rose from the estimated $5 million to $18 million before it was completed.)

Civil service reform has shown some modest accomplishments. For example, competetive examinations were established in 1971 for middle- and lower-level positions in the National Health Service, and other departments were preparing to follow this lead.[28] New auditing procedures have made it more difficult for officials to enrich themselves at public expense—at least, as a consequence of the administration's opening of Liberia's books to impartial audit, and advisory positions in the government to foreign experts, there are limits to the amounts of public money that can go into the wrong pockets. It is difficult to demonstrate the depth or durability of this commitment to "good" government. The Liberians who were being prepared to replace transient foreign advisers in the sixties have apparently yielded to political exigencies as often as they have carried out the reforms introduced by their former mentors.

Some Conclusions . . . and Prospects

Even if the will to reform had been stronger, it could not have overcome the problems of ever-growing budget expenditures, partly the result of heavy external debt obligations. Debt-servicing constituted 20 to 25 percent of the total budget between 1965 and 1970 (reaching $21.5 million in 1970) and was expected to continue at about that level through 1974.[29] The few advances made in hiring and salary procedures have been mitigated by traditional patronage practices, still the keystone of the Liberian political system. One observer estimated that the bureaucracy grew at the rate of 10 percent per annum until 1968. Expenditures for personnel payments over the years 1964 through 1967 show annual increases averaging about $1 million.[30] Hence, though progress has been made in reducing some of the more costly and inefficient modes of government operations, to the extent that the Liberian political system continues to be based upon spoils and patronage (to a widening constituency), administrative and fiscal reform can be expected to proceed haltingly.

We will see in the next chapter how the expansion of secular education brought different groups into the same institutional framework. The public service has likewise drawn together educated people from all strata.[31] Tribal and coastal graduates of European and American univeristies have more in common than, say, the children of the elite will have with their less educated, more parochial parents. As their norms, values, and even modes of expression differ from those of the older generation, they will seek to supplant the values and prerogatives of the old, more conservative leaders with their own.

It must be noted, however, that some of these younger, educated people appear to be as intent as their elder colleagues upon acquiring property and farms, and constructing houses to rent to the government and foreigners. They perceive, perhaps better than the older time-servers, the need for some form of economic insurance if their tours with the government should prove unsatisfactory, or if they should fall from political favor. (Moreover, given the inadequate salaries received even by people with professional training, civil servants often wish to supplement their incomes.)

By contrast, a number of disillusioned younger civil servants have concluded that their hopes for progress in the public service were doomed to founder in Liberia's patronage swamp. Some of them left the government for private business or to seek postgraduate studies abroad during Tubman's last years. These men and women appeared to believe that they would have a greater and more rewarding role to play in a new government after Tubman's passing.

Yet members of both of these groups—when they are not feathering their own nests or planning to emigrate or take jobs in the private sector—as well as other educated Liberians who are entering the public service bring to their jobs skills and values that sustain a modicum of businesslike procedures. The core of Treasury Department personnel, a "workhorse" group, so to speak, attempted to conserve scarce monetary and manpower resources by seeking to balance the priorities for development with the budgetary consequences of development programs. In one instance, at some peril to their own personal security, these officials sought vigorously but unsuccessfully to reverse a personal decision by President Tubman to permit the United States to construct a hospital. Running the hospital added nearly $2 million to Liberia's annual recurrent expenditures.

Such a case is interesting in terms of the implicit tensions it brought into being. On the one hand, Liberians had to reckon with the personal authority of President Tubman, who concluded economic agreements with foreigners and could transfer budget allocations at will. On the other hand, the technical cadres had to find funds to meet the operating costs of activities approved by Tubman. The resulting tensions were felt not only by the "technocrats," who had to serve both political expediency and economic rationality; but the political leaders themselves had to decide whether they were willing to dissipate Liberia's economic growth and lose the opportunity for future development through administrative incompetence and inefficiency, or whether they would yield to the technocrats in certain aspects of decision making.

It appears that President Tubman, in spite of occasional lapses, had moved gingerly in the latter direction before his death. It is far from certain, however, that President Tolbert can continue far in this area and keep the support he needs in order to govern.

The evidence offered here does not make it possible to predict the future role of the bureaucracy in Liberia with confidence. But the public administration of Liberia and the new nations may be the only institution with the capacity to survive, intact, political change (violent or evolutionary) at the very top. Moreover, in much of Africa—single parties notwithstanding—the civil service bears the major responsibility for keeping the wheels of government turning. As Joseph LaPalombara has pointed out, "For the great mass of people in most countries, government is scarcely much more than the specific public officials with whom they come in direct contact."[32] In Liberia, because it is also the most modern public institution, the bureaucracy may become an even more influential political factor in the political system.

9

Education and Communications

The ability of a government to provide secular education to a broad spectrum of the population, and to penetrate the farthest reaches of the country by modern means of communication is regarded as characteristic of—and indeed necessary to—development and modernization. These services, not incidentally, convey and reinforce the values that underlie the existing social order. But they may also produce stresses in existing structures because they stimulate an interest in specifically modern values and amenities and may do so more effectively than do other political institutions.

The Role of Education

Any examination of an educational system must recognize that formal education involves not only the substance of education, but the environment and the manner in which it is transmitted. In addition to imbuing students with the values of their culture in order to create cohesion and loyalty that go beyond any one political regime, education is expected to create a citizenry that can participate in all aspects of economic, social, and political life according to each person's abilities. An educational system that aims only at producing cadres of technically and administratively competent workers may also create dispirited, rootless, rebellious students—particularly if economic and social mobility and political participation are denied them, whether through the absence of suitable job opportunities, or as a result of built-in political limitations. As the following description suggests, after World War II Liberia undertook to expand education with only a fragmentary design: to provide a service that modern nations are expected to provide and, perhaps as an afterthought, to create a more effective work force for the growing modern economy. In retrospect, Liberia's educational system has produced too many dropouts at the primary and secondary level; ill-trained and uncreative secondary school graduates; and alienated university graduates. As in many other developing nations, considerable expenditures in education have not always served the political system, the economy, or the students.

The Expansion of Secular Education

The most notable expansion of public investment in education, health, and other basic social services began in the late fifties—another benefit of economic growth. During the sixties, 15 percent of annual government expenditures was allocated to education—apparently an expression of Liberia's commitment to expand educational opportunities and speed up the incorporation of tribal people into the nation's life.

Before World War II, education had been left almost exclusively to religious missions. Since then, the government has assumed the principal responsibility for education at all levels.[1] Compared with expenditures of $25,000 in 1900 and $33,070 in 1926, the government now spends over $6 million per annum on education. In 1965, a peak year, contributions by concessionaires, missions, and foreign donors brought the total expended on education to $15 million, or about 6 percent of the gross national product.[2] A great part of United States aid in the sixties went to education, particularly for the construction of school buildings in the hinterland.

By 1969, over 130,000 pupils were enrolled in over 900 elementary and pre-primary schools, 11,300 in 85 high schools (grades seven through twelve),[3] and 1,200 in three vocational and two teacher-training institutes. The three institutions of higher (but sub-university) learning, the University of Liberia, Cuttington College, and Our Lady of Fatima College, had a registration of 1,300 students. An additional 471 Liberians were studying abroad on scholarships from the Liberian and foreign governments and United Nations agencies,[4] a level Liberia maintained from 1965 to 1970. The 4,200 teachers in elementary and secondary schools theoretically afford Liberia a ratio of a little over thirty students per teacher.

These statistics, however, do not even faintly suggest the quality of education. For example, in 1965, only 120 of the 800 elementary schools produced students qualified to take national examinations for admission to secondary school; of their 3,088 teachers, nearly a third had not graduated from high school themselves. Of the 379 secondary school teachers, 150 were aliens, such as Peace Corps volunteers; and there were only forty-four new secondary school teachers.[5] Even teacher-student ratios were misleading. An average twelfth-grade class was reported to have six to ten students (for all high schools the average was eight), yet many classrooms throughout Liberia had over 50 students, and some as many as 150.[6] There have been some improvements in recent years, particularly in performances on national examinations. "Passes" at the high school level were 12 percent in 1962, 39 percent in 1964, and 12 and 18 percent at the elementary level for the same years.[7] A report for 1969 shows an astounding 70 percent pass rate for high school examination takers, 63 percent for elementary schools.[8]

However unsuccessful the system has been technically, pedagogically, or in meeting Liberia's trained manpower needs, it has profoundly affected people throughout Liberia: Liberian schools have produced a generation that is seeking, if not permanently finding, a place in the modern economic sector.

Broadening the Education Base

As of 1970 some 38 percent of Liberian young people of school age (5 through 24 years) had at some time experienced Western-type education and instruction in the English language.[9] Most of these children—one source indicates over 80 percent in 1967[10]—were born in rural areas, and may be assumed to be for the most part of tribal background. In 1949 only 619 children outside the coastal counties were attending school; in 1960, there were over 18,000; and by 1970, some 153,000 persons of school age were attending schools *in the rural areas.* This enormous increase was nearly duplicated by the school attendance of tribal children in urban areas. Nearly 60 percent of school children attending urban schools in 1967 had been born in rural areas.[11]

Blue-collar employment and farming account for a substantial proportion of the occupations of the parents of urban students. For example, among sixth-grade national-examination-takers in 1967, 49 percent were children of farmers. This level drops, however, as children reach higher levels of education. Forty-nine percent of ninth-grade examination-takers listed farmers, laborers (mostly in mining), and craftsmen for their father's occupation. White-collar and professional occupations were listed by a majority of twelfth-grade students. As the report from which these data are taken concludes: "Children of farmers, fishermen, hunters and loggers do not continue school long enough while those of professionals, technicians, executives and administrators continue to the high school completion point."[12]

This tendency of urban coastal peoples to dominate the professions and benefit disproportionately from higher education was confirmed by data obtained in a survey of government school students in Monrovia in 1968 (total sample of 2,316 from selected schools in a population of 10,340). Members of the Bassa and Kpelle tribes, for example, constituted 22.9 and 17.9 percent, respectively, of the second- and third-grade populations, but declined to 13.1 and 10.5 percent by tenth and twelfth grades. The coastal Kru, Vai, and "others" (presumably including Americo-Liberians) climbed from 12.9, 4.3, and 4.9 percent in the second and third grades to 14.8, 7.3, and 9.9 percent in the tenth and twelfth.[13] This favored position of coastal people may reflect the inferior education received by hinterland tribal children before reaching Monrovia's secondary schools as much as the achievement orientation among families of higher social and occupational status.

Nonetheless, tribal people predominate in sheer numbers at all levels, including the post-secondary one. Just as important, the bringing together of different ethnic, social, occupational, and regional groups of Liberia's population within one institutional framework has increased their interrelationships and the sharing of a common experience and a common language.[14]

The Social Consequences of Education

This expansion of educational opportunities has reinforced tendencies toward modernization in other spheres. Educational qualifications at least complement, and sometimes displace, personal and family criteria in the selection of candidates for public office and the bureaucracy. It is not only the government's need for efficient administration, but the pressures emanating from the growing body of educated tribal people, that is creating responsible positions for tribesmen in Liberia's social system.

The Liberian government has placed both faith and finances in its goal of "preparing citizens to enter into the mainstream of Liberian economic, social, and political life or enabling them to make a contribution to Liberian society."[15] In terms of the number of employees (mostly the 4,200 teachers in 1969), the Department of Education affects more people and reaches more deeply into the remote areas of the country than any other agency of government. Until recently, education was the fastest growing part of the public sector in the country and the one upon which the greatest popular demands were being placed. Given the difficulties of obtaining reliable information on the number of schools, their location, and the size of their enrollment, it is impossible to document precisely the extent of this pressure.[16] An official publication estimated that in 1966, in Monrovia alone, "over 2,000 potential pupils were placed on the waiting list because they could not be accommodated at the beginning of the year."[17]

Like most African states, Liberia faces staggering problems in developing an educational system consistent with its needs, problems that are compounded by the inflated patronage system and the acute inefficiency and dishonesty that affect most government departments.

Poorly paid teachers have staggering absentee and attrition records;[18] the pocketing of school fees, and the illegal sale of school supplies and books have become part of the extracurricular business activities that so often characterize the civil service in Liberia.

Official Liberian publications and various technical studies conducted by foreign advisers have examined the shortcomings in the educational system and their consequences. For example, owing to the dearth of secondary schools in the interior until the 1960's, most tribal youths who wished to pursue advanced education had no choice but to emigrate to Monrovia. Many primary-school leavers who have attained some degree of literacy have migrated to the capital and compete for the limited school places as well as for housing and employment.

Another consequence of the poor and limited educational facilities in Liberia is a bottleneck at the secondary school level. Most primary school matriculants fail to qualify for higher education. Of the 90,000 children attending primary schools in 1965, only one in ten could expect to reach the secondary level; of this number, only 315 would graduate.[19] Not enough secondary school teachers were being produced to staff existing schools, let alone to handle increased attendance.

Liberia, like many other African nations, has expected too much and produced too little with its educational system—it has not matched the cost to government of public education with a sufficient number of trained Liberians to man the government and commerce. Furthermore, this system is likely to expand quantitatively while operating with an inadequate force of teachers, most of whom are poorly trained and have poor facilities at their disposal. The Liberian school system may simply raise the level of expectations without raising the quality of instruction. At present it has a growing population of semiliterate school leavers who are unprepared for the modern world which they aspire to enter. Just as they are largely unqualified for anything but poorly paid, unskilled labor, so the modern sector is not geared to provide them jobs, housing, or basic social amenities. Finally, education in Liberia tends to disorient students with respect to the rural world in which they have been living, and to which, as a result of urban frustrations and unemployment, they might one day wish to return.

Higher Education

For the 800 students enrolled at Liberia's three higher institutions of learning in 1966, a share of the country's economic wealth and the attainment of relatively high social status were virtually ensured.[20] But as more tribal youths have been admitted to higher levels of education in

Liberia, children of the elite have tended to go abroad to American and European institutions. Thus, the currency of Liberian higher education has been devalued, and local graduates, while they may anticipate the rewards of a government position, are not gaining entry at the high levels graduates expected in the past.[21] The dropout rate for these institutions was 74 percent in the mid-1960's. This figure reflects very liberal admission requirements, the financial difficulties that faced most students, and the choice of a number of students to leave for overseas education before completing studies in Liberia.[22] None of the three institutions' graduates, however, were accorded college-level status abroad. Most universities in the United States and Europe required students to have four years of study at the University of Liberia, or two years at the other two institutions, before admitting them at the first-year university levels.[23]

Although Cuttington and Our Lady of Fatima colleges are not public institutions, both receive government grants. A considerable part of their finances still derives from subventions from missionary organizations and, in Cuttington's case, until recently, from scholarship subsidies from the United States aid program.

The University of Liberia suffers from political interference, a consequence of government control of its budget. The government provided about 45 percent of the university's income in the 1960's; the remainder came from tuition, foreign donors, and private gifts.[24] About 80 percent of the students were supported by government scholarships. Furthermore, legislators, who dominated the Board of Trustees, prescribed rules of conduct, controlled student admissions and dismissals, and influenced faculty appointments.

In February 1967 a so-called scholarship scandal was revealed. It involved the withdrawal of government scholarships from a number of students in order to accommodate others "for undisclosed reasons."[25] Although the names of former and new scholarship holders do not readily indicate the ethnic backgrounds of the students involved, it was widely believed at the time that tribal students had been obliged to give way to Americo-Liberians, probably of lower-class background (most wealthy and influential Americo-Liberians send their children abroad for secondary as well as university education). Thus, even in a program that would seem to be directed at reducing the old social divisions in Liberia, the schism between Americo-Liberians and tribesmen came to the surface. Evidence that this division persists also came to light in an election contest for the president of the Liberian Students Association of the United States and Canada. The election apparently was fought on the basis of the candidates' ethnic and social origins, or, as one student called it, "this Americo-Liberian business."[26]

The increasing sums expended for overseas education by the Liberian government may be regarded both as an investment in the manpower of the country and as another patronage device. The $900,000 to $1 million annual expenditure for overseas education in the mid-1960's (roughly 15 percent of total government expenditure on education) underlines the government's involvement in this field. In 1965 foreign governments spent another $880,000 on scholarships for Liberians, with emphasis on general administration.[27]

Since the government also viewed overseas education as a possible source of dissidence, it ruled in 1962 that all foreign fellowships—whether sponsored by the Liberian or foreign governments—must be channeled through a special committee within the Department of Education. The government maintained that this procedure was necessary in order to ascertain the qualifications and the financial ability of the candidates to support themselves beyond the cost of tuition, which was often the extent of most foreign scholarships. The authorities also hoped to regulate fields of study in order to meet Liberian manpower needs. Yet the persistent financial and academic difficulties encountered by Liberian students abroad, their preference for the humanities rather than technical training, and the sometimes greatly extended periods of residence abroad showed that this aspect of the program was loosely administered.[28] Children of the elite still enjoyed the preponderance of foreign scholarships and higher level jobs upon their return.

However ineffective the government's efforts to control this costly program may have been, the fundamental objective of training Liberians to assume responsible positions in an increasingly complex administration and society was being partly realized. Furthermore, whether the returnees were children of the old elite or were of tribal origin, the technology and values of the developed world left an enduring mark on many of them. It is most frequently among these overseas graduates that one encountered both the determination to do a job well and frustration with a system that impedes efficiency and honesty in the public service. Regrettably, in terms of Liberia's manpower needs, it is also among this element that this frustration often led to withdrawal from public life after completion of an obligatory four years of government service, sometimes by pursuing graduate studies abroad.

Education for Social Integration

Given the dearth of data about the possible "socializing" effects secular education has had upon young Liberians, one can only conjecture about its role in the nation's modernization and integration. One thing appears certain, however: education is a greatly desired commodity, however poor its quality and however slight its relevance to a still largely agricultural nation. This phenomenon suggests that many people who are supposedly enmeshed in traditional life wish that they or their children might obtain the skills and qualifications necessary for entry into the modern life of the country. Poro education, which does not provide such qualifications, is diminishing not only in the length of training, but in relevance to hoped-for life roles. Whether or not the slim evidence concerning the erosion of traditional values and, by implication, social obligations, is completely accurate, the secular educational experience and the new values shared by some 10 percent of the population do point them away from the traditional and toward the modern world.[29] As they pursue their fortunes outside the tribal environment, these young people may further disengage themselves from its social and psychological controls.

On its part, the government has sought to harness this acculturating process. In the past, Liberian history was written (by Americo-Liberians) almost exclusively to praise the heroism of the early settlers against the "uncivilized" aborigines. For example, Liberia celebrates, among other holidays, the birthday of Matilda Newport, whose reputed heroism in the early wars between the settlers and indigenous peoples of Liberia has become a part of Liberia's historical lore. Recently published school books, however, now speak of "misunderstandings" between the two groups and often attribute the cause of clashes between them to "foreigners who increasingly realized the wealth of Liberia and feared a loss of trade" if the country were developed.[30] Such books emphasize the consanguinity of the settler and tribesman; they also note that "there is little doubt that the tribes of Liberia are descended from the inhabitants of the great Central and West African kingdoms." School manuals now admit that "for a long time Liberians who lived along the seacoast assumed complete responsibility for developing the primitive groups of citizens in the hinterland. But this was not a fair arrangement." Finally, these books exhort all students "to insure the unity of your country by helping to hold together your countrymen of various tribal and non-tribal groups."

These modest and relatively recent efforts to reduce the old hostility between the handful of descendants of the settlers and the mass of tribal peoples reflect an awareness on the part of Liberia's leaders that it is foolish and dangerous to teach tribal children about the courage, heroism, and innate superiority of their ancestors' overrulers. However, the same writers are hardly apologetic for having themselves assumed this superiority, for the books are replete with references to "advanced," "Christian," "Western" pioneers as opposed to "backward," "primitive," and "slave-trading" tribal people. In this way, in civics and history classes at least, both the elite child and the tribal child are learning that all men may be equal in Liberia if they emulate the Americo-Liberians, which means that they must be literate in English, Christian in faith, Westernized in behavior, and loyal to the President.

Now these prerequisites may well have been designed to maintain the dominance and values of the ruling class. But it is perhaps significant that they are conveyed at the same time that the means of achieving "civilized" status are being taught to tribal children. The Americo-Liberian way of life, it may be assumed, also offers the prospect of a more equitable sharing of the fruits of Liberia's wealth. Not only is it held to be morally "good," it promises a materially better existence than tribal life ever could have provided. The still unanswered question is: If expectations of a better life are still frustrated at a later stage in the tribesman's life by the system which in effect attracts him out of his tribal environment, will he burn the books or the edifices of the system?

The Liberian National Youth Organization

Further evidence that Liberian leaders sensed the need to manage the acculturation of the new generation of educated youth in the early sixties was the formation in 1962 of the Liberian National Youth Organization as an autonomous agency of government. The LNYO apparently was formed because it was recognized that certain elements of society, if left to their own devices, might become the source of urban conflict and possibly violent opposition.[31] While the accomplishments of the organization must be considered modest, the prescriptions for good citizenship and social and civic consciousness, and the training of youth in both paramilitary and vocational skills under the auspices of Israeli advisers, are tokens, at least, of the government's desire to channel urban youth into "useful" activities. (Most of the LNYO activities are still in Monrovia.) And if the organization serves to inculcate some civic responsibility in the approximately 500 youths per year it aims at reaching, and affords vocational and agricultural training to some of them, it may yet prove to be a significant program.[32]

Communications

In its broadest sense, communication is the "web of human society."[33] *Political* communication may be said to involve the two-way flow of demands, support, and information between a people and their government. The literature that employs these concepts usually relates communication to mobilization of the polity for specific goals, most often in support of programs of economic and political development.[34] Through its control of communications, the government may learn the limits within which the public will support its actions, and attempt to broaden support for itself and its policies. Political communication may also be employed as a control mechanism by which the government informs the population, explicitly or implicitly, of the types of political activities it considers tolerable.

Given the array of official and unofficial informants and the centralization of authority in the office and person of the President, the upward flow of information is difficult to describe. President Tubman's personal contacts with chiefs, elders, and other tribal representatives was greater and more varied than those of any of his predecessors. They ranged from the more formal contacts with members of the Executive Councils of Chiefs, which met in different sections of the country from time to time—and at need in special cases—to informal contacts with the legions of people who took advantage of the "open door" policy at the Executive Mansion. And there were, of course, the more regular presidential representatives, public relations officers, county officials, police, and intelligence officers, who reported to the President.

It is not always apparent what significance or distortion attended the representations of informants and ordinary citizens, given their differing perceptions and interests and the complex cross-cutting influences of person, family, and region. Certainly the interests of political contenders in the modern sector were likely to be served first. Yet, political leaders nowadays need more accurate information about the ordinary people who are producers and consumers, subjects of public law and administration, and taxpayers. Ultimately, it may be these people on whom the survival of the regime will depend.

If Liberian government institutions were more representative, knowledge about popular support for, or opposition to, the government might be more easily obtainable. But in spite of the better geographic balance and the scattering of chiefs and Poro members in the legislature in the Tubman era, the urban and rural tribal people were poorly represented. The nature of Liberia's political system, and the manner in which representatives were chosen, militated against the communication through the legislature of any but the demands of the various elites. One might conjecture that had "pork barrel" politics existed in Liberia, as opposed to dependence on one source for favors, there might have developed a greater degree of give-and-take between various groups. But whether or not the upward flow of information was sufficient for rational decision making, the Tubman government had a corner on the dissemination of ideas. By monopolizing the communications media, it controlled the outflow of information and set the terms upon which the people could understand, interpret, and evaluate political developments and their personal or group relationships to them.[35]

The Press, Radio, and TV

If the control of political ideas and information, and political development in general, were to depend upon the "effective penetration of the mass media into all communal divisions of the nation,"[36] Liberia might be in a state of anarchy. For there are few such media, and they are not directed to the "masses." In spite of a literacy rate of 25 percent,[37] the principal newspapers—two dailies and one biweekly—had a combined circulation of only five to six thousand in 1967. This readership was almost exclusively in Monrovia; fewer than 500 papers were sent to other coastal townships and the hinterland, according to the largest publisher. These journals, as well as a number of rural newspapers published under the auspices of the Department of Information, were, and still are, government- or party-owned or subsidized. Members of their staffs often held government jobs as well. There also were some forty private news sheets, produced by missions, concessions, and other institutions. *New Day*, a monthly in simplified English, with a circulation of 10,000 in 1967, is produced under the auspices of the Department of Education for teachers and for classroom use.

In 1971 there were an estimated 150,000 to 200,000 radio sets throughout the country.[38] Television was limited to Monrovia and its immediate environs; there were some 2,750 sets in 1965, and 5,800 in 1969. Both the radio and television stations are owned by the government and are operated on a commercial basis under the management of the Liberian Broadcasting Company. Almost all radio and TV broadcasts are spoken in English, Liberia's official language (a considerable proportion of the population speaks some English). Some twenty broadcasts per week on Radio Liberia were delivered in tribal languages in 1971. A second radio station, "Eternal Love Winning Africa" (ELWA), sponsored by the Sudan Interior Mission, broadcasts principally religious programs throughout West Africa. The Voice of America has a relay station near Monrovia.

The radio obviously reaches more people in Liberia than any other medium, owing to the availability of battery sets. But the written media are a richer source of information about the social and political life of Liberia.

All these media generally support the government and the President. (The *Daily Listener* once offered the following headline: "The Tribesmen Have Right to Vote for Tubman.")[39]

The *Liberian Star*, a daily with a circulation of about 3,000 in 1967, is the liveliest source of national news. But in spite of its semiindependent status, the *Star* operates under virtually the same restrictions as the government-owned *Liberian Age*, a biweekly with a circulation of two to three thousand. These restrictions reside in the strong libel and slander laws, which protect government officials from nearly any sort of criticism.[40] The *Star* pithily characterized its situation in a column called "Editor's Notebook," in answer to queries about its failure to print editorials. Commenting on the freedom of the press guaranteed by the Liberian Constitution, the editor stated that "in certain situations, what is legal may not be expedient."[41] President Tubman added his own warning: "The press should begin where the press limitations start and not where the limitations end."[42]

Such a warning does not seem necessary, since the radio and press invariably support the government, often act as its mouthpiece, and observe silence in matters of political delicacy. In the 1959 elections, for example, the press did not even mention the names of opposition candidates.[43] On the other hand, there have been occasions upon which either imprudent reports or implicit opposition have caused the proscription of certain newspapers and the imprisonment of their editors—the now defunct *Friend* in 1954; the *Independent* in 1955.[44] In more recent times, the editor and two reporters of the *Liberian Age* were imprisoned for sedition; the editor of the *Star* spent a short stint in jail in 1966 and again in 1970 for "improprieties" for which the *Star* was banned; and the home editor of the *Daily Listener* was dismissed for "irresponsible" reporting in 1963.[45] (The *Listener*, which does not always appear daily, was owned by one of Tubman's close friends, C. C. Dennis.) These episodes indicate that even government- or TWP-supported media are not always discreet or knowledgeable about what they are permitted to print.

On occasion, reports that appeared to be politically sensitive, but in fact were not, were published, presumably at the direction of political leaders. For example, all media have attacked "tax delinquents," among whom the worst offenders are usually "the Honorables" themselves; but no one would mistake the fact that the message was a broad hint to the Lebanese and other aliens that payments to government officials were expected. The press has been used in other ways to pressure foreigners. In 1964, the *Listener* attacked foreign concessionaires for their failure to place Liberians in high-level management positions at a faster rate. Several racial incidents then and later were used to support the complaint that the white foreigners were not respectful or charitable guests in Liberia. These articles often served to warn businessmen that their positions in Liberia were not sacrosanct, and thus indirectly to speed up the renegotiation of whatever concession agreements were under consideration.

The press also issues the President's personal warnings to dissident or excessively independent-minded members of the ruling class or of his own administration. Such notables as former Vice-President C. L. Simpson, Congressman J. J. Mends Cole, and former cabinet official Arthur Sherman have had their loyalty to Tubman questioned by the press in the past.[46] Even Speaker Richard Henries had to defend himself in the press against charges of "plotting" against the President.[47] Though an outsider cannot fully comprehend the nuances of these incidents, it is clear to Liberians, and especially to members of the elite, that unfavorable press comments about senior members of government are sure to have been approved higher up. The final results, in any case, usually were protestations of the accused's devotion to the country and his personal loyalty to the President. Leading Liberians seldom remained long in the wilderness of Tubman's disaffection.

Perhaps the most intriguing chapter in Liberia's recent political history, the treason case of former Ambassador Henry B. Fahnbullah, was the more interesting and confusing because of the extensive press coverage given his trial. The Liberian press reported nearly word-by-word the alleged incriminating statements of the defendant. It was extraordinary to read in a Liberian newspaper about the "rape of the tribal aborigines by the Americo-Liberian ruling class."[48]

In order to control the flow of news, the government set up a Department of Information (formerly called the Liberian Information Service). The Department occupies one of the newer and finer government buildings near the Executive Mansion. After its reorganization it grew to become a major department, with a budget of nearly half a million dollars in 1965.[49] It sponsors the publication of rural newspapers with circulations ranging from several hundred to one thousand. Four such papers existed in 1969, and there were plans to have one in every county. The new Department also houses the Bureau of Cultural Affairs, whose aim is to revive or inaugurate indigenous cultural activities in Liberia, thus affording recognition of the tribal contribution to Liberia's heritage, as well as to focus national attention upon Liberia's "Africanness." All these activities are aimed at performing the function expected of any Liberian institution—to maintain the system and the elite.

— 10 —

The International Factor

From the founding of the colony in 1822, some of the most crucial influences have come from outside Liberia, profoundly affecting the nation's economic growth and decline, the rise and fall of political leaders and regimes, the forms and dynamics of government and politics, and even, at times, its sovereignty. Most important, Liberia's economy is inextricably bound to the international economic system. The foreign ownership of the nation's primary revenue and income producers intensifies this involvement.

Liberia is understandably considered, therefore, to be a typical case of neocolonialism. A defense treaty with the United States, one of the United States' largest per capita AID programs, the use of United States currency, and significant American-Liberian trade links go along with the predominantly American investment in Liberia. Foreign firms—most of which are American—provide some 80 percent of government income, 70 percent of wage employment, and 50 percent of GNP. An apparent alliance between these firms and Liberia's small ruling elite appears to be the foundation and the bulwark of the elite's material and political power.

The Impact of Foreign Investment

The areas and dimensions of foreign investment in Liberia and its economic and social consequences were discussed in Chapters 4 and 5. In this section I will summarize the political impact of foreign domination of the Liberian economy.

Albert O. Hirschman has observed that foreign investment, like most human inventions and institutions, has potential for good and evil.[1] Marx, Lenin, and latter day anti-imperialists have amply predicted and described the evils. Perhaps contemporary economists can provide tools with which we may analyze the salutary consequences of foreign investment. According to Hirschman, foreign investment may (1) provide the "missing factors of production," namely, capital and entrepreneurial management, making it possible for output to increase sharply, and (2) through its teaching function "improve the quality of the local factors of production" and hence spur the "general efficiency of local enterprise." If it does, Hirschman suggests, foreign investment will be "providentially self-limiting." But he asks, What if local businessmen do not respond vigorously, but rather fall to superior foreign competition and further deteriorate or sell out? And what if superior foreign technical, managerial, and administrative skills stunt local development before it gets started?

I must leave it to economists to deal with the economic aspects of these questions. But I will try to pose and answer them in terms of the political consequences to Liberia.

1. Have domestic political structures succumbed to foreign investors who became the principal producers of revenue and users of wage labor?

2. Have the efficiency and economic power of the foreigner set an example for, and hence spurred the efficiency of, indigenous political institutions, or have they overwhelmed and stultified them (and perhaps raided them for able personnel as well)?

3. Has the growing economic power of foreign investors proved irreversible, as individuals or groups in various localities attached themselves to the foreign enterprises? And has the Liberian government lost real sovereignty and become the instrument of foreign domination?

One might also ask whether, apart from the financial and technical contribution, Liberia might not have developed, albeit more slowly, on its own. Implicit in such a question is the suggestion that Liberians might have shared more equitably the fruits of their nation's resources and that perhaps a more democratic leadership might have emerged, had reliance on foreigners been less. Certainly any form of economic development would have unleashed social and political forces that would ultimately require the government to develop responsive mechanisms, hence more open institutions, if it wished to survive.[2] Foreign-generated and foreign-controlled economic growth, I contend, intensified the need to improve and broaden Liberian political institutions in order to keep them under Liberian control. In the process, these institutions developed the capability to resist undue foreign influence on domestic political processes. At the same time, they became more responsive to popular needs and demands.

Moreover, the Liberian government has sought to do more than just give the appearance that foreign investors were in the country at the sufferance of the government and the people. That it has done so without upsetting the very advantageous situation of the concessionaires, and the elite's own advantage from relations with them, does not alter the fact that the government has retained its legal rights and, by merely leasing land, ultimate authority in all of its concession agreements.

It seems possible to conclude that while foreign investment has not yet become "providentially self-limiting" in Liberia, its political aspects have. Thus the Liberians have answered the question "Is foreign investment good or bad for the developing countries?" not merely in economic terms. They have answered it in political terms, according to national and class interests. Because these interests are linked to political stability and continued development, they have adapted formerly narrow-based political institutions to the requirements of a modernizing society.

One can assert, therefore, that foreign investment has been "good" for Liberia, in having been a modernizing force, *if* one accepts the idea that modernization does not necessarily or immediately do away with elites, prevent class formation or, indeed, preempt all foreign economic influence.

Liberia and Africa

Liberia's international posture is generally acceptable to most Western governments. Its public opposition to communist influence in Africa is consistent with the capitalist, elitest ethos of the ruling class. And its cautious support for African unity, particularly when the more radical African states appeared to be its advocates, was also in the self-interest of that class.

Liberia's leaders failed in the past to concern themselves greatly with the rest of Africa or with the question of European imperialism on the continent. For one thing, the Republic's interests centered on Europe and the United States more than on Africa. For another, Liberia had itself been little more than a pawn of foreign diplomacy and ambitions until after World War II. Finally, the class from which Liberian leaders came had practiced a form of colonialism within their own borders.

In his first inaugural address in 1944, President Tubman endorsed the Atlantic Charter, particularly those provisions dealing with freedom and self-determination. But he was more interested in making certain that they applied to Liberia than in suggesting that they should apply as well to other parts of Africa.[3] By his second inauguration in 1952, Tubman had assumed a gradualist approach to independence for fellow Africans. He exhorted all "democratic and freedom-loving nations," under the aegis of the United Nations,

to adopt and to prosecute speedy, adequate and effective measures whereby the teeming millions of mankind inhabiting most of the underdeveloped areas of the world, who because of their peculiar circumstances are considered unprepared presently to assume the responsibility of full sovereignty and independence, may be able to do so in common with us in the shortest possible period of time.[4]

He repeated this statement in his 1956 inaugural.[5] But on the eve of Ghana's independence in 1957, Liberia seemed finally to have recognized that the independence of most African states was inevitable and that concomitant with it would be the political transformation of the continent. Yet, even at that time it was principally contention over African leadership that engaged President Tubman's attention. "I have observed," he said, "that there seem to be three schools of thought on this subject."

> There are those who feel that Liberia should assume leadership based on the fact that she is the oldest African Republic and is riper in political experience; but it will require more than age and political experience to assume leadership of Africa. There are others who hold that Ghana should assume that role because she is physically more developed and embraces larger territories. It will require more than development and larger territory to assume leadership of Africa. And there are yet those who opine that Egypt with its rich traditions dating back to the remotest antiquity, should do so. It will require more than rich traditions of antiquity. It will require, in my opinion, the aggregate of all three of these and more besides. It will require the aggregate of the best of all that Liberia, Ghana, Egypt, Tunisia, Ethiopia, The Sudan, Morocco, South Africa, Nigeria, The Federation of Nyasaland and all other African Territories and States possess, moulded together, to assume the leadership of Africa, compounded in such a manner as to represent the divisibility of Africa indivisible.
>
> I am inclined to the view that each African State must remain independent, entering, of course, into pacts, treaties or international agreements, naturally so as to strengthen and accelerate mutual intercourse and reliable ties of friendship among them, which will be beneficial to themselves and the world.[6]

Despite the pro-independence tone of his speeches, Tubman obviously regarded the tumult attending the birth of African nations as a possible threat to Liberia's independence owing to the apparently revolutionary character of a number of the new regimes, and their efforts to erase Western influence in Africa, an influence that remained important to Liberia's development.

Dreading isolation on the continent, Liberia has emphasized its own African heritage since the late sixties and has asserted a moderating presence in inter-African disputes, for example, through Tubman's personal intervention in the Ghana-Guinea quarrel in 1968; in the

Nigeria-Biafra conciliatory efforts in Niamy in August 1968; and as a
co-plaintiff in the Southwest Africa case before the International Court of
Justice. As the first black African state to sit on the Security Council of the
United Nations (1961), Liberia has sought to press its claim, if not for
leadership, at least for seniority in Africa.

As one of the oldest members of the new African community, Liberia
has served as host to a number of inter-African conferences, such as the
Monrovia Conference of the Heads of African and Malagasy States in May
1961, the largest African meeting up to that time. This meeting endorsed
the Liberian policy of functional cooperation in such areas as trade,
communications, transportation, and the like, rather than unitary political
development for the continent. The latter had been favored by the more
radical Casablanca group of African states (Ghana, Guinea, Mali,
Algeria). Monrovia also provided the locale (in April 1968) for a conference
of nine West African states (including Ghana) that were attempting to
establish a West African economic community.

The present trend in Africa toward economic cooperation represents a
moral victory for Liberia, which had resisted Nkrumah's efforts to lead
Africa into some form of political federation under Ghana's leadership.
Not only was that idea unacceptable to Tubman, but Nkrumah's efforts to
export to other African states his own radical tenets were anathema to the
conservative and Western-oriented Liberians. Relations between Ghana
and Liberia were further strained owing to the alleged Ghanaian
interference in Liberian labor affairs in 1961. Only after Nkrumah's fall in
1966 did the two states resume normal relations.

Although Guinea had been a member of the Casablanca group,
relations between Guinea and Liberia are remarkably friendly. However,
their virtually open and still partly disputed borders have not always made
for good relations between them. Widespread smuggling of Guinean
produce is done through Liberia, depriving Guinea of export revenues.
Some Liberian leaders have expressed the fear that among the large
number of Guineans who have drifted across the border to work in nearby
mines or to trade or settle with their fellow tribesmen in the border area may
be some who would indoctrinate Liberians with Guinea's brand of
Marxism. If the rather steady military build-up in Liberia over the past ten
years has any purpose apart from that of internal security, it is to protect
Liberia from the only neighbor it has any real or imagined reason to fear. In
spite of these strains and the widely differing ideological outlooks between
Sékou Touré and William Tubman, personal relations were warm between
the two. Liberia granted Guinea use of the Port of Monrovia, as well as of
the LAMCO railroad between the Guinean border and the port of
Buchanan.

Relations between Liberia and its other neighbors are also good. There are, in fact, family ties between a number of Creole families in Sierra Leone and Americo-Liberians, as there are between tribesmen who reside on both sides of the boundaries separating Liberia from Sierra Leone, the Ivory Coast, and Guinea. From time to time, the question of federation is raised. But the economies of Liberia, Sierra Leone, and the Ivory Coast do not complement one another. The special links that continue to tie Liberia to the United States, Sierra Leone to Britain, and the Ivory Coast to France, preclude, for the present, more than limited economic cooperation. Nevertheless, Liberia's efforts to forge closer relations with other African states, and its support of the Organization of African Unity's policies on anticolonialism, anti-apartheid, southern African liberation, and even nonalignment in the Cold War, have had an impact upon domestic political life. Some Liberian leaders, many students who had attended school abroad, and others have begun to feel a new identity with, and derive inspiration from, the professedly anti-imperialist people of the Third World.

Liberia in the International Community

Membership in and support of the United Nations and its specialized agencies is another cornerstone of Liberian foreign policy. The desire to play an independent international role may have sprung from Liberia's fear of being overwhelmed by American influence as well as from its past experience as the near-victim of European territorial and economic appetites. For in the UN, the small nations are theoretically equal to the great; and, through the rule of international law, national sovereignty supposedly is respected and guaranteed. The importance attached by Liberia to membership in the international community is reflected in its growing interest and participation in international diplomacy. The government has been devoting 8 to 10 percent of its annual budget in recent years to foreign relations.[7] By 1970, Liberia had direct diplomatic representation in twenty-six capitals, covering thirty-five countries (of which seventeen were in Africa).[8] It is a member of most specialized UN agencies, sent troops to the Congo in 1961 under UN auspices and, as noted, has served as host to a number of inter-African conferences.

It is difficult to assess all the domestic political consequences to Liberia of immersion in international politics after World War II. But it seems safe to say that Liberia can never again cut itself off from the rest of Africa as an island of Western civilization—which it apparently considered itself to be before World War II.

The most obvious domestic consequences of Liberia's membership in international organizations revolved around the government's treatment of the tribal people. Ever since the League of Nations inquiry into slavery in the 1930's, Liberia had been sensitive about charges of maltreatment of tribal people. As national unification became official policy, the Liberians attempted to expunge the old abuses from their country's record. In 1960 Portugal accused Liberia before the International Labor Organization (ILO) of employing forced labor. Although the ILO commission appointed to investigate the Portuguese charge found no evidence that the economy of the Republic was based upon forced labor, it reported that Liberia had been lax in conforming to all terms of the Forced Labor Convention of 1930, as well as those of other international labor agreements.[9]

Liberia has remained vulnerable to charges of unfair labor practices as a result of its efforts to limit the organization of labor. Various international labor bodies have put pressure on the Republic during the last few years. In 1967, the ILO considered charges made by the International Confederation of Free Trade Unions (ICFTU), the International Federation of Plantation, Agricultural, and Allied Workers (IFPAAW), and the Miners International Federation (MIF) regarding legislation that apparently discriminated against Liberian labor unions. Liberia conformed to the recommendations of the ILO Committee on Freedom of Association by removing from its law the alleged discriminatory language regarding trade unions.[10] In a communication to the ILO of September 11, 1967, Liberia stated that "the Government fully recognizes and accepts the right of industrial unions and agricultural unions to affiliate at the national level."[11]

The ICFTU and IFPAAW nevertheless pressed further complaints. They alleged that the Liberian government had formed and selected officials of the Rubber Tappers Association at Harbel after the January 1966 strike, and that Firestone had attempted to take control of the union. The government replied to the ILO that it had merely assisted in supervising elections and provided technical advice; furthermore it claimed to have informed Firestone that it was illegal and contrary to international labor conventions for management to control a union; and the government assured the ILO that the company had thereafter abandoned its attempts to take control of the Tappers Association.[12]

Other ILO pressures concerned the question of what is a "reasonable" time for government arbitration before a strike could legally be called; the forceful suppression of strikes at LAMCO in July 1966 and at Goodrich Plantation the following December; and the punitive arrests and dismissals of strikers. In the case of the arrest and release of a former CIO officer at Monrovia in November 1966, the ILO Committee warned that "it would feel obliged to examine the matter in further detail if the charges were subsequently to be revived."[13]

Where it has not been able to evade the pressures of international organizations, Liberia has demonstrated that it will comply with them—at least on paper. It remains to be seen to what extent this international posture will be accepted among the old guard. But as long as they are committed to reproducing in Liberia those aspects of modernity and economic development which the developed nations possess; as long as they continue the Open Door Policy; and as long as Western-style skills, organization, and institutions are needed to manage their increasingly complex economy and social system, they will not be able to resist the impact of foreign ideas and values—about labor issues as well as others. The country will not be able to function without the Western-educated technicians and administrators who represent and communicate such values.

In summary, the international relationships impose upon Liberia a variety of pressures: economic and political rationality (required and often inadvertently stimulated by foreign investors and technicians); financial obligations (to givers of aid, as part of international or bilateral loan agreements); diplomatic obligations (to special interest agencies, such as the ILO, and regional associations, such as the Organization of African Unity).[14] These external forces were influencing Liberia at the same time that Liberian society was being profoundly transformed from within. It was nearly impossible for Liberian leaders to stem or slow the tide of foreign influence and rapid change if they wished to continue the country's development and establish their prestige in the international community.

Tubman's Last Years: Political Retrenchment

The political consequences of the economic growth and development of the 1950's and early 1960's seemed for a time to be irreversible. Tubman had expanded the nation's political institutions: more broadly based representative bodies, county governments in the hinterland, a more effective and far-reaching bureaucracy, and vastly increased educational facilities, to name the most important instruments of the modernization process. But as Liberia's economic bubble deflated, and the government adopted necessary but unpopular austerity policies, discontent grew within various levels of the population. Americo-Liberians had to restrain their economic appetites; civil servants found their salaries frozen; educated tribal people had their expectations of status and wealth disappointed; and tribal migrants to the towns found the job market declining, housing scarce, and the cost of living high. Tubman came to view expressions of dissent and opposition as ingratitude at best and virtual sedition at worst. He began increasingly to employ economic, social, and political institutions to maintain his own power, and to limit that of all possible contenders. The earlier tentative steps toward broader participation began to give way to political retrenchment by the end of the 1960's.

Tubman must have seen his place in history and perhaps in office threatened by a confluence of adverse circumstances. Liberia at about this time seems to have found an unsought place on the academic map; the surge of post-independence scholarly research in Africa brought attention to Liberia's unique and somehow "un-African" form of political development. Unflattering versions of the Americo-Liberian style of rule circulated abroad.[1] Students began criticizing "the system"; military officers were thought to be involved in plotting against the government; several tribal members of the cabinet appeared to be establishing independent bases of power; labor unions were threatening the country's economic lifeline. Tubman responded by shuffling his cabinet, mainly at the expense of men whose political stars seemed too bright, such as Charles Sherman, Secretary of the Treasury and a favorite of foreign economic interests, members of the official American community, and the Vai; Augustus Caine, abrasive to the old guard and the Americans, but a favorite among young intellectuals; and others of this ilk. Tubman also spoke publicly of foreign as well as local sources of sedition, invoked presidential emergency powers more frequently, especially in putting down strikes, and tightened the press laws.

There was a palpable malaise by the late 1960's. The momentum of modernization was lost, and there was a sort of freezing of things as they were. Institutional vehicles of modernization were not halted, but they were slowed down. Young, educated people were not denied positions in the administration, but they were, and felt themselves to be, ineffectual. Challenges to the system were expressed not only in private, often by people who went abroad for post-graduate studies, but also broke out, however poorly conceived and organized, in opposition or acts of sedition. These events served further to drive Tubman into what appeared to be greater uncertainty regarding the direction in which he now should lead the country.

Following a number of military coups in Africa, Tubman began to suspect his own military establishment. In 1963, the Acting Commander of the Liberian National Guard, Colonel Y. D. Thompson, was accused, along with several members of the Grebo, Vai, and Kru tribes, of plotting to assassinate the President and other officials. Tubman claimed that this intended coup d'etat was a survival of an alleged plot of the previous year involving students from several colleges.[2] As he began increasingly to do, Tubman blamed foreign subversives for introducing

a new, strange, and traducing concept [which] seems to be attracting some of our people, particularly some of the young, impressionable and irresponsible ones who seem still to be obsessed with the idea of tribalism and fall easy prey to the propaganda and indoctrination that is secretly and stealthily being disseminated amongst them that the land and territory of Liberia belong to them and that they have been deprived of their heritage. . . . This doctrine is being disseminated by certain foreign agencies and it is finding its way into some of the schools of the country, particularly Cuttington College, the College of West Africa, the University of Liberia and other schools.[3]

Again in 1966, following widespread labor strikes, Tubman announced another near occurrence of a coup.[4] As in most of these cases, few details of the plotting were made public; a handful of people were sent to jail. In late 1966, Tubman apparently found it necessary to nip possible Montserrado-based opposition in the bud. The *Liberian Star*, obviously with official blessing, implicated former Vice-President C. L. Simpson and former Attorney General Joseph F. Chesson in "plotting" against the President.[5] The charges were never pursued or proven.

Tubman apparently believed that students were responsible for posting a sign, during his visit to the United States in 1968, which stated, "The shameless dog has gone to lick his master's feet."[6] Upon his return he labeled Cuttington College and the University of Liberia "hotbeds of revolution,"[7] and made known his determination to suppress any manifestations of student dissent. He could, of course, do so by terminating government scholarships, or by arresting student leaders. He jailed one organizer of a student committee at the University of Liberia, Tarpeh Tweseh, who allegedly circulated a document advocating a socialist movement in Liberia.[8] Further, he warned the students that those who did not favor Liberia's free enterprise system would suffer economic sanctions after graduation—primarily the denial of government employment.[9] As if to confirm Tubman's suspicions about them, students attended the treason trial of Edwin Fahnbullah in such numbers that the administration of the University of Liberia found it necessary to forbid them to cut classes to attend the trial.

The Treason Trial of 1968

The government sought to portray Fahnbullah's alleged attempt to mount a tribal movement aimed at overthrowing Americo-Liberian rule (according to the press) as a lesson in the futility of conspiratorial politics based on imagined tribal solidarity. The government charged that Fahnbullah had been dealing with communist embassies in Nairobi, where he was Ambassador from Liberia, and had sought support from Kwame Nkrumah and the envoy of the People's Republic of China in Conakry. But no evidence was presented at the trial to suggest that he had in fact constructed an underground organization in Liberia, apart from perhaps a handful of sympathizers. Instead, the Attorney General castigated Fahnbullah for attempting to "barter away the heritage of the youths of this land to satisfy the evil ambitions" of himself and "a few disgruntled members" of his tribe.[10] Government spokesmen attempted further to isolate Fahnbullah by pointing out that his section of the Vai tribe originated in Sierra Leone.

The Fahnbullah trial was reported daily by the *Liberian Star* in June and July 1968. The government further alleged that the county superintendents of Lofa, Bong, and Nimba counties had been involved in the affair. These three men were dismissed from their jobs and charged with treason. They were also charged with misappropriating public monies; the Superintendent of Lofa County, for example, was said to have collected $6 million for the purchase of arms from the People's Republic of China and France! These arrests occurred at a time when anonymous letters expressing grievances of the "aborigines" were circulating in the country. It is impossible to discuss these episodes conclusively. I have profound doubts about the "plotting" of the county officials. It would appear that Tubman was using the occasion to shake up local county factions and to keep certain ambitious individuals off balance. At the same time, the government organized manifestations of loyalty to the President from chiefs, county officials, and school children.

If there was not, in fact, serious or united tribal opposition to the regime in Liberia, why did the government make such a public issue of the Fahnbullah case? And why, after so many years of exhorting Liberians to forget the divisions between Americo-Liberians and the tribal people, did Tubman permit the press to recount Fahnbullah's apparent writings, which indicted the Americo-Liberians by name for exploiting the tribal people and expropriating their land? Only a government fairly confident that such publicity could not excite opposition would permit it.

Part of the answer to these questions may lie, first, in the government's courtroom summation against Fahnbullah. It emphasized his ingratitude to his "benefactors," who had made him an ambassador. It pointed out that he had been receiving a salary higher than that of many "descendants of the Pioneers who also served with [him] in the Foreign Service."[11] The message, it would seem, was directed to the educated tribal youth: High positions in the government were available to those who cooperated with the leadership; attempts to obtain those positions by overthrowing that leadership were therefore unnecessary (but if made, would be dealt with harshly). Fahnbullah was found quilty and imprisoned, and his personal property was confiscated.

Second, Tubman appeared also to be addressing his own constituency, which in fact he identified as "the element to which I belong."[12] He apparently perceived growing opposition from some members of the old guard, who feared that the balance of power had been shifting away from them. I believe he was informing them that if they sought to revert to the old ways, and deny tribal people participation in Liberia's political and economic development, they would face more Fahnbullahs. He also appeared to be warning them that only their unity would keep the Fahnbullahs at bay. That unity, based on class, wealth, and values, and bolstered by patronage, had been, from the beginning, the basis of Tubman's power.

Tubman may have hoped to use the Fahnbullah case to force a resolution of the conflict between his need for (1) the support of the old elite, who were unwilling to yield more of their own powers and (2) more flexibility in dealing with new contenders for influence if the potential opposition were to be suppressed. Ideally, educated tribal people and trade union leaders who were admitted into the system would abide by its rules, and the conservative old guard would reduce their hostility to assimiles who had accepted their rules, as well as their values and behavior. Tubman may have feared that on the eve of the anticipated struggle for succession, the maneuvering among the various contenders for power would threaten to rend the historical unity of the coastal elite. But the activities and the trial of Fahnbullah apparently were not the most significant indicators of deep stresses in Liberian society.

Labor as Potential Opposition

Increasingly frequent labor strikes reflected both societal stresses and organizational capabilities that could be turned to broad-based political opposition. For even though the strike in Liberia had thus far been an economic act, it was also a demand upon the state. It was an implicit challenge to the existing allocation of resources, since not only was the ruling elite partner to the largest employers, but individual members of the government were themselves employers. Labor plays a critical role in Liberia's major economic institutions. Thus, it has the potential, far in excess of its size, to disrupt both private and public economic activities.

The government's concern over the CIO's growing strength was evident in its refusal to support union efforts to adopt a "check off" system, whereby union dues are automatically withheld from wages and paid by management to the local union. The authorities also continued to harass the CIO leaders and impede their efforts to organize workers. At the end of 1966, the Secretary General of the CIO was imprisoned, indicted for sedition, and held in jail for several months under the Emergency Powers Act.[13] Bass's arrest followed two other incidents: In November 1966, an American representative of the International Federation of Plantation, Agricultural, and Allied Workers union sought to assist workers at Firestone's Harbel plantation in organizing their union; and a British representative of the Miners International Federation (MIF) attempted to advise the CIO in its wage negotiations with the Liberian Mining Company. The representative was ordered to leave Harbel by the Attorney General. (The CIO disassociated itself from his visit, observing that they were forbidden by law to organize agricultural workers.) The MIF was barred from the mine negotiations by the Secretary of Commerce.[14]

The Liberian government's resentment of foreign intervention, its fears of the growth of an independent economic interest group outside the ruling establishment, and its sense of responsibility for the welfare of at least those workers employed by foreign concessionaires resulted in a hotchpotch of labor laws which neither restrained nor effectively regulated labor organization. On the one hand, the government supported union claims for wage increases at LMC, and in one case directed that LAMCO pay $175,000 in back wages to workers employed by one of its now defunct contractors.[15] On the other hand, the government warned organized labor: "Don't bite the hand that feeds you" (meaning the government) and "Don't kill the hen [sic] that lays the golden eggs."[16] When such warnings failed, the government apparently was able to influence the choice of CIO leadership. Mrs. Susan Berry, a minor True Whig Party official, retained the figurehead presidency, but two able and active CIO officials were not returned to office in the April 1968 CIO elections.

While Tubman sought to restrain organized labor, a number of politicians showed more than casual interest in establishing communications with it. Then Vice-President Tolbert, for one, conveyed the impression of being sympathetic to the CIO, and perhaps more.[17] In another instance, a county superintendent wrote to the CIO indicating that he would "cherish" the establishment of a CIO office in his county capital.[18] Strange as this act may seem, it illustrated the beginning of political maneuvering by appointed officials who saw in organized labor a potential ally for the time when their patron, W. V. S. Tubman, would leave the scene. Other politicians at times also paid court to labor. Shad Tubman, Jr., for example, still ostensibly champions the working man.

Feelings about organized labor within the Tubman administration were more or less divided between those who would contain and those who would use its political potential. The government had, perhaps unwittingly, assumed a significant role in the field of labor relations, a role more familiar to mobilization-oriented or welfare states. The activities of the Labor Bureau, which undertook to place workers in jobs, and the Labor Practices Review Board, which adjudicated wage demands, illustrate the growth of government involvement. The Labor Bureau successfully found jobs for nearly half of its 3,270 applicants over a twelve-month period in 1965–66.[19] It also adjudicated claims for workers' compensation, and awarded workers nearly $40,000 in 1966. When the Bureau was reorganized in 1967, L. Dash Wilson, Jr., who enjoyed the respect of organized labor for his fairness and understanding of their problems, was appointed its chief.

Owing to its careful public separation of itself from the interests of foreign, white employers, the government retains a trump card in its relations with both workers and concessionaires. In spite of its corporate partnership with foreign concessionaires and its leaders' private interests, the government, as arbiter of the nation's welfare, could be responsive to workers' demands, and might, in a crisis, seek to escape opprobrium by blaming its failures upon the largest employers, who are aliens by nationality and race—a tactic that has been used in Liberia before. Such a solution would, of course, be economically risky; but it would be one means of buying time for any regime that feared the politicization of social and economic demands.

Urban Problems

Whereas there are institutional devices for suppressing or absorbing the tensions created by organized labor, potential discontent among Monrovia's underemployed and unemployed slum-dwelling *sous proletariat* was and is a greater menace to Liberia's rulers, and one that is less amenable to solution by legislation, arbitration, and shifting of responsibility. Steady migration to Monrovia in the late sixties aggravated already high unemployment. At the same time, the consumer price index for Monrovia showed a steady and fairly rapid rise: from 100.2 in December 1965 to 125.0 in 1969. The greatest increases in prices were for food (especially rice), clothing, rent, fuel and light, household goods and furniture, and health care.[20]

The response of the government to its growing urban problems appears to have been to awe urban dwellers with the power of the state, partly by erecting many imposing public buildings in Monrovia, and partly by stationing most of Liberia's security forces in and near Monrovia. On the whole, the Liberian government has not sought to reach the growing population of townsmen other than through the established, formally regulated channels of town chiefs and tribal associations.

An Era Ends

It is difficult to date—or even to describe—the phenomenon I characterize as retrenchment. But as the 1960's drew to a close, a feeling of stagnation had set in. The government's failure to continue to pursue rational administrative policies was reflected in the civil service rolls, once again burgeoning, and the continuing exodus, abroad and to private industry, of a number of abler employees. Its insecurity was reflected in the expanding size, budgets, and influence of the police and security agencies, including the Public Relations Officer program. And education received only a paltry increase of less than half a million dollars betewen 1966 and 1969.

To some observers the fading of the Tubman era was symbolized by the "old man's" halting gait, blurred speech, and general loss of physical vigor in the closing days of his reign. What struck me on my last visit, in the summer of 1971, several weeks before the President's death, were the open and frequent discussions of the question of succession. I remember when I broached that subject in 1964, and Tubman was already 69 years of age, one old hand observed, "You are making a false assumption. What makes you think the old man is ever going to die?"

Yet, Tubman's obviously poor state of health in the summer of 1971 was apparently not considered by Liberian leaders to be a license to maneuver to become the heir apparent. In spite of his father's obvious desire to place him in the line of succession, "Shad" Tubman, Jr., had failed to win support from the old guard. If Secretary of State Rudolph Grimes had harbored presidential ambitions, he apparently placed his constitutional responsibility first, as it was he who assiduously searched for the vacationing Vice-President to inform him of Tubman's death. After Tolbert's accession to the presidency, Liberians extolled their adherence to the law of the land. But I suspect that the political paralysis created by even a dying Tubman prevented illegal moves for power. Out of this paralysis and his own undistinguished vice-presidency, William Tolbert emerged to pick up the still tight reins of power and the direction of the faltering processes of modernization.

— 12 —

Conclusions

This study has traced Liberia's development from the early history of the nation, when a small coast-bound community of American settlers were the active polity, through the Tubman era, when the nation-state came to include the indigenous people of the country.

The political system established in the early years of the Republic was adequate to manage the nation's affairs when its politically active class was small and socially homogeneous,[1] and when the vast majority of the hinterland tribal people lived apart from the Americo-Liberians and were governed indirectly through tribal authorities. The need for strong central authority and for modern and efficient institutions was relatively small. But phenomenal economic growth after World War II precipitated abrupt, profound changes whose consequences are still felt. In only twenty years (1950 to 1970), the gross domestic product rose from $48 million to over $400 million. Foreign investment and aid plunged $1 billion into what had been a largely agricultural, subsistence economy. The state budget rose from some $4 million to over $60 million. Other indicators of change— numbers of schools, miles of roads, consumption of power—underscored the near tumult attending Liberia's development. Monrovia grew rapidly from a small, torpid town of 12,000 people at the outset of World War II to a hub of commerce and government with a population of 134,000 in 1970. Tribesmen in the tens of thousands moved to other towns, rubber plantations, and iron ore mines, where they apparently found life materially better than in the villages. Perhaps one-quarter of the 1.5 million people left their villages for the relatively modern Western environment. Government activities and expenditures expanded, the bureaucracy proliferated, and the web of governmental administration spread throughout the country. Markets, schools, and local government offices sprang up in remote areas; a two-way traffic of goods, people, and ideas flowed between the coast and the hinterland on a growing system of all-weather roads.

During this period of economic and social transformation, one president reigned, one party ruled, and one class dominated the political life of the nation. The legislature, the True Whig Party, the judiciary, and the bureaucracy remained, in effect, subsystems of the crucial social-political institution: the Americo-Liberian family and regional network. Even when representation at various levels of government was broadened, it remained essentially an instrument of government, and not "the 'right' of the governed."[2] Nepotism and cronyism persisted, even while standards of efficiency were being introduced into public administration. Cultural and ethnic divisions remained significant even in urban and other modern environments.

How could a political system freighted with the values and behavior of a hundred years of elitist rule remain stable during this period? The military and security forces, though intimidating, would not have been adequate to suppress serious or widespread disorder, had it occurred. Most government leaders were not popular with the mass of the people, although Tubman personally enjoyed wide support. How could a political system that served first and foremost a small elite class develop the capacity to regulate political and economic demands and win support from a wider and more diverse polity?

It may be concluded, I think, that Liberia has enjoyed relative stability because its political system has proved to be sufficiently flexible to absorb the strains produced by extensive and complex economic and social change. Under Tubman's administration a stronger and more pervasive government, including traditional forms of authority, supplanted indirect rule. Family, class, and other ascriptive criteria, which had been the sole basis for the recruitment of leadership, began giving way, albeit slowly, owing to the need for merit and achievement in governing institutions.

In this process, the monopoly of power once held by the coastal elite was breached. The narrow base of Liberian politics was greatly broadened after Tubman's accession to power and after massive foreign investment and economic and technical assistance launched economic development. The old elite is no longer coterminous with political authority *and* the polity. Though its members still dominate the political arena and use their power in their own interests, they now have to be conciliatory toward others. As a consequence, political leaders have begun to seek broader popular approval and support and have become more accountable to the groups of their constituents who have begun to demand a greater share of economic resources and social and political rights. The bureaucracy, once based purely on patronage, has begun to adopt more rational procedures. Men with technical competence are being given more responsibilities as purely political determinants are modified by economic exigencies.

Identification with the nation rather than the tribe is becoming more relevant as more people come to depend upon the state for their economic survival, political rights, and social mobility.

Integration

What can be called, conceptually, broadening participation is in part a product of a carefully regulated process of assimilating tribal people into the modern, Westernized culture of the Americo-Liberians. As noted earlier, while economic growth has produced wealth for the country and launched its modernization, economic development and modernization together have produced and accentuated inequalities in the society. Indeed, according to Irving Louis Horowitz, "modernization serves to reinforce the existing social structure by showing how it is possible for a small section of the population to share in the goods of the scientific-technological world, without altering the forms of human relations or the character of social production."[3] Nevertheless, the Liberian elite, in seeking to maintain the existing social structure and their own preeminence, sought not to exclude tribesmen but to enmesh them in the system. In earlier days it was done on a very small scale by adopting tribal children who worked as servants but were otherwise treated as members of the family. Now, eminent tribesmen who hold positions in the legislature, the government, or the True Whig Party usually do so as a result of sponsorship (or at least acceptance) by older members of the elite. They do not yet hold independent political power, nor do they enjoy social parity with the older members of the elite, although most newcomers have willingly adopted their values and behavior, and adhere to their social, political, and bureaucratic rules.

Newcomers have strengthened the ruling class numerically. On the other hand, they have broadened its multi-ethnic membership and altered its character. Even the more conservative members of the elite acknowledge the right of qualified tribal people to participate in government. Americo-Liberian norms persist. But the rewards attending their acceptance no longer are the exclusive preserve of the Americo-Liberians' descendants.

Some critics contend that this form of integration has arrested the country's political development. I believe that such a view underestimates the powerful push which economic forces have given to modernization. It overestimates the ability of the elite to contain these forces, as well as the desire, haste, and ability of the new members of the modern sector to assume greater political responsibilities. In any case, the ordinary tribal people's participation in the political life of the nation apparently lags far behind their important contribution to economic development.

Thus far, the quest of urban and agricultural workers has been for horizontal mobility and a greater share of the rewards that accompany membership in the modern sector, not political power. Are there no stirrings of opposition? History provides much evidence that disinherited people do not always remain passive; that those who begin to receive greater economic rewards and political influence tend to want more; and that there are usually alienated elements in all strata of a society that has undergone rapid and profound change, as Liberia has. I will review, briefly, the apparent political attitudes and behavior of those groups which are the most likely source of opposition to the system that has developed over the last twenty years.

Tribes

Some students of Liberia's political development seem to summon up images of hordes of tribal people descending on the centers of politics and commerce in order to seize power from their oppressors. There is little evidence that the tribal people are, collectively, aware of any such oppression, or that they would or could seize power. How can there be, if the tribes are themselves divided, both internally and from one another, and when their potential leaders have access to and may even become part of the ruling establishment. Tribal groups do not constitute an alternative to the present partly integrated government.

Workers, Urban and Rural

Owing to the recent economic opportunities in commerce and wage labor, the availability of new social services, such as in public education and health, and the diminution of the former customary excesses of officials and the military, most Liberians are better off than ever before in the history of the Republic. Liberians—unlike the revolutionary Frenchmen described by Tocqueville—apparently do not yet find their situation more intolerable the better it becomes. While discontent undoubtedly exists in the slums of Monrovia, these poor urban-dwellers are partially insulated from a shared sense of deprivation by urban tribal associations and the relationships they maintain with their tribal homelands. Even if workers are aware of their class membership, they do not yet express class interests in political terms. Rather, they seek individually to obtain the status, symbols, and rights of participation in the economic life of the modern sector, and only indirectly in its political life.

Organized Labor

If, as seems likely, Liberia's economic development continues to be based on export production, on the alienation of land for plantations, and on extractive industries, a large stable wage labor force will become imperative. The role of labor unions therefore seems likely to become increasingly significant, though it is not apparent whether they will be independent or will become virtually an arm of government. If, as has occurred elsewhere in Africa, the leaders of organized labor are incorporated into the ruling establishment, their independence will be lost. Whether it retains its independence or not, organized labor will be more likely to press for greater economic rewards in return for its political cooperation than to seek an alternative to the present system.

Youth

Will opposition form on the basis of differences in the political orientation of the generations? These differences are not so harsh in Liberia as in other underdeveloped countries. In many of the former colonies, a young, Western-educated generation displaced their fathers as indigenous rulers at the time of the transfer of power. In Liberia, by contrast, the old elite as well as the educated younger generation are Westernized. Though less well-educated than their children, they are still able to enforce their claim to continue their effective rule.

Among the educated young Liberians are some who believe Liberia has been denied a fair share of the fruits of its commercial exploitation. Thus, they tend to favor greater state intervention in economic affairs, and consider themselves the appropriate leaders to direct this intervention. But though some of them fear that they will not be able to assume the roles they merit by right of education and ability as long as Liberia's traditional system persists, the perquisites which await them if they work within the system, and the inevitability of the passing of power to them, both as biological heirs and as the technological managers of a modernizing economy, tend to bind most potential radicals to the existing system. Even among those educated youths and students who felt a strong antipathy to the Tubman regime, the most immediate goal appears to have been to gain admission into the system, not to destroy it.

The Military

As events in Africa and elsewhere readily show, the military forces often have the capability to seize (if not to hold) power, almost at will. It is difficult to predict whether such an event could occur in Liberia. Given the attachment of the military to the existing political authority, and its fairly careful development as an instrument of the ruling class, I would not expect the army or police—apart from a few ambitious individuals—to intervene in politics unless the present ruling class were threatened from without or unless no single person could muster enough support to govern. As in the bureaucracy, even the younger tribal officers appear to identify themselves with the elite. If there are among these men ideological or reformist impulses, they remain undetected by the observers I have interviewed in Liberia.

*   *   *   *

Adaptation, not opposition, appears to describe best the response of Liberians to modernization and integration. Neither Americo-Liberians, tribal farmers, tribal workers, tribal associations, nor tribal elites, either separately or in concert, have seriously opposed the government and endangered its capacity to rule. There have been no attempts, say, to organize a nationwide strike or rebellion. And occasional efforts to build a new political party have failed. Indeed, most of these elements appear to have accommodated themselves to the established system. That they have not been denied access to positions of influence and improved economic status underscores the successful adaptation by the ruling elite to their demands. This mutual accommodation, which undeniably includes sanctions against recalcitrants, has blunted the prospect of serious upheavals and formal opposition.

This changing system has produced a new array of potential power brokers, such as union officials, unofficial workers' leaders, and educated tribal people in the central and county governments. For example, just as the Paramount Chief became the focus of tribal politics and the instrument of administrative centralization during "pacification" in the 1930's, so the county seat has become an intermediate arena of county and central politics. It has been suggested that some hinterland county leaders "have formed groupings to compete for resources of the government in competition with the powerful coastal forces."[4] I have seen no evidence of this; and were it to occur, it would be unlikely to take this form of direct competition. Rather than hold out for regional advantage, local leaders would be more likely to trade their constituencies' support for aspiring national politicians for the many favors potentially at the disposal of the latter once they assumed power. This type of arrangement would improve communication between the center and the periphery and would serve to integrate government and party organs at both levels.

Yet, modernization and integration have ambiguous consequences and, indeed, create new stresses in societies. A new form of rural stratification may be finding roots in this combination of national integration, which opens participation in national politics to hinterland people through their local and congressional representatives, and the country's assimilation practices, which serve to select those individuals for leadership who emulate, and cooperate with, the coastal elite. It is possible that the result of this form of patron politics will be exploitation at the local level by local leaders. However, in view of the continuing rural exodus to modern economic enclaves, there may also be a quest for sound and mutually beneficial relationships in the rural areas in order to keep people at home.

In short, modernization does not produce the millennium. It only provides a greater capacity to contend with problems of change than traditional systems have. It does not eliminate classes, traditionalism, recidivism, pernicious and avaricious behavior, or conflict. How things come out, what sort of conflict is likely, and who ends up on top depend to a great extent upon the system's leaders, their goals, and the political tactics they employ. Thus far, Liberia's leaders have been slowly introducing modernization and, at the same time, preserving certain inherited characteristics of the political system relatively intact. And they have done so in a plural setting marked by the emergence of new forces in society alongside—at times integrated with, and at times pressing their claims against—older ones. Old institutions with new functions provide a structural link between the past and the present. They are no longer traditional, yet they are not completely modern. This type of development resembles the Western modernizing experience, in which "historically evolved institutions" were important factors in maintaining continuity and stability during those nations' modernization.[5]

In spite of, or indeed because of, its historical foundations, Liberia's political system has become relatively more elastic, inclusive, and amenable to peaceful change. Liberia may not escape political upheavals during its continuing modernization. It is possible that if its leaders had been less defensive they could have done much more to enhance the nation's development and to develop more democratic processes. But had they been less traditional, they might have lost the support of the more conservative elements in the country—both Americo-Liberians and tribal. Had they been less modern, Liberia would not enjoy the economic growth *and* development, or the stability, it does today.

One might turn this last statement around and argue that economic growth purchased stability. Certainly, phenomenal economic growth did serve as a handmaiden to Tubman and other politicians in the 1950's. Substantially increased revenues and patronage provided the "political goods" and material rewards which made manageable the rising demands of new tribal leaders, workers, and students, among others. However, the leveling off to about five percent in the late 1960's of some fifteen years of expanding GNP, personal income levels in all strata of society, and the state's budgetary resources, has in effect forced the government to rely more on the institutional features of the political system, and less on its capacity to distribute financial and other economic rewards. Thus, in a period of fiscal austerity, evolving institutions apparently succeeded in not merely withstanding but facilitating modernization. While there were tell-tale signs of resistance to extensive political change in the last few years of Tubman's rule, the government did not greatly increase its reliance on political repression. Decay did not set in.

Liberia has taken some cautious steps toward more democratic government. One new member of the elite may have expressed, both in his person and his words, this emerging new politics in Liberia. Thanking President Tubman and the True Whig Party for "elevating" him "from the butcher shop to the Legislature," he offered Liberians the following analysis and implied prescription for avoiding the coups d'etat that have beset Africa in recent years:

> There would have been no coup if the poor man has an opportunity of eating smoked fish while the leader eats ham and eggs. But if the poor man has nothing to eat while you eat ham and eggs, he will surely do something against you.[6]

Postscript

"To Higher Heights" *

Vice-President William Richard Tolbert became the nineteenth president of Liberia in July 1971 when Tubman died, in England, at the age of 75. As Vice-President-elect—elections had been held in April 1971—he began in January 1972 what would have been Tubman's full four-year term. Contrary to the expectations of many observers, and in spite of deep uncertainty in the country during the first weeks, there were no serious challenges to his accession to power. The transition occurred in an atmosphere of deep mourning. The nation's leaders offered prayers for peace and unity. Tolbert invoked Tubman's spirit, world stature, and policies in promising continuity.

While he may have sought the spiritual guidance of his predecessor, he did not depend upon the organizational apparatus he inherited. Not, at least, upon the military and security services. Within days of his assumption of office, Tolbert visited military units on several occasions, a practice he continues to perform regularly. Across-the-board pay raises were granted in 1972, and selective promotions and retirements in the officer ranks followed. Tolbert's first personnel action as President was to appoint a new director of the formerly autonomous security agencies, and he shortly thereafter chose a new police director.

Although a number of cabinet officials who had been considered contenders for the presidency were removed, such as Secretary of State Grimes, several new cabinet officials were drawn from the heart of the Tubman machine: Mrs. Mai Padmore, former Special Assistant to the President, who was appointed Minister of Health and Welfare (she left office in 1973 for reasons of health); William E. Dennis, son of Tubman's old friend C. C. Dennis, to the Ministry of Commerce and Industry; and an "outside" contender for the presidency, Dr. Rochefort Weeks, President of the University of Liberia, as Secretary of State (he was replaced in mid-1973 by C. C. Dennis, Jr.).

Tolbert also appointed three former officials who had been out of favor in Tubman's last administration: James Gbarbea, former Superintendent

---

*The subtitles in the postscript are the slogans coined by President Tolbert to mark his administration.

of Bong County, as Deputy Director of the Bureau of National Resources
and Surveys; former Ambassador Henry Fahnbullah, whom Tolbert
pardoned in December 1972, as Assistant Minister of State for Presidential
Affairs; and Albert T. White, former Commanding Officer of the Liberian
National Guard, as Superintendent of Grand Gedeh County (to which
Tubman had "rusticated" him in 1966). Tolbert also restored two younger
men whose fortunes had declined in Tubman's last year: former
Secretaries of Education John P. Mitchell and Augustus Caine.

Clearly the most important new cabinet member is Stephen Tolbert,
younger brother of the President.* A Secretary of Agriculture under
Tubman, and more recently a millionaire businessman, Tolbert assumed
the important Treasury portfolio (subsequently renamed the Ministry of
Finance). The younger Tolbert's commanding position in the new
government became evident in mid-1972 during broad-ranging concession
renegotiations between the government and foreign investors. His
activities were reported widely in the press, taking second place only to
those of the President, who had undertaken a heavy schedule of foreign
visits through Africa in 1972 and to Europe and the United States in 1973.

By the end of 1972 Tolbert's cabinet, while not yet de-Tubmanized,
had a fresh look. For one thing, it was considerably younger than
Tubman's last cabinet, consisting of a number of men who had advanced
degrees from foreign universities. Perhaps more important, it reflected
Liberian geography better than any previous cabinet. As one newspaper
columnist observed, the cabinet had its roots in "the various segments of
society," reducing by a little Montserrado's historical dominance of key
government positions.[1] Hence, Lofa County gave a young Ph.D., Edward
Kessely, Minister of Information, Cultural Affairs, and Tourism, its first
cabinet post. D. Franklin Neal, a Marylander, replaced Montserrado's
Cyril Bright at the Ministry of Planning in November 1972. Finally,
Tolbert honored Sinoe County, an area in which Tubman had always been
politically insecure, by picking Senator James Greene for his Vice-
President, to which office he was returned in a special election in January
1972. Tolbert could afford to reduce Montserrado's domination in government. Unlike Tubman, he is from Montserrado County; his brother Frank
is a powerful senior Senator from that county; and his brother Stephen's
multifarious business ventures accord him power and prestige in the nation's capital and dominant region.

Tolbert's early actions, then, were aimed at securing his position.
They marked his administration as at once the heir of Tubman (in the
persons of a number of Tubman's cronies, e.g., Speaker Henries, Post

---

*Stephen Tolbert died in a plane accident in April 1975.

Master General and TWP Chairman DeShield) and as distinctly his own, in the persons of his brother Stephen and a band of younger and non-Montserrado men. These tactics are characteristic of Tubman's early and middle years. But there were crucial differences in terms of economic and political policies. Here Tolbert appears to have picked up the momentum that Tubman let falter in the mid-1960's. It is too early in the Tolbert administration to assume that the "tendencies" described below are in fact trends. Yet there is evidence that Tolbert has sought to strike out in the direction of reform and revitalization of certain institutions, even while he has responded "traditionally" to some of the consequences of the reforms he has instigated.

"A Wholesome Functioning Society"

Reform may serve the reformers as much as—or more than—the people it purports to help. Reform can also reshape institutions. Shortly after his inauguration, Tolbert announced that deductions from salaries of civil servants for the True Whig Party would be abolished.[2] Although this relief was not immediate in coming, its promise heartened civil servants, who remain the bedrock of the government. In May 1972, Tolbert announced the termination of the Public Relations Officer (PRO) program instituted by his predecessor, a costly and onerous institution. Disclosing that over $1 million would otherwise have been expended in fiscal 1972, Tolbert recommended the establishment of a pension scheme to be paid for with funds already appropriated for the PRO program. He proceeded thereafter to "pension off" a number of PRO's.[3] He also announced his intention to establish a social security program.

In seeking to rationalize the civil service system, Tolbert revived the moribund Civil Service Commission. He instructed the commission to develop an examination system for all government employees and to standardize salary scales. The military did not have to wait, however. Soldiers' pay was raised $5 per month for privates, $3 for all other ranks in April 1972. Tolbert's efforts to reorient military and security services to himself were augmented by a United States loan of $2 million for the purchase of military equipment in order to "increase the mobility and civic action capabilities of the armed forces."[4] In 1973, nothing less than a purge of the armed forces occurred. Seven hundred officers and enlisted men of the 4,000-man army were retired from active duty for "old age, tenure of service, physical disability, general worthlessness and for the convenience of the government."[5]

By these actions, Tolbert uprooted much of Tubman's personal patronage system and his network of informers and defenders, whose loyalties he could not confidently transfer to himself. At the same time he avoided alienating those who lost their positions (PRO's, retired civil servants, and military officers) by increasing the available pension funds. Whether these arrangements, the increase in salary scales for the armed forces, and the improvement of civil servants' (including teachers') pay and working conditions have succeeded in securing their loyalties to Tolbert can only be conjectured. What *is* clear is that Tolbert clearly sought, in the name of reform, both to weaken and to appease these possible sources of opposition.

"From Mats to Mattresses"

The customary annual celebration of President Tubman's birthday, the responsibility for which had devolved in turn upon each county, was transformed in Tolbert's first year into a "National Fund Raising Rally." Though designated for certain national projects and, as Tubman's fêtes supposedly were, aimed at raising funds for development in the counties, the rally is just as likely to end up as local slush funds or as funds for "development projects" that would benefit relatively few people, such as the 500-seat football stadium, administration building, airfield, motel-hotel, cinema, and clubhouse, announced by Lofa County's Superintendent as its effort in the "development race."[6] It may be hoped that some of the $4.8 million collected by July 1974 (the goal was $10 million) will go, as announced, to the relocation and improvement of the University of Liberia, and to development of education, housing, roads, and health.

In view of the fact that the central government has announced a new $5 per person (or per hut) development tax, it appears that the bulk of Liberia's development will still depend upon the national budget.[7] Of the $83 million budgeted in 1973, $23 million was for external and domestic debt-servicing; $28.8 million was for personnel services, or about 47 percent after debt-servicing. It is fair to add that education receives the greatest share of government expenditures after debt servicing.[8]

"Total Commitment"

The Tolbert administration, then, has not broken with the past. But it has, even while retaining old institutions and practices, revitalized some of them. While Tolbert's casting off of suit jacket and tie in favor of informal, open-necked garb does not constitute a revolution, it is an expression of a new, more informal style in Liberian politics. The President's earlier practice of appearing at his ministers' offices at 8 a.m., and publicly chastising (and in one case firing) senior officials not on the job, did not immediately wipe out diffident work habits, but it expressed a seriousness about government that may produce salutary results over time.

There has been substance, too, in Tolbert's efforts to bring economic reform to Liberia. The campaign to review and rationalize the country's concession agreements testifies to Tolbert's determination to correct inequities in these agreements. As he stated in his Independence Day address in July 1972, he intended to rectify a situation in which Liberian resources were being depleted, the environment was being polluted, and the people received "comparatively insufficient direct or indirect, immediate or future compensation." He went on: "At present, benefits have accrued to a few individuals, but not to the nation. . . . Government is obligated to ensure that benefits derived from her policies accrue to the masses, and not to a privileged few."[9]

Tolbert's call for a more equitable partnership between Liberians and foreign investors echoed in the press and in subsequent public statements, such as one calling for the "liberation" of the economy from foreign domination.[10] Finance Minister Stephen Tolbert, who led negotiations between the government and the largest concessions (and in 1973 became Chairman of Board of Directors of LAMCO) announced his intention to devise a model concession agreement; but he warned that while new agreements would be beneficial, they were not aimed at diminishing Liberia's hospitality to foreign investment. Clearly the renegotiations have not produced a hostile climate, as foreign investors continue to find attractive opportunities in Liberia. According to one informed source, while the new agreements have gone some way in reducing past inequities, the Liberians should have held out for more: "They were too timid."

At the same time, in keeping with the President's announced wish that Liberians distribute the advantages and burdens of citizenship more equitably among themselves, tax and other revenue collections were stepped up. Revenues received from income tax collections increased by 16 percent in 1972. Tolbert also ordered Tubman's luxury yacht to be sold, saving $250,000 per year in maintenance costs. And he abolished the monopoly of rice imports held by a firm that was headed by a member of the Tubman family. The government also established a public corporation to "aid, assist, encourage and develop private entrepreneurship" for the benefit of Liberian traders, and proposed the establishment of an Agricultural Credit Bank to aid small farmers.[11] As in the Tubman era, such gestures of reform and help for the little man often were not implemented as promised. But new government bureaus did create economic opportunities and jobs for the elite.

Perhaps overestimating the liberalizing intentions of the Tolbert administration and the more open climate for free expression, some young people took up the cry of reform. Students at the University of Liberia voted to change the national motto, "The Love of Liberty Brought Us Here," claiming that it applied only to the Americo-Liberian settlers, not to the indigenous people.[12] Then, in January 1973, a nationwide youth movement was formed by students at the University of Liberia to involve young people in national affairs "in order to effect major socioeconomic and political changes in our national structures."[13]

In response, Tolbert announced that he wanted nine additional seats in the legislature set aside for representation of people under the age of twenty-eight (later twenty-five) from each county.[14] The youth movement, reconstituted as the People's Progressive Movement, challenged the President's proposal on the grounds that legislative representation did not accurately reflect the constitutional provision for distribution by population; and that the movement would not accept "gifts" from, nor a loss of its independence to, the True Whig Party. At about this time, students at the University of Liberia verbally assaulted and insulted Vice-President James Greene, who was addressing them on behalf of the National Fund Raising Rally. They complained of "hard times" generally, the high price of rice, and his personal extravagances, urging him to replace his expensive car with a Volkswagen.[15]

The press resounded with attacks upon the pretensions of the youth movement, its claim to represent all youth, its members' bad manners, and its expectation that the nine seats would automatically go to members of the movement.[16] By the middle of 1973 the youth movement had fallen on hard times, as open disputes for leadership split the organization into three factions.

While this source of opposition appeared to have been dampened (university students apologized to the Vice-President), a plot to subvert the Tolbert government was revealed later in 1973. The plot was alleged to have involved the Assistant Minister of Defense for Coast Guard Affairs and two army officers. During the trial, at which it was revealed that President Tolbert, Minister Tolbert, and Senator Tolbert (President Pro-Tempore of the Senate) were to have been assassinated, several additional army officers were implicated. It was further alleged that the plotters intended to place Senator Harrison Grigsby, from Sinoe County, in the presidency, but to maintain military dominance in the country.[17] Grigsby denied knowledge of the plot, and averred that he would not have accepted the presidency had it been offered to him. He was not prosecuted. The chief plotters received heavy jail sentences, but Tolbert pardoned and freed them in July 1974.

This alleged military-sponsored plot, the restiveness of students, and persistent labor troubles, surfacing in frequent strikes, may have blunted the more reformist and revitalizing tendencies of the Tolbert administration. Tolbert was granted "emergency powers" by the legislature in May 1973, at about the time of the alleged military plot, and further powers in March 1974, acts that hark back to Tubman's last years.[18] Potential opponents and political recalcitrants have begun to feel the sting of government disapproval. For example, the Liberian Congress of Industrial Organizations lost its monopoly in the labor field when the United Workers of Liberia was formed in 1974, possibly at the government's instigation. The UWL won over several formerly CIO-affiliated unions in Monrovia and by mid-1974 was challenging the CIO for the affiliation of the important LAMCO mine workers.[19]

The press has been harshly reminded of the limits to its freedom. In July 1974, the editors of the *Liberian Star* and the *Liberian Age* were arrested, allegedly for "promoting gambling," after President Tolbert had vetoed legislation that would legalize it. A *Star* columnist, in assessing the arrests and the loss of his own position as assistant editor, observed that the government was acting against those who dared to express unacceptable opinions on issues of national concern.[20]

Perhaps to underline his capacity to punish offenders, President Tolbert personally broke ground for a new $1.3 million prison, to be known as the "Palace for Correction and Rehabilitation." The prison will hold up to a thousand inmates.[21] In the meantime, according to Tolbert, troublemakers would be sent to Bella Yella prison.[22]

Students, too, were reminded of the limits the government placed on their political behavior. President Tolbert personally ordered the closing of Booker Washington Institute in July 1974, and school authorities, probably at government instruction, closed Cuttington College the following month, in both cases because of student agitation.[23]

At the end of 1974 the government banned public meetings in connection with a libel case brought by Stephen Tolbert against an inveterate pamphleteer, Albert Porte. The case, involving Porte's accusation that Tolbert had used his office for personal profit, was turned into a political cause célèbre by supporters of both Tolbert and Porte. Porte's supporters, college professors and journalists, were cited for contempt of court for having convened mass meetings and for making public speeches and publications "with a view to inciting and exciting the public."[24]

These apparently repressive acts are not unusual in the Liberian context. Nor do they necessarily signal a resumption of Tubman's retrenchment policies. For there is also evidence of fresh movement at the top: there are new faces, new styles, and new official goals. Tolbert appears to wish to broaden the political system to include more representatives of the hinterland, youth, and labor, but not as political adversaries. Thus, he has sought to resume the modernizing tendencies of the early 1960's; and he has linked them to a new emphasis on nationalist sentiments and some tinkering with the power structure and distributive mechanisms of the state. Taken together, these tactics would seem to offer enough political and economic payoffs to older members of the elite and new aspirants for wealth and influence to forestall serious opposition, in the near future at least.

In his efforts to maintain a balance between tradition and the forces of modernization—or between the old ruling class and new contenders—Tolbert is so far, like Tubman, a defensive modernizer. His new style and rhetoric, however, may have unleashed forces for change that he will have to give scope to, or he may be forced to give way to others who will.

Notes

1: Introduction

1. C.T.O. King, Liberian Ambassador to the United Nations, 1957, complained that this had been a disadvantage. Robert Clower et al., *Growth Without Development: An Economic Survey of Liberia* (Evanston: Northwestern University Press, 1966), p. 3.
2. Clower et al., *Growth*, and J. Gus Liebenow, *Liberia: The Evolution of Privilege* (Ithaca: Cornell University Press, 1969).
3. See also Elliot J. Berg's excellent discussion of the growth-development argument, in "Growth, Development and All That: Thoughts on the Liberian Experience" (Center for Research on Economic Development, University of Michigan, March 1969), esp. pp. 3–19. The population of Liberia, formerly put at 1.1 million, has recently been resurveyed. Department of Planning and Economic Affairs, *Demographic Annual of the Population Growth Survey, 1970*, Monrovia, Dec. 1970.
4. The Liberian Legislature amended the laws which provided for the separate administration of the hinterland. The counties system, until 1964 effective only at the coast, replaced the three provinces of the hinterland. This act began the administrative integration of the tribal peoples.
5. A. N. Allott, "Draft Report on Advisory Visit to the School of Law, University of Liberia," [1967].
6. Aristide Zolberg, "The Structure of Political Conflict in the New States of Tropical Africa," *The American Political Science Review*, vol. 62, no. 1 (March 1968), p. 77.
7. The UN Statistical Yearbook, 1973, puts life expectancy at 45.8 years for men, 44.0 for women. It reports 159.2 deaths per 1,000 live births.
8. All societies, of course, are in some form of transition, as are the two principal sectors in Liberia. The transition expressed here is one from subsistence farmer to sometime member of the modern sector.
9. The principal works that have inspired the conceptual approach used in this book are: Samuel P. Huntington, *Political Order in Changing Societies* (New Haven: Yale University Press, 1968); Aristide R. Zolberg, *Creating Political Order* (Chicago: Rand McNally, 1966); Claude E. Welch, ed., *Political Modernization* (Belmont: Wadsworth, 1967); C. E. Black, *The Dynamics of Modernization* (New York: Harper & Row, 1966); Dankwart A. Rustow, *A World of Nations* (Washington, D.C.: 1967); David E. Apter, *The Politics of Modernization* (Berkeley: University of California Press, 1965); J. Roland

Pennock, "Political Development, Political Systems and Polit-ical Goods," *World Politics*, vol. 18, no. 3 (April 1966); "New Nations: The Problems of Political Development," Karl von Vorys, ed., *The Annals of the American Academy of Political and Social Science*, vol. 358 (March 1965); and S. N. Eisenstadt, *Modernization: Protest and Change* (Englewood Cliffs: Prentice-Hall, 1966).

10. Martin Kilson aptly describes "rationalization" as the establishment of structures and procedures "appropriate to the performance of the major needs of a social system," in *Political Change in a West African State: A Study of the Modernization Process in Sierra Leone* (Cambridge, Mass.: Harvard University Press, 1966), p. 281.

11. Huntington, *Order in Changing Societies*, pp. 34–36.

12. Charles W. Anderson et al., *Issues of Political Development* (Englewood Cliffs: Prentice-Hall, 1967), p. 8.

13. Charles W. Anderson, *Politics and Economic Change in Latin America* (New York: D. Van Nostrand, 1967), p. 34.

14. Huntington, *Order in Changing Societies*, Ch. 1. See also Irving Louis Horowitz, *Three Worlds of Development* (New York: Oxford University Press, 1966), and Lloyd I. and Susanne H. Rudolph, *The Modernity of Tradition: Political Development in India* (Chicago: University of Chicago Press, 1967).

15. Amatai Etzioni, *Political Unification* (New York: Holt, Rinehart and Winston, 1965), p. 330.

16. Claude Ake, "Political Integration and Political Stability," *World Politics*, vol. 19, no. 3 (April 1967), p. 486. See also A.F.K. Organski, *The Stages of Political Development* (New York: Knopf, 1965); Myron Weiner, "Political Integration and Political Development," in Welch, ed., *Political Moderniza-tion*, pp. 150–66; and Aristide R. Zolberg, "Patterns of National Integra-tion," *The Journal of Modern African Studies*, vol. 5, no. 4 (December 1967), pp. 449–67.

17. Karl W. Deutsch, *Nationalism and Social Communication*, 2nd edition (Cambridge, Mass.: M.I.T. Press, 1966).

18. Zolberg, "Patterns of National Integration," p. 451. Clifford Geertz, "The Integrative Revolution: Primordial Sentiments and Civic Politics in the New States," in Geertz, ed., *Old Societies and New States: The Quest for Modernity in Asia and Africa* (Glencoe: The Free Press, 1963).

19. Paul Mercier, "Remarques sur la signification du 'Tribalisme' actuel en Afrique Noire," *Cahiers Internationaux de Sociologie*, July–December 1961, pp. 61–80. See also Immanuel Wallerstein, "Ethnicity and National Integration," in H. Eckstein and David Apter, eds., *Comparative Politics* (New York: Free Press of Glencoe, 1963).

20. James S. Coleman, "Political Modernization," in *International Ency-clopedia of the Social Sciences*, vol. 10.

21. Robert Graves, "Introduction" to Alexander Liberman, *Greece, Gods, and Art* (New York: The Viking Press, 1968), p. 8.

22. Anderson, *Politics*, Ch. 4, discusses the concept of power capability. See also

Louis J. Halle, *The Society of Man* (New York: Harper & Row, [1965?]), p. 120: "The corruption of all doctrinaire thought is that it becomes a vested interest, bound up with personal power and security, more than a representation of what is conceived to be true." See also Apter, *The Politics of Modernization*, p. 2.

23. See Frantz Fanon, *The Wretched of the Earth* (London: Penguin Books, 1967).

24. Albert O. Hirschman, *Journeys Toward Progress* (Garden City: Doubleday, Anchor, 1965), p. 23.

2: The History and People

1. A start has been made by Warren L. d'Azevedo, in his five-part study, "A Tribal Reaction to Nationalism," which has appeared serially in the *Liberian Studies Journal*, vols. 1, 2, and 3; Svend E. Holsoe, editor of the above journal, author of several historiographic studies appearing therein, and author of an unpublished Ph.D. dissertation, "The Cassava-Leaf People: An Ethno-historical Study of the Vai People with Particular Emphasis on the Tewo Chiefdom" (Boston University, 1967); and Zamba C. Liberty, "The Growth of the Liberian State: An Analysis of Its Historiography" (draft, Stanford University, 1972). There are other Liberian historians, but the above authors are making sustained efforts in the field.

2. Hannah Abeodu Bowen Jones, "The Struggle for Political and Cultural Unification in Liberia, 1847–1930" (unpublished Ph.D. diss., Northwestern University, 1962), p. 89.

3. Liebenow, *Liberia*.

4. Seymour Martin Lipset, *The First New Nation* (New York: Basic Books, 1963), p. 174.

5. P. J. Staudenraus, *The African Colonization Movement, 1816–1865* (New York: Columbia University Press, 1961), pp. 12, 29–35.

6. U.S. Congress, Senate, "Roll of Emigrants That Have Been Sent to the Colony of Liberia, West Africa by the American Colonization Society and Its Auxiliaries, to September 1843 &c," 28th Cong., 2d sess., 1845, *Public Documents*, vol. 9, docs. 150–171 and 173. Much of the following data and analysis derive from this source. See also Huberich, *History of Liberia*, vol. I.

7. Huberich, *History of Liberia*, vol. 1, pp. 568–615.

8. Staudenraus, *Colonization Movement*; Merran Fraenkel, *Tribe and Class in Monrovia* (New York: Oxford University Press, 1964), pp. 5–7.

9. U.S. Congress, Senate, "Roll of Emigrants." Huberich, *History of Liberia*, vol. 1, p. 818, records several ships arriving after that period, but notes a sharp decline after 1843.

10. U.S. Congress, Senate, "Roll of Emigrants."

11. *Ibid.* See also Tom W. Shick, "A Quantitative Analysis of Liberian Colonization from 1820–1843, with Special Reference to Mortality," *Journal of African History*, vol. 12, no. 1 (1971), who records 2,198 deaths and 520 persons having left the colony for other parts of Africa or to return to the United States.

12. U.S. Congress, Senate, "Roll of Emigrants."

13. Jane J. Martin, "How to Build a Nation: Liberian Ideas about National Integration in the Later Nineteenth Century," *Liberian Studies Journal*, vol. 2, no. 1 (1969), p. 30. Martin points out that among certain Americo-Liberians, intermarriage with Africans was encouraged, and notes that President Anthony Gardiner's son married an African of tribal background.

14. Huberich, *History of Liberia*, vol. 1, p. 77.

15. *Ibid.*, p. 146.

16. *Ibid.*, p. 333.

17. *Ibid.*, pp. 319–20, 362–63.

18. *Ibid.*, p. 568.

19. *Ibid.*, pp. 638–54.

20. George W. Brown, *The Economic History of Liberia* (Washington, D.C.: Associated Publishers, 1941), pp. 138–70 *passim.* See also Huberich, *History of Liberia*, vol. 1, pp. 768–69, for the relatively greater importance of commerce (in African products) than agriculture.

21. U.S. Congress, Senate, "Roll of Emigrants."

22. Staudenraus, *Colonization Movement*, p. 150.

23. Report of M. C. Perry, Commanding U.S. Naval Forces in West Africa, 1844, *Senate Documents*, vol. 9, no. 150, pp. 149–50.

24. Brown, *Economic History*, pp. 129–30.

25. For the Constitution of 1847, see Huberich, *History of Liberia*, vol. 2.

26. *U.S. (United States) Army Handbook for Liberia* (Washington, D.C., 1964), pp. 16–17.

27. Edith Holden, *Blyden of Liberia* (New York: Vantage Press, 1966), p. 350.

28. Jones, "Struggle for Unification," quoting George R. Stetson, *The Liberian Republic As It Is* (Boston: A. Williams and Co., 1881).

29. Brown, *Economic History*, p. 141.

30. *Ibid.*, pp. 134–35, and Benjamin Nnamdi Azikiwe, *Liberia in World Politics* (London: Arthur H. Stockwell, 1934), pp. 112–13.

31. Harry Johnston, *Liberia* (New York: Dodd, Mead, 1906), vol. 1, pp. 402, 410.

32. Brown, *Economic History*, pp. 142–43, attributes this new look at the interior to the serious depletion of the Treasury owing in part to mishandling of public funds. Expeditions were sent to measure the hinterland's potential in 1868 and 1874. Johnston, *Liberia*, pp. 250–54. See also Benjamin J. K. Anderson, *Narrative of a Journey to Musardu, the Capital of the Western Mandingoes* (New York: S. W. Green, 1870).

33. Johnston, *Liberia*, p. 262. For other versions of this loan, see Raymond L. Buell, *The Native Problem in Africa* (Hamden, Conn.: Archon Books, The Shoe String Press, 1965), vol. 2, pp. 796–97; Frederick Starr, *Liberia: Description, History, and Problems* (Chicago: [Author], 1913), p. 200; and

Brown, *Economic History*, p. 143, who states that only $40,000 reached the Treasury.

34. Buell, *The Native Problem*, pp. 797–817. Buell describes the several Liberian efforts to bail the country out of its chronic financial difficulties by foreign loans in 1906, 1912, 1917, and 1920.

35. Speaker of the Liberian House of Representatives, Richard Henries, *New York Times*, 19 December 1966. The notion of a populist accession to power of the darker-skinned Americo-Liberians appears to be part of contemporary Liberian history (or mythology). See, for example, Mary Fiske, "History of the True Whig Party, 1869–1967" (Monrovia, mimeographed, 1967), and C. L. Simpson, *The Memoirs of C. L. Simpson* (London: The Diplomatic Press and Publishing Co., 1961), p. 61, who describes the final accession to power of the True Whig Party in 1883 as follows: "The True Whigs were anxious to replace the Republican caste system with a more democratic and liberal administration . . . under which the poorer classes would have a voice in politics."

36. Gardiner, a mulatto, launched the TWP's still unbroken tenure in office by gaining the support of Congoes and indigenous Africans through promises of seats for their candidates in the House of Representatives. Jones, "Struggle for Unification," p. 143.

37. Raymond L. Buell, *Liberia, A Century of Survival, 1847–1947* (Philadelphia: University of Pennsylvania, African Handbooks, no. 7, 1947), p. 60.

38. Maurice Duverger, *The Idea of Politics* (London: Methuen, University Paperbacks, 1966), p. 76.

39. I. Schapera, *Government and Politics in Tribal Societies* (London: Watts, 1956), p. 8, defines this community.

40. The problem of selecting what is relevant is complicated by the dearth of basic ethnographic studies on Liberia. This problem is beginning to be remedied by such anthropologists as d'Azevedo on the Gola and Gibbs on the Kpelle (see below). A number of younger scholars are also beginning to fill the gaps. For sources see Svend Holsoe, comp., "A Bibliography on Liberian Government Publications," *African Studies Bulletin*, 11 (1968); "A Bibliography on Liberia" (in two parts), *Liberian Studies Research Working Papers*, no. 1 and no. 3 (1971). For earlier studies see George Schwab, *Tribes of the Liberian Hinterland*, edited with additional material by George W. Harley (Peabody Museum Papers, vol. 31, 1947).

41. Liberia's experience is consistent with Mair's observation that tribes do not act in common as a single institution. Lucy P. Mair, *Primitive Government* (Baltimore: Penguin, 1962), p. 157. Confederations including large elements of one or more tribes have existed in Liberia, however (see below).

42. *U.S. Army Handbook*, p. 55.

43. *Census of Population, 1962*, Summary Report (Bureau of Statistics, Monrovia, 1964), Table 12.

44. Fraenkel, *Tribe and Class*, pp. 83–84.

45. J. Genevray, *Eléments d'une monographie d'une division administrative Libérienne (Grand Bassa County)* (Dakar: I. F. A. N., 1952).

46. Fraenkel, *Tribe and Class*, p. 88. The type of stereotype which consigns certain tribal groups to certain occupations seems to be validated by the Bassa. The same may be said for the Loma, who appear to dominate the military numerically.

47. Merran Fraenkel, "Social Change on the Kru Coast of Liberia," *Africa*, vol. 36, no. 2 (April 1966), pp. 154–72.

48. *Ibid.*, p. 171.

49. *U.S. Army Handbook*, p. 53.

50. Warren d'Azevedo, "Some Historical Problems in the Delineation of a Central West Atlantic Region," *Annals of the New York Academy of Sciences*, vol. 96 (January 20, 1962), p. 514.

51. *Ibid.*, p. 515.

52. See George W. Harley, *Notes on the Poro in Liberia* (Peabody Museum Papers, vol. 19, no. 2, 1941); Schwab, *Tribes of the Hinterland*; and James L. Gibbs, "The Kpelle of Liberia, in Gibbs, ed., *Peoples of Africa* (New York: Holt, Rinehart and Winston, 1965).

53. D'Azevedo, "Historical Problems," p. 516. One student, who worked among the Kpelle, observed that Poro and Sande leadership "are strictly hereditary prerogatives of one family. Any son of a poro zo is called a zo [priest]." Beryl L. Bellman, "Some Constitutive Features of Secrecy Among the Fala Kpelle of Sucromu, Liberia" (paper presented at the First Conference on Social Science Research in Liberia, Stanford University, August 1969).

54. Gibbs, "The Kpelle," p. 219. Gibbs continues: "Several bits of field data confirm the view that political power and Poro tend to be lodged in the hands of the same individuals, and it is not unlikely that chiefs utilize Poro mechanisms to underscore their political decisions." Kenneth Little, "The Political Function of the Poro" (Part II), *Africa*, vol. 36, no. 1 (January 1966), p. 69, writes of the Poro in Sierra Leone: "Political power was normally balanced between the Poro and the chieftainship."

55. Gibbs, "The Kpelle," p. 220. D'Azevedo points out that many tribal Liberians are convinced that "the Masons represented the Liberian [i.e., Americo-Liberian] equivalent of Poro, and in explaining Poro to Liberians they frequently made the analogy." The Americo-Liberians in turn referred to Poro as an "African Masonry" and held it in "a degree of awe." Warren d'Azevedo, "A Tribal Reaction to Nationalism" (Part I), *Liberian Studies Journal*, vol. 1 (Spring 1969), p. 20.

56. Kenneth Little, "The Political Function of the Poro" (Part I), *Africa*, vol. 35 (October 1965), p. 358. "By joining the society they established their status as men."

57. D'Azevedo, "Historical Problems," p. 515.

58. D'Azevedo, "A Tribal Reaction" (Part I), p. 10.

59. John Gay and Michael Cole, *The New Mathematics and an Old Culture: A Study of Learning Among the Kpelle of Liberia* (New York: Holt, Rinehart and Winston, 1967), p. 14.

60. D'Azevedo, "A Tribal Reaction" (Part I), p. 12.
61. *U.S. Army Handbook*, p. 76. Little, "Function of the Poro" (Part I), attributes the 1898 Mende rising in Sierra Leone to Poro, and believes that there may have been some links between Poro and the disturbances in that country in 1955–56.
62. Warren d'Azevedo, "A Tribal Reaction to Nationalism" (Part II), *Liberian Studies Journal*, vol. 2, no. 1 (1969).
63. D'Azevedo, "A Tribal Reaction" (Part I), pp. 4–5.
64. *Ibid.*, p. 6. See also Svend E. Holsoe, "The Condo Federation in Western Liberia," *The Liberian Historical Review*, vol. 3, no. 1 (1966), pp. 1–28.
65. D'Azevedo, "A Tribal Reaction" (Part I), p. 7.
66. Jones, "Struggle for Unification," pp. 127ff.
67. Martin, "How to Build a Nation," p. 31. Martin points out, however, that there was awareness that tribal peoples "could drive the Americo-Liberians into the sea—a commonly used expression." *Ibid.*, p. 23.
68. Jones, "Struggle for Unification," pp. 229–32. See also Buell, *The Native Problem*, pp. 738–39.
69. G. M. Haliburton, "The Prophet Harris and the Grebo Rising of 1910," *Liberian Studies Journal*, vol. 3, no. 1 (1970–71), esp. pp. 34–37.
70. D'Azevedo, "A Tribal Reaction" (Part II), p. 47.
71. *Liberian Code of Laws of 1956*, 5 vols. (Ithaca: Cornell University Press, 1957, 1958, 1960). See Martin, "How to Build a Nation," pp. 15–22, for a good discussion of the tangled skein which is the question of availability of citizenship to indigenous Liberians in the nineteenth and early twentieth centuries. See also Huberich, *History of Liberia*, vol. 2, pp. 1015–53.
72. D'Azevedo, "A Tribal Reaction" (Part II), p. 51.
73. *Ibid.*, p. 52.
74. Jones, "Struggle for Unification," pp. 222–32. Buell, *The Native Problem*, pp. 740–43.
75. Buell, *The Native Problem*, pp. 740–41. American officials forwarded the request to the U.S. State Department, recommending that help was "necessary to prevent the destruction of U.S. interests." These interests were not described, but may have involved U.S. bank loans to Liberia in 1912.
76. D'Azevedo, "A Tribal Reaction" (Part II), pp. 52–53.
77. *Ibid.*, p. 55.
78. Graham Greene, *Journey Without Maps* (New York: Doubleday, Doran & Co., 1936), and Henry J. Greenwall and Roland Wild, *Unknown Liberia* (London: Hutchison & Co., 1936).
79. Department of Interior, *Departmental Regulations Governing the Administration of the Interior of the Republic of Liberia*, Monrovia, January 21, 1921. See also Buell, *The Native Problem*, pp. 744–45.
80. Brown, *Economic History*, p. 150.
81. Clower et al., *Growth*, p. 8.
82. Buell, *The Native Problem*, p. 751.
83. Huberich, *History of Liberia*, vol. 2, pp. 898–916.

84. D'Azevedo, "A Tribal Reaction" (Part II), p. 59.
85. Warren d'Azevedo, "A Tribal Reaction to Nationalism" (Part III), *Liberian Studies Journal*, vol. 3, no. 1, pp. 4–5.
86. Buell, *Century of Survival*, p. 24.
87. *Ibid.*, pp. 3–6, and 20–46 *passim*, describes U.S. involvement in internal Liberian affairs.
88. *U.S. Army Handbook*, p. 20. For example, from World War I to 1951 the receiver of customs was an official appointed by the United States. He administered the servicing of Liberia's foreign debts.
89. Buell, *Century of Survival*, pp. 31–32.
90. Buell, *The Native Problem*, pp. 818–52 *passim*, discusses the circumstances attending the Firestone agreements. See also Frank Chalk, "The Anatomy of an Investment: Firestone's 1927 Loan to Liberia," *The Canadian Journal of African Studies*, no. 1 (March 1967), esp. pp. 28–31.
91. Azikiwe, *Liberia in World Politics*, p. 132.
92. Chalk, "Firestone's Loan," p. 32.
93. Azikiwe, *Liberia in World Politics*, pp. 334–35.
94. Buell, *Century of Survival*, pp. 3–5.
95. Speech by President Tubman at the inaugural ceremonies opening the Port of Monrovia, Government Printing Office, Monrovia.
96. J. W. Cason, "The Growth of Christianity in the Liberian Environment" (Unpublished Ph.D. diss., Columbia University, 1962), p. 225.
97. Cason, "Christianity"; *U.S. Army Handbook*, pp. 143–53.
98. United Christian Fellowship Conference of Liberia, *Changing Liberia, A Challenge to the Christian*, Report of meetings in Monrovia, December 1957 and July 1958, [Switzerland, 1959], p. 22.
99. Simpson, *Memoirs*, p. 104.
100. Martin, "How to Build a Nation," p. 32.
101. Inaugural Address, January 1, 1912, Government Printing Office, Monrovia.

3: The Tubman Era

1. Simpson, *Memoirs*, pp. 240–41.
2. "First Inaugural Address," in E. Reginald Townsend, ed., *President Tubman of Liberia Speaks* (London: Consolidated Publications Co., 1959), p. 16.
3. Robert A. Smith, *William V. S. Tubman* (Amsterdam: Van Ditmar, 1966), p. 70. Smith discusses at length this break with Montserrado County's long-standing hold on the presidency, pp. 64–70.
4. Simpson, *Memoirs*, p. 237.
5. J. Gus Liebenow, "The Republic of Liberia," in Gwendolen M. Carter, ed., *African One-Party States* (Ithaca: Cornell University Press, 1962), p. 361.
6. Clower et al., *Growth*, pp. 145–47; and Brown, *Economic History*, p. 212. Liberian growers, however, produced only 3 percent of total rubber output.

7. Henry B. Cole, ed., *The Liberian Yearbook, 1962* (Monrovia: A Liberian Review Publication), pp. 213–18.

8. David Easton, *A Framework for Political Analysis* (Englewood Cliffs: Prentice-Hall, 1965), p. 78.

9. Black, *The Dynamics of Modernization*, p. 4.

10. The two presidents Barclay (1904–1912; 1930–1944) were of West Indian origins. President King (1920–1930) was from a Sierra Leone immigrant family. Liebenow, *Liberia*, p. 28.

11. Among the extra-governmental associations, the Masonic Order is the bedrock of social *cum* political loyalties. The Order was and is practically one with the government (the new Masonic Temple in Monrovia was constructed with public funds), and membership therein is tantamount to membership in the elite. Senator Frank E. Tolbert was Grand Master; President Tolbert, Deputy Grand Master; Postmaster General and former TWP General Secretary McKinley DeShield, Senior Grand Warden; and Tubman held the highest rank, as a 33d-degree Mason. (Cole, ed., *Liberian Yearbook, 1962*, pp. 248–49.) Most senior Masons hold government office or serve in the legislature. Leadership in the YMCA and the Protestant Churches (especially the Methodist and Baptist denominations) also offers some hints of a man's political status. Former Secretary of the Treasury Charles Sherman was President of the World Alliance, and former Secretary of Education John Payne Mitchell was President of the National Board of the YMCA. President Tolbert was the Vice-President of the Baptist World Alliance.

12. Fraenkel, *Tribe and Class*, pp. 197–200; Liebenow, *Liberia*, pp. 137–40.

13. Buell, *The Native Problem*, p. 722. This occurred in 1904.

14. Simpson, *Memoirs*, pp. 91–92.

15. Liebenow, "The Republic of Liberia," p. 368.

16. *Ibid.*, pp. 368–70.

17. Townsend, ed., *Tubman Speaks*, pp. 21–22.

18. *Ibid.*, pp. 27–28.

19. Cole, ed., *Liberian Yearbook, 1962*, pp. 56–59; Liberian Cartographic Services, *Geographic Names*, Monrovia, Oct. 16, 1955 (mimeographed); Fraenkel, *Tribe and Class*, Appendix C, p. 236, estimates a total of 100 paramount chiefdoms. The figure fifty for the hinterland was provided, after extensive inquiries, by the Department of Internal Affairs.

20. Cole, ed., *Liberian Yearbook, 1962*, p. 56.

21. *Ibid.*, p. 57. Some also became wealthy farmers and large private landowners.

22. Liebenow, "The Republic of Liberia," p. 336.

23. D'Azevedo, "A Tribal Reaction" (Part III), p. 1.

24. Gibbs, "The Kpelle," p. 216.

25. *Ibid.*, p. 214.

26. *Ibid.*, p. 216.

27. Tubman held numerous Executive Councils throughout the country, especially in his first two terms in office.

28. But it does not appear that the Liberian version of indirect rule supported

influences that were opposed to "necessary change" (see Mair, *Primitive Government*, p. 255), or that it entrenched sentiments of tribal separatism, which in some new nations have become disruptive.

29. The British suppression of Kikuyu customs in the 1920's comes to mind here. Carl G. Rosberg, Jr., and John Nottingham, *The Myth of the "Mau Mau": Nationalism in Kenya* (New York: Praeger, 1966), trace the development of Kikuyu and Kenyan nationalism in part to this period.

30. Brown, *Economic History*, pp. 184–85; Buell, *The Native Problem*, pp. 724–27.

31. U.S., Agency for International Development, "Revenue Collections by Major Source," *Quarterly Progress Reports*, by Public Administration Service, Chicago, Ill., submitted to AID over the period 1962–67. Mimeographed.

32. Marion J. Levy, "Patterns (Structures) of Modernization and Political Development," *The Annals of the American Academy of Social and Political Science*, vol. 358 (March 1965), p. 35. Levy observed that rural folk accept as a way of life rents, taxes, and the flow of interest and profits to urban centers.

33. Buell, *The Native Problem*, p. 721. The militia numbered some 3,000 men in 1928, but was of questionable competence. It was not, in any case, needed for active duty during the period in question. Pacification of the interior was not completed until the 1930's.

34. *Ibid.*, pp. 746–47. The change Buell anticipated was related to the great expectations held in many quarters about the Firestone rubber enterprise. The hoped-for economic impact did not occur, however, until World War II.

35. Quoted in Lawrence Marinelli, *The New Liberia* (New York: Praeger, 1964), p. 64.

36. Townsend, ed., *Tubman Speaks*, pp. 106–8.

37. *Ibid.*, p. 236.

38. Department of Interior, Bureau of Folkways, *Laws and Administrative Regulations Governing the Poro and Sande Societies*. Compiled by V. J. Fahnbullah, Monrovia, 1962.

39. Richard M. Fulton, "Primitive Government: The Case of the Kpelle of Liberia," unpublished manuscript, 1968.

40. Townsend, ed., *Tubman Speaks*, p. 99.

41. *The Budget of the Government of Liberia, 1967*, Executive Mansion, Monrovia.

42. Smith, *Tubman*, pp. 170–72.

43. *Ibid.*

44. Townsend, ed., *Tubman Speaks*, pp. 111–12.

45. *Ibid.*, pp. 113–15.

46. Smith, *Tubman*, pp. 170–72. See also Liberian Information Service, *The Plot That Failed: The Story of the Attempted Assassination of President Tubman* (Monrovia, 1959), for the official version of the events surrounding the assassination attempt.

47. Townsend, ed., *Tubman Speaks*, p. 148. In other speeches in November 1955

Tubman scored local and sectional prejudices, particularly those emanating from Monrovia. *Ibid.*, pp. 140–41.

4: The Economic Factor

1. See Igor Kopytoff, "Socialism and Traditional African Societies," in William H. Friedland and Carl G. Rosberg, eds., *African Socialism* (Stanford, Ca.: Stanford University Press for the Hoover Institution, 1964).
2. Elliot J. Berg, "Socialism and Economic Development in Tropical Africa," *Quarterly Journal of Economics* 78 (1964).
3. Brown, *Economic History*, pp. 172–74; see also Buell, *The Native Problem*, pp. 766–68.
4. Buell, *The Native Problem*, pp. 724, 729, 765.
5. Clower et al., *Growth*, pp. 23–24.
6. After World War II a portion of Liberia's income began to come from "flag of convenience" shipping. Ranking first in the world in registered merchant ship tonnage—38.5 million tons for 2,060 ships in 1971—Liberia earns about $3 million per year in registry fees and taxes. *Lloyds Register of Shipping, 1971* (London: Lloyds, 1971).
7. Department of Planning and Economic Affairs, *Population Growth Survey, 1970*, p. 10.
8. U.S., AID, "Summary of Basic Data," in *Liberia: Economic Background Highlights*, 1971.
9. U.S., AID, The U.S. Economic Aid Program for Liberia, August 1967 and September 1970. The total includes all forms of aid, loans, and grants, except military assistance, which amounted to over $10 million in the postwar period. Other donors together now outspend the United States in Liberia; e.g., Western Europe, UN agencies, and the International Bank for Reconstruction and Development have made loans and grants amounting to some $60 million in recent years. Liberia has also received allocations from the International Monetary Fund Special Drawing Fund Accounts since 1963 to meet its debt-servicing burden. There has also been a substantial shift in trade and investment to Europe, Japan, and Israel.
10. Russell U. McLaughlin, *Foreign Investment and Development in Liberia* (New York: Praeger, 1966), pp. 65–66. The $8.5 million represents Liberian government equity of $5 million, and some $3 million invested by a special Liberian company.
11. *The Liberian Code of Laws of 1956* (Ithaca: Cornell University Press, 1957, 1958, 1960) 27:263, provides penalties, from fines to deportation, for racial discrimination. The law is clearly pointed at foreign employers. Section 19:72 also deals with "abusive language" on the part of foreign employers. In his first inaugural address, Tubman attacked certain personnel for "overawing and overlording everybody and everything," and threatened them with deportation. (See Townsend, ed., *Tubman Speaks*, p. 29.) Foreigners have

been arrested and deported or fined in the past (see LAMCO's complaint, *Liberian Star*, May 29, 1968, for example).

12. Several concession agreements have been rewritten by mutual consent since 1964, and some of the more serious abuses have been remedied. Several concessions even made advance payments against future taxes to help Liberia through its financial difficulties in the mid-1960's. This information on the concessions comes from reliable private sources.

13. Clower et al., *Growth*, pp. 133–34. McLaughlin, *Foreign Investment*, pp. 25–26, lists Firestone's investment at $32 million, and suggests doubling its value at 1962 levels, as much of the investment took place when the value of the dollar was higher. This would still give Firestone a 20 percent annual profit-to-investment ratio.

14. A rough estimate based on Clower et al., *Growth*, p. 133. This figure is probably on the conservative side as LMC did not reach full production until the late 1950's.

15. Liberian Iron Ore Limited (LIOL), *Annual Report, 1966*. LIOL is an equal partner with the Liberian Government in LAMCO. The Bethlehem Steel Corporation, a participant in the LAMCO joint venture, also pays income tax to Liberia. Grängesberg (now called Gränges A.B.) of Sweden is a major stockholder in LIOL. It is responsible for managing the LAMCO joint venture and conducts sales for LAMCO. Torsten Gårdlund, *LAMCO in Liberia* (Stockholm: Almquist and Wiksell, 1967), pp. 18–20.

16. United Christian Fellowship Conference, *Changing Liberia*, p. 51.

17. Several banks reported in 1967 that such credit no longer was readily available to Liberian political leaders. The banks preferred to limit noncommercial loans to middle-level civil servants upon whose salaries they could effect liens.

18. Anderson, *Politics and Economic Change in Latin America*, p. 82, describes a similar phenomenon in Latin America.

19. Simpson's reason for doing so, he declared, was to avoid being "dependent for his daily existence on Government posts, with all that this implies." Simpson, *Memoirs*, p. 139.

20. *Rubber Planters Bulletin*, vol. 1, no. 4, (November 1965), p. 5. The Rubber Planters Association of Liberia, Inc. (RPAL) is an association of foreign concessionaires and Liberian rubber growers whose estates are greater than a hundred acres. There were sixty-four members in 1967, including the President, Vice-President, Chief Justice, House Speaker, and other Liberian leaders, past and present. Data for 1970 are from *Liberia: Economic Trends*, U.S. Embassy, Monrovia, November 26, 1970. See also address by William E. Dennis, President of the RPAL, March 14, 1967, quoted in *Rubber Planters Bulletin*, vol. 3, nos. 1 and 2 (January-April 1967).

21. RPAL, Inc., *Membership List* (as of May 1967).

22. Even Firestone works only 90,000 acres of the original one million acres it leased for ninety-nine years in 1926. *Rubber Planters Bulletin*, vol. 1, no. 4 (November 29, 1965), and information provided by the RPAL.

23. From a manager of a private Liberian rubber estate. Also, "Rubber Farms

and Roads in Liberia," working paper, February 1962. Department of Planning and Economic Affairs, *Economic Survey, 1969*, Monrovia, June 1970. Hereafter cited as *Economic Survey, 1969*.

24. International Monetary Fund, *Staff Report for the 1970 Article XIV Consultation*, approved by Mamoudou Touré and Timothy Sweeney, January 28, 1971.

25. *Ibid.*, and *Economic Survey, 1969*.

26. Elliot J. Berg, "Growth, Development and All That: Thoughts on the Liberian Experience" (University of Michigan, mimeographed, 1969), pp. 41–42, points out that Liberia has experienced not so much enclave expansion as enclave multiplication. Thus, where there was but one such enclave in 1950 (Firestone), today there are about fifteen.

27. See Adam Curle, *The Role of Education in Developing Societies* (Accra: Ghana University Press, 1961), pp. 7–8.

28. Office of National Planning, *Some Aspects of Recent Economic Development and Possible Implications*, by Y. H. Diddens, Monrovia, March 1966 (mimeographed). Diddens remarks that foreign aid largely follows the distribution of the Liberian budget. See a comparable phenomenon in Samir Amin, *Le dévelopment du capitalisme en Côte d'Ivoire* (Paris: Editions de Minuit, 1967), pp. 267–68.

29. Personal income tax was instituted during the Tubman era (in 1950). After a basic deduction of $1,500 on declared income, rates of taxation progress from 2 percent to 8 percent on taxable income up to $8,000; 11 percent on taxable income from $8,000 to $10,000; 15 percent between $10,000 and $20,000; and 20 percent up to $50,000. Net taxable income over $100,000 is taxed at 35 percent. Cole, ed., *Liberian Yearbook, 1962*, pp. 116–17. In 1965, the duty on luxury goods and maximum rate on corporate profits were raised. In 1967, income taxes on wage earners were made somewhat more progressive. Berg, "Growth, Development, and All That," p. 48. Apart from the gradual progression of tax rates is the more important problem of tax collection: it is difficult to find out upon what bases the ruling class is taxed, and how regularly taxes are collected. It is noteworthy, however, that personal income tax collections have increased from $2 million in 1960 to $11 million in 1970. U.S., AID, "Consolidated Statement of Central Government Finances," September 12, 1970.

30. Clower et al., *Growth*, p. 232.

31. McLaughlin, *Foreign Investment*, pp. 18–19.

32. Andrew M. Kamarck, "Economics and Economic Development," in Robert A. Lystad, ed., *The African World* (New York: Praeger, 1966), p. 232.

33. Fourth Annual Message to the First Session of the Forty-Fifth Legislature, December 23, 1963, in Townsend, ed., *Official Papers*.

34. Department of Agriculture, *Annual Report, 1966*. Also, Department of Planning and Economic Affairs, *Public Sector Accounts, 1965*, Table 25, p. 39.

35. The project ultimately succumbed to superior competition from a Liberian commercial venture.

36. *Liberia Journal of Commerce and Industry*, vol. 1, no. 2 (July-September 1966).
37. Department of Agriculture, *Draft Development Plan, 1967–70*, December 15, 1966.
38. International Monetary Fund, Staff Papers, *The Liberian Economy*, by M. A. Qureshi, Yoshio Mizoe, and F. d'A. Collings, July 1964, pp. 291–92. See also Special Commission on Government Operations (SCOGO), *Executive Branch Organization and Operations: A Survey Report*, Monrovia, August 1964, p. 270. Hereafter cited as *SCOGO Report*.
39. *SCOGO Report*, p. 270.
40. Sources for this and much of the following information about roads: William R. Stanley, "Changing Patterns of Transportation Development in Liberia" (Ph.D. diss., University of Pittsburgh, 1966) and "Evaluating Construction Priorities of Farm-to-Market Roads in Developing Countries: A Case Study," *Journal of Developing Areas*, vol. 5, no. 3 (April 1971); Office of National Planning, *Transport and Communications in Liberia*, by Harvey Klemmer, December 15, 1964; "Rubber Farms and Roads in Liberia."
41. Stanley, "Transportation Development," p. 27. The favored position of the hinterland counties has been overcome by the completion of roads bending back toward the coast. See Stanley, "Construction Priorities."
42. Clower et al., *Growth*, p. 33.
43. See M. G. Smith, *The Plural Society in the British West Indies* (Berkeley: University of California Press, 1965), p. 80; see also *ibid.*, pp. 66 and 79.
44. "Rubber Farms and Roads in Liberia," Tables 1 and 10.
45. *Ibid.*, p. 2.
46. Art. V, Sec. 14 of the Constitution of 1847. Any such purchase is to be considered null and void. Huberich, *History of Liberia*, vol. 2, p. 863.
47. Clower et al., *Growth*, pp. 248–54.
48. Buell, *The Native Problem*, pp. 735–36, describes the numerous ways land had been acquired in the past, and the discretion enjoyed by county land commissioners.
49. Leon Weintraub, "Land and Power in Liberia," paper presented at the Second Conference on Social Science Research in Liberia, Indiana University, May 1970.
50. Clower et al., *Growth*, p. 249.
51. Firestone still suffers seasonal shortages, but it does not rely on obligatory labor as it did in the past, although some private Liberian growers still do so.
52. Office of National Planning, *Transport and Communications*, p. 91.
53. McLaughlin, *Foreign Investment*, p. 19, and Clower et al., *Growth*, p. 59.
54. McLaughlin, *Foreign Investment*. Rice imports cost Liberia $8.6 million in 1968, $5.2 million in 1969. *Economic Survey, 1969*, p. 68; U.S. Department of Agriculture, *Liberia: Agricultural Situation*, Monrovia, January 26, 1971.
55. Department of Agriculture, *Annual Report, 1966*, p. 17.
56. McLaughlin, *Foreign Investment*, p. 21.
57. This contention by Clower et al., *Growth*, has been questioned in a study in which it was found that exactions of crops tended to be applied equally, that is,

surplus producers were not penalized. Charles E. Lindblom, *Diffusing Economic Development in Liberia*, for U.S. AID, Liberia, May 1968, p. 36n, mimeographed.

58. Most of the following information is based on a study carried out in the Wolota clan area of the Mano tribe by David Blanchard, who lived in the area for a total of five years and continued to study it thereafter. Blanchard, *The Study of Small Farm Agriculture in Liberia*, for U.S. AID, Liberia, July 31, 1967.
59. *Ibid.*, p. 12.
60. *Ibid.*
61. *Ibid.*, p. 13.
62. *Ibid.*, p. 22.
63. *Ibid.*, p. 15.
64. A good part of the land "is now divided into private plots and secured by tribal certificates" (*Ibid.*, p. 26).
65. *Ibid.*, p. 25. See also Gibbs, "The Kpelle," p. 222, who says that the *kuu* is possibly "the most time-consuming, if not the most important, corporate group in Kpelle life."
66. Communication from H. D. Seibel. Seibel, a social anthropologist, informed me that he had uncovered several other cases in which rudimentary modern cooperative activities had been developed from traditional cooperative groups in Liberia. See also his "Arbeitsgenossen-Shaften bei den Mano in Liberia," *Africa Heute*, vol. 10, June 1968, suppl. This transformation of the *kuu* from a labor activity to one in which money is pooled and invested resembles the "money company" that heretofore had existed among wage earners in the towns. Called *susu* (Mandingo) or *esusu* (Yoruba), the "money companies" pool portions of their members' earnings and turn over lump sums to each member periodically. Fraenkel, *Tribe and Class*, p. 176. McLaughlin, *Foreign Investment*, p. 116, notes that the income of the *kuu* is sometimes used for the purchase of a capital asset, such as a truck. For other forms of the *susu* see Kenneth Little, *West African City* (London: Cambridge University Press, 1965), pp. 51–52.
67. Blanchard, *Small Farm Agriculture*, p. 34.
68. *Ibid.*, p. 22.

5: Labor and Society

1. Daniel Lerner, "Comparative Analysis of Processes of Modernization," in Horace Miner, ed., *The City in Modern Africa* (London: Pall Mall Press, 1967), p. 27.
2. Fraenkel, *Tribe and Class*, pp. 33–34, cites the principal sources of these earlier population figures. See also Office of National Planning, Bureau of Statistics, *Census of Population, 1962*, Monrovia, 1964 (hereafter cited as *Census, 1962*); and Department of Planning and Economic Development, *Demographic Annual of the Population Growth Survey, 1970*, Monrovia, 1970.

3. Fraenkel, *Tribe and Class*, p. 36.
4. *Census, 1962*.
5. Data provided by Firestone spokesmen.
6. Office of National Planning, *Transport and Communication in Liberia*, by Harvey Klemmer, Monrovia, 1964, p. 91; and LMC spokesmen.
7. Clower et al., *Growth*, p. 308.
8. *Census, 1962*, Summary Report and Area Report for Montserrado County. This age group constituted 32.4 percent of the total urban population (i.e., areas of over 2,000 people) in 1970. Department of Planning and Economic Development, *Population Growth Survey, 1970*, p. 37.
9. Horowitz, *Three Worlds of Development*, p. 338. Cf. Kenneth Little, *West African Urbanization: A Study of Voluntary Associations in Social Change* (Cambridge, Eng.: Cambridge University Press, 1965), p. 12. See also Jeanette E. Carter, "The Rural Loma and Monrovia: Ties with an Urban Center," *Liberian Studies Journal*, vol. 2, no. 2 (1970), p. 145.
10. Little, *West African Urbanization*, p. 9. On the other hand, James C. Riddell, "Mano Labor Migration and Cash-Cropping," *Liberian Studies Journal*, vol. 2, no. 2 (1970), points out that new opportunities for cash-cropping have drawn many Manos back to their home areas.
11. *Census, 1962*.
12. Fraenkel discusses the requirements of urban life at length in *Tribe and Class*, pp. 196–229.
13. I. M. Lewis, "Nationalism, Urbanism and Tribalism in Contemporary Africa" (paper presented at the University of East Africa Social Science Conference, December 1966). In this excellent paper, Professor Lewis also observes that urban migrants who live within easy reach of their tribal homelands can "afford" to become more strongly urbanized than tribesmen from more distant areas because they are better able to maintain effective links with the rural area. Igolima T. D. Amachree finds much evidence to support this generalization in " 'Detribalization' and Urban Residence: A Study of Some Liberian Urban Dwellers" (paper presented at the Third Annual Conference on Liberian Social Science Research, University of Delaware, June 1971). See also Carter, "The Rural Loma and Monrovia."
14. Miner, *City in Modern Africa*, p. 1.
15. The stereotype that usually associates certain tribes with certain occupations seems to be borne out by the Bassa, who generally appear to work as petty clerks, unskilled workers, and servants of the wealthy. Fraenkel, *Tribe and Class*, p. 88. Even prominent Bassas suffer this sort of prejudice. According to one well-educated son of an Americo-Liberian father and Bassa mother, his own political future was limited because of his Bassa antecedents.
16. See Fraenkel, *Tribe and Class*, pp. 83–84, for data on the late 1950's.
17. *Ibid.*, pp. 52 and 70.
18. *Ibid.*, pp. 53 and 224–25. The *lappa*, a single piece of colorful printed cloth with which tribal women drape themselves, appears to have become more popular among "civilized" women in recent years, especially when they go abroad and wish to demonstrate their Africanness.

19. Aidan Southall, ed., *Social Change in Modern Africa* (London: Oxford University Press, 1961).
20. Fraenkel, *Tribe and Class*, p. 69. See also United Christian Fellowship Conference, *Changing Liberia*, p. 43, which discusses the economic liability of a large family in the town (as opposed to the rural setting), and the decline of polygamy. One home I visited was occupied by three young men, all white-collar workers, a lower-class Americo-Liberian, a Vai, and a Loma. Their apartment was furnished with, among other things, a radio, a refrigerator, a bar, and modern furniture.
21. Fraenkel, *Tribe and Class*, p. 158.
22. Leo Kuper, "Sociology: Some Aspects of Urban Plural Societies," in Robert A. Lystad, ed., *The African World* (New York: Praeger, 1965), pp. 125–126.
23. Fraenkel, *Tribe and Class*, p. 94.
24. Claude E. Welch, Jr., "The Comparative Study of Political Modernization," in Welch, ed., *Political Modernization* (Belmont: Wadsworth, 1967), p. 10. Cf. Liebenow, "The Republic of Liberia," and Robert Melson, "Ideology and Inconsistency: The Cross-Pressured Nigerian Worker," *American Political Science Review*, vol. 65, no. 1 (March 1971), for similar phenomena.
25. See Kuper, "Sociology," in Lystad, *African World*, pp. 109–110.
26. I. M. Lewis, "Nationalism, Urbanism, and Tribalism." See also Little, *West African Urbanization*, p. 164.
27. See Little, *West African Urbanization*, p. 20.
28. Fraenkel, *Tribe and Class*, p. 151.
29. Cole, ed., *Liberian Yearbook, 1962*, p. 228.
30. Fraenkel, *Tribe and Class*, p. 184.
31. *Liberian Star*, January 10, 1966. I have been unable to learn whether the association was active after 1967.
32. See I. M. Lewis, "Nationalism, Urbanism, and Tribalism," who regards the town and rural areas as forming "parts of a single (but by no means simple) social continuum," partly because many townsmen look to their rural home areas as their ultimate place of retirement. See also Riddell, "Mano Labor Migration."
33. Fraenkel, *Tribe and Class*, pp. 70–83.
34. *Ibid.*, pp. 81–83.
35. *Ibid.*, pp. 175–78.
36. Immanuel Wallerstein, "Ethnicity and National Integration in West Africa," in Harry Eckstein and David Apter, eds., *Comparative Politics* (New York: Free Press of Glencoe, 1963). Cf. Little, *West African Urbanization*, pp. 151–53, who shows that certain types of associations crystallize feelings of social class membership.
37. Fraenkel, *Tribe and Class*, p. 189.
38. The *Liberian Star*, April 5, 1968, reported that the Association expressed "grave concern" over cuts and disparities in salaries, and strong resentment over levies by the True Whig Party.
39. Fraenkel, *Tribe and Class*, p. 158.

40. *Ibid.*, p. 171.
41. *Ibid.*, pp. 171–75. Cf. M. P. Banton, *West African City: A Study of Tribal Life in Freetown* (London: Oxford University Press, 1965).
42. Clower et al., *Growth*, p. 259.
43. Andrew M. Kamarck, "Economics and Economic Development," in Robert A. Lystad, ed., *The African World* (New York: Praeger, 1965), pp. 226–28.
44. *Ibid.*
45. Department of Planning and Economic Affairs, *Annual Report, 1966*, pp. 63–72.
46. *U.S. Army Handbook*, p. 310.
47. Clower et al., *Growth*, p. 306, and Firestone spokesmen, 1967.
48. Firestone spokesmen, 1967.
49. LAMCO spokesman, 1967.
50. LMC spokesmen, 1964.
51. Gårdlund, *LAMCO in Liberia*, p. 78.
52. *Ibid.*, p. 79.
53. Information on educational levels of Liberian workers from *Census, 1962*.
54. *Ibid.*
55. International Monetary Fund, Staff Papers, *Staff Report for the 1970 Article XIV Consultation*, p. 5.
56. *Ibid.*, pp. 3–4.
57. *Ibid.*
58. Berg, "Growth, Development and All That," p. 44.
59. *Ibid.*, p. 42.
60. Brown, *Economic History*, p. 206, writes that while many Liberian officials welcomed Firestone's entry in the twenties, they dreaded American wage rates, and "solicited Mr. Firestone . . . not to pay wages in excess of twenty-five cents a day."
61. Interviews with CIO officials.
62. See Ioan Davies, *African Trade Unions* (Baltimore: Penguin Books, 1966), p. 219.
63. Clower et al., *Growth*, p. 281.
64. Fraenkel, *Tribe and Class*, p. 82.
65. Clower et al., *Growth*, p. 281; *U.S. Army Handbook*, p. 321.
66. *U.S. Army Handbook*, p. 322.
67. Clower et al., *Growth*, p. 281.
68. *Ibid.*, p. 282. See also "An Act to Restore and Enlarge Emergency Powers Granted the President of Liberia," Ch. I, *Acts Passed by the Legislature, 1962–63*.
69. "An Act to Amend the Labor Practices Law with Respect to Employment in General," May 30, 1966.
70. Dated February 14, 1966.
71. The AFC workers' letter to President Tubman was dated February 26, 1966.
72. No date, signed by two leading growers, William E. Dennis and R.S.S. Bright, President and Vice-President, respectively, of the RPAL.
73. "Decision of the Labor Practices Review Board in connection with the

complaint of African Fruit Company workers against the company which led to the recent strike in Sinoe," April 29, 1966.

74. It is quite possible that local leaders had called the strike to divert attention from charges by national CIO leaders that they had misused union funds. See Gårdlund, *LAMCO in Liberia*, pp. 61–65.

75. *ILO Official Bulletin*, Supplement 11, vol. 50 (no. 3, July 1967), pp. 75–86.

6: Political Modernization

1. The title but not the same interpretation used by Liebenow in *Liberia: The Evolution of Privilege*.

2. Liebenow, "The Republic of Liberia," p. 362.

3. Grigsby is quoted quite often in a significant document prepared by a group of young, liberal (by Liberian standards) Liberians who sought to investigate some of the social and political problems facing Liberia. United Christian Fellowship Conference, *Changing Liberia*.

4. According to my informant, prominent Krus informed Tubman that their people resented Grigsby's ouster from government.

5. J. Genevray, *Eléments d'une monographie d'une division administrative Libérienne (Grand Bassa County)* (Dakar: I.F.A.N., 1952), p. 60.

6. This is the only case of which I know in which Tubman was virtually forced to withdraw a decision. Were the source of this information (a private informant) not so reliable, I might doubt that it even took place. On the basis of this incident it would seem that Tubman was not invulnerable.

7. *Bong County News*, March 31, 1967.

8. The jailed persons were released shortly thereafter. Another incident in which the Tubman administration defended a tribal County Superintendent against alleged abuse from persons of coastal origins occurred at the LAMCO mine in 1967. The government imprisoned several senior Liberian employees for allegedly insulting the Nimba County Superintendent.

9. Brown, *Economic History*, p. 62.

10. Buell, *The Native Problem*, pp. 714–15.

11. Liebenow, "The Republic of Liberia," pp. 357–63.

12. *Liberian Star*, May 8, 1967.

13. *Census, 1962*, pp. 1–4, Summary Report, PC-B.

14. Ambassador G. Padmore, quoted and paraphrased in the *Liberian Age*, May 30, 1967.

15. Buell, *The Native Problem*, pp. 717–18.

16. Liebenow, "The Republic of Liberia," p. 375.

17. Buell, *The Native Problem*, pp. 717–18.

18. Genevray, *Eléments*, p. 60. My translation. County superintendents now earn $3,000 to $4,000 per annum. They have separate budget categories, and are not listed in the budget of the Department of Internal Affairs.

19. Richard Fulton, "From Colonization to Nationhood: President Tubman and the Political Development of the Interior" (Paper presented at the

Conference on Social Science Research in Liberia, Stanford University, August 1969). In his fifth inaugural address, January 1964, Tubman stated, "the Superintendent is solely responsible for the successful administration of his county, and he is not obliged to accept all advice given by the members of his council." E. Reginald Townsend, ed., *The Official Papers of W.V.S. Tubman, 1960–67* (London: Longmans, Green, 1968), p. 117.
20. *Liberian Star*, February 6, 1973.
21. Huntington, *Political Order*, p. 219.
22. *Ibid.*, p. 194.
23. It is criminal libel to "defame, degrade . . . or expose to public ridicule and contempt" the President. *Code of Laws, 1956*, 27:55.
24. *Budget, 1970*. The 1967 budget listed sixty-five agents, and a total of ninety-one officials in this branch.
25. One military adviser stated in 1967 that no one knows exactly how many men are in the LNG.
26. Evidence of the alleged plots was very thin. In the 1966 "plot," a "neighboring country" was alleged to have offered some $85,000 to persons in the LNG. *West Africa*, October 22, 1966, p. 1224.
27. *The Budget of Liberia*, 1970 and 1971.
28. Huntington, *Political Order*, pp. 34–35.

7: The True Whig Party

1. *Election Law*, 2LCL, Title 12, Ch. 1, Sec. 2 (Definitions).
2. *Annual Report and Opinions* of the Attorney General, October 1965 to September 1966, pp. 11–12. The Independent True Whigs were outlawed in 1955.
3. Mary Fiske, "History of the True Whig Party, 1869–1967," Monrovia, [1967], p. 14. (Mimeographed.)
4. Liebenow, *Liberia: The Evolution of Privilege*, p. 2.
5. Fiske, "True Whig Party," p. 14.
6. Maurice Duverger, *Political Parties* (London: Methuen, 1959), p. xv.
7. *Ibid.*, p. 64.
8. *True Whig Party of Liberia: General Rules and Regulations*, Revised and adopted by the National Convention at the City of Monrovia, February 7, 1963.
9. Quoted in Fraenkel, *Tribe and Class*, p. 58; Buell, *The Native Problem*, p. 712, describes the practice of deducting 10 percent of salaries of government employees in 1925, when the TWP sought funds to pay for the costs of the 1923 election. The practice also existed under President Edwin Barclay.
10. *General Rules and Regulations* do provide for an auditor and a budget, but there is no evidence that audits were carried out.
11. *West Africa*, April 29, 1967, p. 574, reported the estimated cost to be $2.87 million. Party Secretary-General DeShield noted that the TWP headquarters was "not a party project as such but a national project which will be of

immense benefit to the entire nation." (*Liberian Age*, March 28, 1967.) This announcement suggests that government funds may have been used in financing construction. DeShield informed me that the building would not house a new party bureaucracy but would provide meeting halls and offices for conferences and the like.

12. Fraenkel, *Tribe and Class*, p. 67.
13. Fraenkel describes the administration of the tribal communities in Monrovia at length, *ibid.*, pp. 70–109 *passim*.
14. An excerpt from a poem by Delsena Draper, the leader of the President Tubman Sinoe Women Social and Political group, published in the *Liberian Star*, May 8, 1968:

    If you love paved streets, you must love Tubman
    Who has paved the dirty streets of every city.
    If you love modern Buildings, you must love Tubman
    The designer of modern Liberia.
    If you love flying from county to county,
    You must love Tubman who gave us the first National Airline.
    If you love Electricity, Running Water, Telephone, Television and
        Radio Systems, you must love Tubman the producer of these
        systems.
    If you love travelling, relaxed in your car,
    You must love Tubman who has linked the counties.
    Tubman Sinoe Girls, and every sound minded, true,
    Loyal, godfearing Liberian, men, women, girls, boys,
    Young, old and crippled dearly love and honour
    Tubman because we love Liberia.

15. Liebenow, "Liberia," p. 561.
16. Duverger, *Political Parties*, p. 18, describes a caucus as consisting of a small number of members, and seeking no expansion. Membership in it "is achieved only by a kind of tacit co-option or by formal nomination. . . . Its strength does not depend on the number of its members but on their quality."
17. Such contests were frequently reported in the press, e.g.: "The Left Bank seat contested by nearly ten candidates . . ." (*Liberian Star*, February 24, 1967); "Owensgrove, situ ⁀d in Grand Bassa County, has not been represented in the Legislature for the past seventy-five years" (*ibid.*, February 27, 1967).
18. Liebenow, "Liberia," p. 464–65.
19. *Liberian Star*, February 24, 1967.
20. Tubman specifically stated that the limiting of party support to two terms is designed to give others a chance to serve. *West Africa*, March 11, 1967, p. 355.
21. *Liberian Star*, February 22, 1967.
22. *Liberian Star*, February 24, 1967.
23. Some members of this same group had accused the District Commissioner of maladministration of Gbarnga District in 1963. When the counties system was instituted, one of their leaders, James Gbarbea, a Kpelle, became the first Superintendent of Bong County.
24. This is an important theme in James S. Coleman and Carl G. Rosberg, eds.,

Political Parties and National Integration in Tropical Africa (Berkeley: University of California Press, 1964).

8: The Bureaucracy

1. *SCOGO Report*, pp. 187 and 210.
2. *The Budget of the Government of Liberia for 1967*, January 1967 (budgets generally emanated from the Executive Mansion); *Economic Survey, 1969*, p. 42. Public sector employees in Liberia account for a smaller proportion of the wage labor force than in many other African countries, but take a larger share of the budget.
3. Department of Agriculture, *Annual Report, 1964–65*, October 11, 1965.
4. *Budget, 1967*. "Other services" (not explained) accounted for $24,610; "Materials and supplies" accounted for $26,070.
5. Department of Planning and Economic Affairs, *Public Sector Accounts of Liberia, 1965*, compiled by Richard M. Barkay, Monrovia, 1965, *The Budget of the Government of Liberia for 1970*.
6. *Budget, 1967*.
7. I saw public works equipment on the farms of several Liberian leaders. The Department of Public Works decried one aspect of this practice in its *Annual Report, 1966*, and stated: "Friends desiring personal favors [such] as a driveway to be built into [sic] their front door, etc., have to be instructed to seek a private contractor specializing in such small jobs" (p. 80).
8. Elliot J. Berg, Harvard Advisory Project, *First Report, October 1964– February 1965*, Monrovia, March 1965, p. 2. (Mimeographed.)
9. *Ibid*. See also, Department of Planning and Economic Affairs, *Public Sector Accounts, 1965*. Another important patronage device, in the form of a promise of future reward, is the pension. The legislature votes pensions for individual civil servants upon their retirement. There is no perceivable regularity in amounts paid to such pensioners. Occasional papers describing the proceedings of the Liberian Legislature, Law School Library, University of Liberia, Monrovia.
10. *Budget, 1967*; *SCOGO Report*, p. 54.
11. Clower et al., *Growth*, pp. 15–22, describes these and other practices.
12. *Budget, 1967*.
13. *SCOGO Report*, p. 186.
14. James S. Coleman, "Political Science and Economic Development" (paper presented at the University of East Africa Social Science Conference, Nairobi, December 1966).
15. *SCOGO Report*, p. 25.
16. International Monetary Fund, Staff Paper, *The Liberian Economy*, pp. 305–7.
17. Berg, Harvard Advisory Project Report, pp. 1–2.
18. *Ibid*., p. 3.

19. U.S. Embassy, Monrovia, "Economic Trends and Their Implications for the U.S.," October 17, 1967 (italics mine).
20. Department of Planning and Economic Affairs, *Public Sector Accounts, 1965*, and *Annual Report, 1966*, p. 10; U.S. Embassy, "Economic Trends," 1967.
21. International Monetary Fund, *Staff Report for the 1970 Article XIV Consultation*; U.S., AID, "Consolidated Statement of [Liberian] Central Government Finances," September 12, 1970. See also Carl Shoup et al., *The Tax System of Liberia* (New York: Columbia University Press, 1969).
22. For example, Executive Order No. II, March 2, 1964, ordered that no department or agency of government should commit funds for new projects or programs without having received the approval of the National Planning Council. Executive Order No. IV, April 24, 1964, ruled that there would be no salary increases or hiring of new personnel except in cases of urgent need, as approved by the Bureau of the Budget.
23. *Liberian Star*, October 7, 1971.
24. Berg observed in 1965 that it would probably be difficult for the government to hold such people (Harvard Advisory Project Report, pp. 16–17).
25. *Ibid.*, p. 4.
26. President Tolbert made the Bureau of Internal Revenue a target of "clean up" and reform activities. The *Liberian Star*, October 5, 1971, reported a charge against Bureau personnel of misappropriating $132,000.
27. *SCOGO Report*, pp. 210–11.
28. *Liberian Star*, October 6, 1971, announced a civil service reform and reorganization program with United Nations assistance.
29. U.S. Embassy, Monrovia, "Liberia: Economic Trends," November 26, 1970.
30. These figures do not include pensions and annuities paid to retired civil servants, which amounted to $450,000 in 1965, and $491,000 in 1971. Department of Planning and Economic Affairs, *Public Sector Accounts, 1965*; *The Budget of the Government of Liberia for 1971*, Monrovia, February 9, 1971.
31. See V. Subramaniam, "Representative Bureaucracy: A Reassessment," *American Political Science Review*, vol. 61, no. 4 (December 1967), who argues that the bureaucracy provides the lower (working) classes access to important representational roles (pp. 1010–19).
32. Joseph LaPalombara, ed., *Bureaucracy and Political Development* (Princeton, N.J.: Princeton University Press, 1963), p. 7.

9: Education and Communications

1. Nevertheless, of the 824 primary and secondary schools operating in 1966, 192 were still run by missions, and 81 by private organizations or concessionaires. Department of Education, *Annual Report, 1966*, p. 92.

2. Educational Policy and Planning Committee, "A Critical Analysis of the Present Situation in Education in Liberia," prepared by the Educational Secretariat, Monrovia, June 21, 1966 (mimeographed), p. 1. Owing to a decrease in foreign aid contributions to education, total investment dropped to $8.7 million in 1969, or 11 percent of total government expenditures. *Economic Survey, 1969*, p. 107.

3. Only about 50 percent of secondary school students were in government-operated schools. Bertha B. Azango, *Liberian Star*, March 28, 1969; *Economic Survey, 1969*, pp. 107–9.

4. *Economic Survey, 1969*.

5. Educational Policy and Planning Committee, "Critical Analysis," p. 24; Department of Education, *Annual Report, 1966*, p. 21.

6. Igolima T. D. Amachree and S. Jabaru Carlon, *Report on Teacher Manpower Study in Liberia* (Monrovia: University of Liberia, January 1969), pp. 31–32.

7. Department of Education, *Annual Report, 1964–65*, p. 124.

8. *Economic Survey, 1969*, p. 108. Some observers have suggested that the high pass rates for 1968 and 1969 were an administrative response to presidential criticism of poor performance in previous years.

9. Department of Planning and Economic Affairs, *Population Growth Survey, 1970*, p. 28. These data indicate that some 240,000 children of school age attend schools, a figure well above any other estimates. It must be taken very skeptically, therefore.

10. Department of Education, *Socioeconomic Characteristics for the Liberian National Examination, 1967*, by Bertha Baker Azango, Monrovia, September 1968, p. 6.

11. *Ibid*.

12. *Ibid*., p. 37.

13. James C. Borg, "Language and Tribe among Government School Students in Monrovia" (Paper presented at the First Conference on Social Science Research in Liberia, Stanford University, August 1969).

14. S. N. Eisenstadt, *Modernization: Protest and Change* (Englewood Cliffs, N.J.: Prentice-Hall, 1966), p. 18.

15. Department of Education, *Annual Report, 1966*, pp. 65–66.

16. *SCOGO Report*, p. 149.

17. Educational Policy and Planning Committee, "Critical Analysis," p. 4. This figure is probably greater now, and the problem exists outside Monrovia as well. For example, only three new high school teachers took up positions between 1966 and 1968, while the student population at that level increased 20 percent. Amachree and Carlon, *Report on Teacher Manpower*, pp. 5–7.

18. *SCOGO Report*, p. 185, reports teacher absentee rates as high as 25 percent in many schools. Amachree and Carlon, *Report on Teacher Manpower*, report a 14 to 20 percent annual attrition rate in recent years.

19. Educational Policy and Planning Committee, "Supplementary Report to the Critical Analysis," p. 1. Almost 20 percent of primary school students were over fourteen years of age. "Critical Analysis," p. 3.

20. The University of Liberia in Monrovia had 540 students; Cuttington College

in Gbarnga had 214, some of whom were non-Liberian Africans on scholarships; and Maryland College of Our Lady of Fatima had 43. Educational Policy and Planning Committee, "Critical Analysis," pp. 13–14. Post-secondary enrollment was 1,199 in 1971, Department of Education, *Annual Report, 1971*, p. 66.

21. Liebenow, *Liberia: The Evolution of Privilege*, p. 105, notes that 80 percent of the surviving members of the graduating classes of 1934 through 1949 (of the University of Liberia) not only had government jobs but held the most senior posts in the government in 1968.

22. *U.S. Army Handbook*, p. 126; Educational Policy and Planning Committee, "Critical Analysis," p. 6. There are few other data on job placement of graduates. Booker T. Washington Institute, a vocational high school, had 137 graduates in 1966, all of whom found jobs; less is known about its dropouts, who comprised 61 percent of all entrants between 1958 and 1965. Department of Education, *Annual Report, 1966*, pp. 32–33.

23. *U.S. Army Handbook*, p. 127.

24. Educational Policy and Planning Committee, "Critical Analysis," p. 15. The recent decline in foreign aid has obliged the government to increase its share of university income.

25. *Liberian Age*, March 23 and 24, 1967.

26. *Liberian Star*, June 16, 1966.

27. Department of Planning and Economic Affairs, *Public Sector Accounts of Liberia, 1965*, p. 65.

28. Educational Policy and Planning Committee, "Critical Analysis," p. 19; Department of Education, *Annual Report, 1966*, pp. 46–55; *U.S. Army Handbook*, pp. 130–32. By 1969, science and technology had overtaken the social sciences.

29. Cf. J. M. Lonsdale, "Some Origins of Nationalism in East Africa," *Journal of African History*, vol. 9, no. 1 (1968), p. 138.

30. Richard and Doris Henries, *Liberia: The African Republic* (London: Macmillan, 1966), p. 42. Also A. Doris Banks Henries, *Civics for Liberian Schools* (New York: Collier-Macmillan, 1966). Both books are used in Liberian schools (Richard Henries is Speaker of the Liberian House of Representatives.)

31. Liberian National Youth Organization (LNYO), *Annual Report*, Monrovia, October 5, 1966. In his letter transmitting the report, the Director of the LNYO, S. Augustu P. Horton, who was appointed by President Tubman, warned that unless the problem of juvenile delinquency "is tackled at this stage of fermentation the stage of explosion, which is in the not too distant future, will prove most devastating."

32. *Ibid.*, p. 6. The LNYO is, of course, also another patronage device. Of the appropriation of $154,000 for 1966, nearly $118,000 (76 percent) was allocated for salaries of adult advisers and office staff. Only $15,000 was appropriated for materials and supplies.

33. Lucian W. Pye, *Communications and Political Development* (Princeton: Princeton University Press, 1963), p. 4.

34. *Ibid.*, p. 13. Pye speaks of the need to "awaken" the bulk of the people to new ideas.
35. Lucian W. Pye, "Communication Patterns and Problems of Representative Government in Non-Western Societies," *Public Opinion Quarterly*, vol. 20 (Spring 1956), pp. 249–57. See also Dankwart A. Rustow, *A World of Nations* (Washington, D.C.: Brookings Institution, 1967), p. 96.
36. Lucian W. Pye, *Politics, Personality and Nation Building* (New Haven: Yale University Press, 1962), pp. 20–21.
37. Department of Planning and Economic Development, *Population Growth Survey, 1970*, p. 24. This high literacy rate, based on self-appraisal, reflects a great advance over 1962 when the literacy rate was recorded at 10 percent.
38. Estimate given by the Department of Information and Cultural Affairs, 1971; in 1973 the estimate was 132 receivers per 1,000 population. *U.S. Army Handbook*, p. 220, estimated that there were 60,000 radios in 1964.
39. *Daily Listener*, February 8, 1955. The press has begun to support and extol President Tolbert in similar ways.
40. *Code of Laws, 1956*, 27:55, "Criminal Libel."
41. *Liberian Star*, February 17, 1967.
42. *Ibid.*, April 22, 1967.
43. Liebenow, "The Republic of Liberia," p. 360.
44. Liebenow, *Evolution of Privilege*, p. 114–15.
45. *Liberian Age*, July 17 and July 24, 1964. *West Africa*, February 25, 1967. The *Star* came under new management and resumed publication shortly after its closing. The former editor, upon his release from jail, became press adviser to President Tubman.
46. *Liberian Star*, February 22, 1963; July 2 and 3, and August 31, 1965.
47. *Liberian Star*, November 17, 1966.
48. The *Liberian Star* provided daily coverage of this trial throughout July 1968. See pp. 164–66 for full discussion of the Fahnbullah case.
49. Department of Planning and Economic Affairs, *Public Sector Accounts, 1965*.

10: The International Factor

1. Albert O. Hirschman, *A Bias for Hope* (New Haven: Yale University Press, 1971). This statement and the following excerpts are from Ch. 11, esp. pp. 226–33.
2. Samuel P. Huntington, *Political Order in Changing Societies* (New Haven: Yale University Press, 1968), discusses this aspect of modernization.
3. Townsend, ed., *President Tubman Speaks*, p. 17.
4. *Ibid.*, p. 103.
5. *Ibid.*, p. 150.
6. *Ibid.*, p. 185–86.
7. *Budget*, 1967 and 1971.
8. Department of State, *Annual Report, 1970*.

9. See *U.S. Army Handbook*, p. 313. For a report of the Commission see *ILO Official Bulletin, Supplement*, vol. 46, no. 2 (April 1963).
10. In the "Act Extending Emergency Powers to the President of Liberia," March 21, 1967.
11. "Report of the Governing Body on Freedom of Association," *ILO Official Bulletin, Supplement*, vol. 51, no. 1 (January 1968), pp. 68–75.
12. *Ibid.*, p. 73.
13. *Ibid.*, pp. 75–86. See Chapter 11 for Tubman's handling of labor problems.
14. Anderson, *Politics and Economic Change in Latin America*, p. 36, points out that characteristics of modernization are "most pronounced in those areas where the nation-state and the international exchange economy have become most explicitly interdependent." See also Rustow, *A World of Nations*, pp. 241–44.

11: Tubman's Last Years

1. Liberian leaders apparently took offense at J. Gus Liebenow's two studies, "The Republic of Liberia," in Carter, ed., *African One-Party States*, and "Liberia," in Coleman and Rosberg, eds., *Political Parties and National Integration in Tropical Africa*; and at the book by Clower, et al., *Growth*. These serious studies, however, are not to be confused with books of the genre of E. J. D. Furbay's *Top Hats and Tom Toms* (San Francisco: Ziff-Davis [Prentice-Hall], 1943), a comic opera version of Liberia; or Fletcher Knebel's *The Zin Zin Road* (Garden City: Doubleday, 1966), a thinly disguised fictional account of a Peace Corps volunteer's misadventures in Liberia.
2. Townsend, ed., *Official Papers*, p. 209.
3. Speech at Third Biennial Unification Council, Kolahun, February 14, 1963, Government Printing Office, Monrovia.
4. Townsend, ed., *Official Papers*, p. 297.
5. *Liberian Age*, November 15, 1966.
6. *New York Times*, May 12, 1968.
7. *Liberian Star*, May 3, 1968.
8. *Liberian Star*, May 2, 1968.
9. *Ibid.*
10. *Liberian Star*, July 9, 1968.
11. *Ibid.*
12. *Liberian Star*, August 1, 1968.
13. *Liberian Age*, December 27, 1966. The "Act of 9 February 1966 to Restore, Supplement and Enlarge the Emergency Powers Granted to the President of Liberia" states that labor unions had been connected with "detestable persons" who were infiltrating the country, and that illegal strikes were a threat to the security of the state.
14. *Liberian Age*, November 22, 1966; *Liberian Star*, November 19, 1966.
15. *Liberian Star*, March 26, 1968.

16. Editorial in the *Liberian Age*, February 24, 1967; address of the President of
    the Rubber Planters Association of Liberia, quoted in *Rubber Planters
    Bulletin*, vol. 3, nos. 1 and 2 (March 1967). *The Liberian Star*, October 20,
    1971, warned in an editorial that a strike at LAMCO's Buchanan operations
    might oblige the government to enact a "no-strike law."
17. I was told by an observer in 1967 that labor was one area which Tolbert was
    exploring for popular support for his claim to succeed Tubman.
18. I saw this letter, written in June 1967.
19. Department of Commerce and Industry, *Annual Report, October 1965–
    September 1966*, p. 135.
20. *The Liberian Journal of Commerce and Industry*, vol. 1, no. 2 (July–
    September, 1966).

12: Conclusions

1. See Gabriel A. Almond and Bingham G. Powell, Jr., *Comparative Politics*
   (Boston: Little, Brown, 1966), p. 11, for the use of this concept.
2. Bernard Crick, *In Defence of Politics* (Chicago: University of Chicago Press,
   1962), p. 62.
3. Irving Louis Horowitz, *Three Worlds of Development* (New York: Oxford
   University Press, 1966), p. 308.
4. Richard Fulton, "From Colonization to Nationhood: President Tubman and
   the Political Development of the Interior" (Paper presented at the First
   Conference on Social Science Research in Liberia, Stanford University,
   August 1969), pp. 18–19.
5. Cyril E. Black, *The Dynamics of Modernization* (New York: Harper and
   Row, 1966), p. 162.
6. *Liberian Age*, February 28, 1967.

Postscript

1. *Liberian Star*, January 4, 1973. Much of the following information is from this
   newspaper.
2. *Liberian Star*, January 26, 1972. Tolbert had, in fact, suspended such
   deductions upon taking office in 1971. But he reimposed them in this statement
   to cover party debts, promising that 1972 would be the last year for such
   collections.
3. U.S. Embassy, Monrovia. The government of Liberia began to implement the
   scheme in June 1973. It covers retired civil servants (including teachers,
   Liberian Star, March 30, 1973), as well as indigent and disabled persons, and
   replaces the previous arrangement, which required special acts of the
   legislature or the dispensing of PRO funds by President Tubman. The
   government announced that 2,000 persons were on government pensions in

1973, including former PRO's, civil servants, ex-soldiers, and senior citizens. *Liberian Star*, July 27, 1973.

4. *Liberian Star*, July 3, 1972.
5. *Liberian Star*, February 26, 1973.
6. *Liberian Star*, April 3, 1972.
7. *Liberian Star*, July 29, 1974.
8. *Liberian Star*, February 9, 1973. The IBRD puts the 1973 *net* debt service at $17.3 million.
9. *Liberian Star*, August 10, 1972.
10. *Liberian Star*, July 28, 1972. One Liberian economist went so far as to recommend public ownership of major economic activities. *Liberian Star*, April 27, 1973.
11. *Liberian Star*, June 28, 1973.
12. *Liberian Star*, October 10, 1972.
13. *Liberian Star*, January 19, 1973.
14. *Liberian Star*, January 24, 1973.
15. *Liberian Star*, March 22, 1973.
16. *Liberian Star*, March 27, 1973.
17. Characteristically, this case was covered extensively in the press in March, April, and May of 1973.
18. The 1974 amendment to the Penal Law broadened the definition of sedition so much that it came under severe criticism in the press. Claiming that the new law "smells of tribalism," R. M. Darpoh observed that it also appeared to be aimed at silencing "critics, critical journals as well as putting fear into anyone who nurtures political ambitions because 1975, a year of elections, is drawing near." *Liberian Star*, March 19, 1974. Such political ambitions had, in fact, been expressed by a former Attorney General, C. Abayomi Cassell, who called for "two determined and fearless men in each county" to join him in forming a national opposition party. *Liberian Star*, December 13, 1973.
19. *Liberian Star*, August 23 and 28, 1974.
20. *Liberian Star*, July 19, 1974.
21. *Liberian Star*, July 30, 1974.
22. *Liberian Star*, December 27, 1974.
23. *Liberian Star*, August 14, 1974.
24. *Liberian Star*, December 13, 1974. Tolbert's supporters had also held a loyalty rally, but indoors at a hotel. They also used the press extensively for guest columns to support Tolbert and attack Porte.

Bibliography

General

Ake, Claude. "Political Integration and Political Stability." *World Politics* 19, no. 3 (April 1967).

Almond, Gabriel A. "A Development Approach to Political Systems." *World Politics* 17, no. 2 (January 1965).

Almond, Gabriel A., and Powell, Bingham G., Jr. *Comparative Politics*. Boston: Little, Brown, 1966.

Almond, Gabriel A., and Verba, Sidney. *The Civic Culture*. Boston: Little, Brown, 1965.

Amin, Samir. *Le développement du capitalisme en Côte d'Ivoire*. Paris: Editions de Minuit, 1967.

Anderson, Charles W. *Politics and Economic Change in Latin America*. Princeton: D. Van Nostrand, 1967.

Anderson, Charles W., von der Mehden, Fred, and Young, Crawford. *Issues of Political Development*. Englewood Cliffs, N.J.: Prentice-Hall, 1967.

Annals of the American Academy of Political and Social Science 358 (March 1965). "New Nations: The Problems of Political Development," edited by Karl von Vorys.

Apter, David E. "Political Systems and Developmental Change." Paper presented at the International Political Science Association, Seventh World Congress, Brussels, September 18–23, 1967.

————. *The Politics of Modernization*. Berkeley: University of California Press, 1965.

Banton, M. P. *West African City: A Study of Tribal Life in Freetown*. London: Oxford University Press, 1957.

Bendix, Reinhard. *Nation Building and Citizenship: Studies of Our Changing Social Order*. New York: Wiley, 1964.

Berg, Elliot J. "Socialism and Economic Development in Tropical Africa." *Quarterly Journal of Economics* 78 (1964).

Black, Cyril E. *The Dynamics of Modernization*. New York: Harper and Row, 1966.

Cliffe, Lionel, ed. *One Party Democracy: The 1965 Tanzania General Elections*. Nairobi: East Africa Publishing House, 1965.

Coleman, James S. "Political Modernization." *International Encyclopedia of the Social Sciences*, vol. 10. New York: Crowell Collier and Macmillan, 1968.

————. "Political Science and Economic Development." Paper presented at the University of East Africa Social Science Conference, Nairobi, December 1966.

Coleman, James S., and Rosberg, Carl G., eds. *Political Parties and National Integration in Tropical Africa*. Berkeley: University of California Press, 1964.

Crick, Bernard. *In Defense of Politics*. Chicago: University of Chicago Press, 1962.

Curle, Adam. *The Role of Education in Developing Societies*. Accra: Ghana University Press, 1961.

Curtin, Philip D. *The Image of Africa: British Ideas and Action, 1780–1850*. Madison: University of Wisconsin Press, 1964.

Davies, Ioan. *African Trade Unions*. Baltimore, Md.: Penguin Books, 1966.

Deutsch, Karl W. *Nationalism and Social Communication*. 2d edition. Cambridge, Mass.: M.I.T. Press, 1966.

Duverger, Maurice. *The Idea of Politics*. London: Methuen, 1966.

———. *Political Parties*. London: Methuen, 1959.

Easton, David. *A Framework for Political Analysis*. Englewood Cliffs, N.J.: Prentice-Hall, 1965.

Eisenstadt, S. N. "Bureaucracy and Political Development." In *Bureaucracy and Political Development*, edited by Joseph LaPalombara. Princeton: Princeton University Press, 1963.

———. "Initial Institutional Patterns of Political Modernization." In *Political Modernization*, edited by Claude E. Welch, Jr. Belmont, Ca.: Wadsworth Publishing Co., 1967.

———. *Modernization: Protest and Change*. Englewood Cliffs, N.J.: Prentice-Hall, 1966.

Etzioni, Amatai. *Political Unification*. New York: Holt, Rinehart and Winston, 1965.

Fallers, Lloyd A. "Social Stratification and Economic Processes." In *Economic Transition in Africa*, edited by Melville J. Herskovits and Mitchell Harwitz. Evanston, Ill.: Northwestern University Press, 1964.

Fanon, Frantz. *The Wretched of the Earth*. London: Penguin Books, 1967.

Friedrich, Carl J. "Nation-Building?" In *Nation Building*, edited by Karl W. Deutsch and William J. Foltz. New York: Atherton Press, 1966.

Geertz, Clifford. "The Integrative Revolution: Primordial Sentiments and Civic Politics in the New States." In *Old Societies and New States: The Quest for Modernity in Asia and Africa*, edited by Clifford Geertz. New York: Free Press of Glencoe, 1963.

Hagen, E. E. *On the Theory of Social Change*. Homewood, Ill.: Dorsey Press, 1962.

Halle, Louis J. *The Society of Man*. New York: Harper & Row, 1965.

Halpern, Manfred. "The Rate and Costs of Political Development." *The Annals of the American Academy of Social and Political Science* 358 (March 1965).

———. "Toward Further Modernization of the Study of the New Nations." *World Politics* 17, no. 1 (October 1964).

Hirschman, Albert O. *A Bias for Hope*. New Haven: Yale University Press, 1971.

————. *Journeys Toward Progress*. Garden City, N.Y.: Doubleday, Anchor, 1965.

Horowitz, Irving Louis. *Three Worlds of Development*. New York: Oxford University Press, 1966.

Huntington, Samuel P. "Political Development and Political Decay." In *Political Modernization*, edited by Claude E. Welch, Jr. Belmont, Ca.: Wadsworth Publishing Co., 1967.

————. "Political Modernization: America vs. Europe." *World Politics* 18, no. 3 (April 1966).

————. *Political Order in Changing Societies*. New Haven: Yale University Press, 1968.

Kamarck, Andrew M. "Economics and Economic Development." In *The African World*, edited by Robert A. Lystad. New York: Praeger, 1965.

Kautsky, John H. *Political Change in Underdeveloped Countries: Nationalism and Communism*. New York: Wiley, 1962.

Kilson, Martin. *Political Change in a West African State: A Study of the Modernization Process in Sierra Leone*. Cambridge, Mass.: Harvard University Press, 1966.

Kopytoff, Igor. "Socialism and Traditional African Societies." In *African Socialism*, edited by William H. Friedland and Carl C. Rosberg. Stanford, Ca.: Stanford University Press for the Hoover Institution, 1964.

Kuper, Leo. "Sociology: Some Aspects of Urban Plural Societies." In *The African World*, edited by Robert A. Lystad. New York: Praeger, 1965.

LaPalombara, Joseph, ed. *Bureaucracy and Political Development*. Princeton: Princeton University Press, 1963.

Lerner, Daniel. "Comparative Analysis of Processes of Modernization." In *The City in Modern Africa*, edited by Horace Miner. London: Pall Mall, 1967.

Levy, Marion J. *Modernization and the Structure of Societies*. Princeton: Princeton University Press, 1966.

————. "Patterns (Structures) of Modernization and Political Development." *The Annals of the American Academy of Social and Political Science* 358 (March 1965).

Lewis, I. M. "Nationalism, Urbanism and Tribalism in Contemporary Africa." Paper presented at the University of East Africa Social Science Conference, Nairobi. December 1966. Mimeographed.

Lewis, W. Arthur. "Beyond African Dictatorship." *Encounter* 25, no. 2 (August 1965).

Lipset, Seymour Martin. *The First New Nation*. New York: Basic Books, 1963.

Little, Kenneth. *West African Urbanization: A Study of Voluntary Associations in Social Change*. Cambridge, Eng.: Cambridge University Press, 1965.

Lloyd, Peter C. *The New Elites of Tropical Africa*. London: Oxford University Press, 1966.

Lloyds Register of Shipping. London, 1971.

Lonsdale, J. M. "Some Origins of Nationalism in East Africa." *Journal of African History* 9, no. 1 (1968).

Mair, Lucy P. *Primitive Government*. Baltimore, Md.: Penguin Books, 1962.

Malenbaum, Wilfred. "Economic Factors and Political Development." *The Annals of the American Academy of Social and Political Science* 358 (March 1965).

Melson, Robert. "Ideology and Inconsistency: The Cross-Pressured Nigerian Worker." *American Political Science Review* 65, no. 1 (March 1971).

Mercier, Paul. "Remarques sur la signification du 'Tribalisme' actuel en Afrique Noire." *Cahiers Internationaux de Sociologie*, July–December, 1961.

Miner, Horace, ed. *The City in Modern Africa*. London: Pall Mall, 1967.

Needler, Martin C. "Political Development and Socioeconomic Development: The Case of Latin America." *The American Political Science Review* 62, no. 3 (September 1968).

Organski, A. F. K. *The Stages of Political Development*. New York: Knopf, 1965.

Pareto, Vilfredo. *Sociological Writings*, selected and introduced by S. E. Finer. New York: Praeger, 1966.

Pennock, J. Roland. "Political Development, Political Systems and Political Goods." *World Politics* 18, no. 3 (April 1966).

Pfaff, Richard H. "Disengagement from Traditionalism in Turkey and Iran." In *Political Modernization*, edited by Claude E. Welch, Jr. Belmont, Ca.: Wadsworth Publishing Co., 1967.

Pye, Lucian W. "Communication Patterns and the Problems of Representative Government in Non-Western Societies." *Public Opinion Quarterly* 20 (Spring 1956).

―――. *Communications and Political Development*. Princeton: Princeton University Press, 1963.

―――. *Politics, Personality and Nation Building*. New Haven: Yale University Press, 1962.

Rosberg, Carl G., Jr., and Nottingham, John. *The Myth of the "Mau Mau": Nationalism in Kenya*. New York: Praeger, 1966.

Rudebeck, Lars. *Party and People: A Study of Political Change in Tunisia*. Stockholm: Almquist and Wiksell, 1967.

Rudolph, Lloyd I. and Susanne H. *The Modernity of Tradition: Political Development in India*. Chicago: University of Chicago Press, 1967.

Rustow, Dankwart A. *A World of Nations: Problems of Political Modernization*. Washington, D. C.: Brookings Institution, 1967.

Scanlon, David. "Education." In *The African World*, edited by Robert A. Lystad. New York: Praeger, 1965.

Schapera, I. *Government and Politics in Tribal Societies*. London: Watts, 1956.

Shils, Edward. *Political Development*. The Hague: Mouton, 1962.

Sinai, I. R. *The Challenge of Modernization*. New York: W. W. Norton, 1964.

Smith, M. G. *The Plural Society in the British West Indies*. Berkeley: University of California Press, 1965.

Southall, Aidan, ed. *Social Change in Modern Africa*. London: Oxford University Press, 1961.

Subramaniam, V. "Representative Bureaucracy: A Reassessment." *The American Political Science Review* 61, no. 4 (December 1967).

Wallerstein, Immanuel. "Ethnicity and National Integration in West Africa." In *Comparative Politics*, edited by H. Eckstein and David Apter. New York: Free Press of Glencoe, 1963.

Ward, Robert E., and Rustow, Dankwart A., eds. *Political Modernization in Japan and Turkey*. Princeton: Princeton Unviersity Press, 1964.

Weber, Max. *The Theory of Social and Economic Organization*. New York: The Free Press, 1957.

Weiner, Myron. "Political Integration and Political Development." In *Political Modernization*, edited by Claude E. Welch, Jr. Belmont, Ca.: Wadsworth Publishing Co., 1967.

Welch, Claude E., Jr. "The Comparative Study of Political Modernization." In *Political Modernization*, edited by Claude E. Welch, Jr. Belmont, Ca.: Wadsworth Publishing Co., 1967.

Welch, Claude E., Jr., ed. *Political Modernization*. Belmont, Ca.: Wadsworth Publishing Co., 1967.

Whitaker, C. S., Jr. "A Disrhythmic Process of Political Change." *World Politics* 19 (January 1967).

Wood, Eric W. "Migrant Labour and Urban Social Systems." *Cahiers d'Etudes Africaines* 8, premier cahier (1968).

Wrong, Dennis H. "Economic Development and Democracy." In *A Dissenter's Guide to Foreign Policy*, edited by Irving Howe. Garden City, N.Y.: Doubleday, Anchor, 1968.

Zolberg, Aristide R. *Creating Political Order: The Party States of West Africa*. Chicago: Rand McNally, 1966.

―――. "Patterns of National Integration." *The Journal of Modern African Studies* 5, no. 4 (December 1967).

―――. "The Structure of Political Conflict in the New States of Tropical Africa." *The American Political Science Revew* 62, no. 1 (March 1968).

Works on Liberia

Amachree, Igolima T. D. " 'Detribalization' and Urban Residence: A Study of Some Liberian Urban Dwellers." Paper presented at Third Annual Conference on Liberian Social Science Research, University of Delaware, June 1971.

Amachree, Igolima T. D., and Carlon, S. Jabaru. *Report on Teacher Manpower Study in Liberia*. Monrovia: University of Liberia, January 1969. Mimeographed.

Anderson, Benjamin J. K. *Narrative of a Journey to Musardu, the Capital of the Western Mandingoes.* New York: S. W. Green, 1870.

Azikiwe, Nnamdi. *Liberia in World Politics.* London: Arthur H. Stockwell, 1934.

Beleky, Louis P. "The Development of Liberia." *Journal of Modern African Studies* 2, no. 1 (March 1973).

Bellman, Beryl L. "Some Constitutive Features of Secrecy Among the Fala Kpelle of Sucromu, Liberia." Paper presented at the First Conference on Social Science Research in Liberia, Stanford University, August 1969.

Berg, Elliot J. Harvard Advisory Project, Liberia. First Report, October 1964–February 1965. Monrovia, March 1965. Mimeographed.

————. "Growth, Development and All That: Thoughts on the Liberian Experience." Center for Research on Economic Development, University of Michigan, March 1969. Mimeographed.

Blanchard, David. *The Study of Small Farm Agriculture in Liberia.* For U.S. AID, Monrovia, Liberia, July 31, 1967. Mimeographed.

Borg, James C. "Language and Tribe Among Government School Students in Monrovia." Paper presented at the First Conference on Social Science Research in Liberia, Stanford University, August 1969.

Brown, George W. *The Economic History of Liberia.* Washington, D.C.: Associated Publishers, 1941.

Buell, Raymond Leslie. *Liberia, A Century of Survival, 1847–1947.* Philadelphia: University of Pennsylvania, African Handbooks, no. 7, 1947.

————. *The Native Problem in Africa.* Hamden, Conn.: Archon Books, Shoe String Press, 1965.

Carter, Jeanette E. "The Rural Loma and Monrovia: Ties with an Urban Center." *Liberian Studies Journal* 2, no. 2 (1970).

Cason, J. W. "The Growth of Christianity in the Liberian Environment." Unpublished Ph.D. dissertation, Columbia University, 1962.

Chalk, Frank. "The Anatomy of an Investment: Firestone's 1927 Loan to Liberia." *The Canadian Journal of African Studies*, no. 1 (March 1967).

Clower, Robert; Dalton, George; Mitchell, Harwitz; and Walters, A. A. *Growth Without Development: An Economic Survey of Liberia.* Evanston, Ill.: Northwestern University Press, 1966.

Cole, Henry B., ed. *The Liberian Yearbook, 1962.* Monrovia: A Liberian Review Publication, n. d.

D'Azevedo, Warren. "Some Historical Problems in the Delineation of a Central West Atlantic Region." *Annals of the New York Academy of Sciences* 96 (January 1962).

————. "Tribal Development and a New Territory." Paper given at the African Studies Association Conference, Los Angeles, Ca., October 16–19, 1968.

————. "A Tribal Reaction to Nationalism." *Liberian Studies Journal*, vols. 1–3 (1969–71).

Fiske, Mary. "History of the True Whig Party, 1869–1967." Monrovia, [1967]. Mimeographed.

Fraenkel, Merran. "Social Change on the Kru Coast of Liberia." *Africa* 36, no. 2 (April 1966).

———. *Tribe and Class in Monrovia*. New York: Oxford University Press, 1964.

Fulton, Richard M. "From Colonization to Nationhood: President Tubman and the Political Development of the Interior." Paper presented at the First Conference on Social Science Research in Liberia, Stanford University, August 1969.

———. "Primitive Government: The Case of the Kpelle of Liberia." Unpublished draft of working paper for Ph.D. dissertation, 1968.

Furbay, E. J. D. *Top Hats and Tom-Toms*. San Francisco: Ziff-Davis, 1943.

Gårdlund, Torsten. *LAMCO in Liberia*. Stockholm: Almquist and Wiksell, 1967. (Authorized translation of *LAMCO i Liberia*.)

Gay, John, and Cole, Michael. *The New Mathematics and an Old Culture: A Study of Learning Among the Kpelle of Liberia*. New York: Holt, Rinehart and Winston, 1967.

Genevray, J. *Eléments d'une monographie d'une division administrative Libérienne (Grand Bassa County)*. Dakar: I.F.A.N., 1952.

Gibbs, James L. "The Kpelle of Liberia." In *Peoples of Africa*, edited by James L. Gibbs. New York: Holt, Rinehart and Winston, 1965.

Greene, Graham. *Journey Without Maps*. New York: Doubleday, Doren & Co., 1936.

Greenwall, Henry J., and Wild, Roland. *Unknown Liberia*. London: Hutchison & Co., 1936.

Haliburton, G. M. "The Prophet Harris and the Grebo Rising of 1910." *Liberian Studies Journal* 3, no. 1 (1970–71).

Harley, George W. *Notes on the Poro in Liberia*. Peabody Museum Papers, vol. 19, no. 2, 1941.

Henries, A. Doris Banks. *Civics for Liberian Schools*. New York: Collier-Macmillan, 1966.

Henries, Richard and Doris. *Liberia: The West African Republic*. London: Macmillan, 1966.

Holden, Edith. *Blyden of Liberia*. New York: Vantage Press, 1966.

Holsoe, Svend E. "The Cassava-Leaf People: An Ethno-historical Study of the Vai People with Particular Emphasis of the Tewo Chiefdom." Unpublished Ph.D. dissertation, Boston University, 1967.

———. "The Condo Federation in Western Liberia." *The Liberian Historical Review* 3, no. 1 (1966).

Huberich, Charles H. *The Political and Legislative History of Liberia*. 2 vols. New York: Central Books, 1947.

International Labor Organization (ILO). "Report of the Governing Body on Freedom of Association." *Official Bulletin*, Supplement, vol. 50, no. 3 (July 1967), and vol. 51, no. 1 (January 1968).

International Monetary Fund. *Staff Report for the 1970 Article XIV Consultation*. Approved by Mamadou Touré and Timothy Sweeny, January 28, 1971.

International Monetary Fund Staff Papers. *The Liberian Economy*. By M. A. Qureshi, Yoshio Mizoe, and F. d'A. Collings. N. p., July 1964.

Johnston, Harry. *Liberia*. New York: Dodd, Mead, 1906. Vol. 1.

Jones, Hannah Abeodu Bowen. "The Struggle for Political and Cultural Unification in Liberia, 1847–1930." Unpublished Ph.D. dissertation, Northwestern University, 1962.

Knebel, Fletcher. *The Zin Zin Road*. Garden City, N.Y.: Doubleday, 1966.

Liberian Iron Ore Limited. *Annual Report, 1966*. [Charlottetown, Prince Edward Island, Canada: Liberian Iron Ore Ltd.]

Liberian Annual Review. London and Monrovia: Consolidated Publications, 1960–61.

Liberty, C. Zamba. "The Rise of the Commercial Faction of the Emigrant Group in Liberia, 1822–1842." Paper presented at the African Studies Association Conference, Los Angeles, Ca., October 16–19, 1968.

———. "The Growth of the Liberian State: An Analysis of Its Historiography." Draft, Stanford University, 1972.

Liebenow, J. Gus. *Liberia: The Evolution of Privilege*. Ithaca, N.Y.: Cornell University Press, 1969.

———. "Liberia." In *Political Parties and National Integration in Tropical Africa*, edited by James S. Coleman and Carl G. Rosberg. Berkeley: University of California Press, 1964.

———. "The Republic of Liberia." In *African One-Party States*, edited by Gwendolen M. Carter. Ithaca, N.Y.: Cornell University Press, 1962.

Lindblom, Charles E. *Diffusing Economic Development for Liberia*. For U.S. AID, Liberia, May 1968. Mimeographed.

Little, Kenneth. "The Political Function of the Poro" (Part I). *Africa* 35, no. 4 (October 1965).

———. "The Political Function of the Poro" (Part II). *Africa* 36, no. 1 (January 1966).

Marinelli, Lawrence. *The New Liberia*. New York: Praeger, 1964.

Martin, Jane J. "How to Build a Nation: Liberian Ideas about National Integration in the Later Nineteenth Century." *Liberian Studies Journal* 2, no. 1 (1969).

McLaughlin, Russell U. *Foreign Investment and Development in Liberia*. New York: Praeger, 1966.

Public Administration Service. "Revenue Collections by Major Source," *Quarterly Progress Reports*. For U.S. Agency for International Development, 1962–67. Chicago: Public Administration Service. Mimeographed.

Riddell, James C. "Mano Labor Migration and Cash-Cropping." *Liberian Studies Journal* 2, no. 2 (1970).

Schwab, George. *Tribes of the Liberian Hinterland.* Edited, with additional material by George W. Harley. Report of the Peabody Mission to Liberia. Peabody Museum Papers, vol. 31, 1947.

Seibel, H. D. "Arbeitsgenossen-Shaften bei den Mano in Liberia." *Africa Heute* 10, June 1968.

Shick, Tom W. "A Quantitative Analysis of Liberian Colonization from 1820–1843, with Special Reference to Mortality." *Journal of African History* 12, no. 1 (1971).

Shoup, Carl, et al. *The Tax System of Liberia.* New York: Columbia University Press, 1969.

Simpson, C. L. *The Memoirs of C. L. Simpson.* London: The Diplomatic Press and Publishing Co. (Diprepu Co.), 1961.

Smith, Robert A. *William V. S. Tubman.* Amsterdam: Van Ditmar, 1966.

Stanley, William R. "Changing Patterns of Transportation Development in Liberia." Unpublished Ph.D. dissertation, University of Pittsburgh, 1966.

————. "Evaluating Construction Priorities of Farm-to-Market Roads in Developing Countries: A Case Study." *Journal of Developing Areas* 5, no. 3 (April 1971).

Starr, Frederick. *Liberia: Description, History, and Problems.* Chicago: 1913.

Staudenraus, P. J. *The African Colonization Movement, 1816–1865.* New York: Columbia University Press, 1961.

Stetson, George R. *The Liberian Republic As It Is.* Boston: A. Williams and Co., 1881.

Townsend, E. Reginald, ed. *The Official Papers of William V. S. Tubman.* London: Longmans Green and Co., 1968.

Townsend, E. Reginald, ed. *President Tubman of Liberia Speaks.* London: Consolidated Publications, 1959.

True Whig Party of Liberia: General Rules and Regulations. Revised and adopted by the National Convention, Monrovia, February 7, 1963.

United Christian Fellowship Conference of Liberia. *Changing Liberia: A Challenge to the Christian.* Report of meetings held in Monrovia in December 1957 and July 1958. N. p., 1959.

United States. Agency for International Development. "Summary of Basic Data." In *Liberia: Economic Background Highlights.* 1967, 1971.

————. Agency for International Development. *Consolidated Statement of [Liberian] Central Government Finances.* September 12, 1970.

————. Agency for International Development. *The U.S. Economic Aid Program for Liberia.* August 1967, September 1970 and 1971.

————. Congress. Senate. "Roll of Emigrants That Have Been Sent to the Colony of Liberia, West Africa, by the American Colonization Society and Its

Auxiliaries, to September, 1843, &c." 28th Cong., 2d sess., 1845. *Public Documents*, vol. 9, docs. 150–171, 173.

———. Department of Agriculture. *Liberia: Agricultural Situation*. Monrovia, January 26, 1971.

———. Department of the Army. *United States Army Handbook for Liberia*. Prepared by Foreign Areas Studies Division, Special Operations Research Office. Washington, D. C.: American University, 1964.

United States Embassy. "Liberia: Economic Trends." Monrovia, November 26, 1970.

United States Embassy. "Liberia: Economic Trends and Their Implications for the United States." Monrovia, October 17, 1967.

Weintraub, Leon. "Land and Power in Liberia." Paper presented at the Second Conference on Social Science Research in Liberia, University of Indiana, May 1970.

Official Liberian Documents and Reports

"Act Extending Emergency Powers to the President of Liberia," March 21, 1967.

"An Act to Amend the Labor Practices Law with Respect to Employment in General, May 30, 1966." *Acts Passed by the Legislature*, 1966.

"An Act to Restore and Enlarge Emergency Powers Granted the President of Liberia." *Acts Passed by the Legislature*, Ch. 1, 1962–63.

Department of Agriculture. *Annual Report, 1966*. Monrovia, 1966.

———. Draft Development Plan, 1967–70.

Department of Commerce and Industry. *Annual Report, 1965–66*. Monrovia, 1966.

Department of Education. *Annual Report* for 1964–65, 1966, and 1971. Monrovia.

———. "Socioeconomic Characteristics for the Liberian National Examination, 1967." By Bertha Baker Azango. Monrovia, September 1968.

———. Educational Policy and Planning Committee. "A Critical Analysis of the Present Situation in Education in Liberia." Prepared by the Educational Secretariat. Monrovia, June 21, 1966. Mimeographed. "Supplementary Report to the Critical Analysis, 1966." Mimeographed.

Department of Interior. *Departmental Regulations Governing the Administration of the Interior of the Republic of Liberia*. Monrovia, January 21, 1921.

———. Bureau of Folkways. *Laws and Administrative Regulations Governing the Poro and Sande Societies*. Compiled by V. J. Fahnbullah. Monrovia, 1962.

Department of Planning and Economic Affairs. *Annual Report, 1966*. Monrovia, 1966.

———. *Demographic Annual of the Population Growth Survey, 1970*. Monrovia, December 1970.

———. *Economic Survey, 1969*. Monrovia, June 1970.

———. *Public Sector Accounts of Liberia*. Compiled by Richard M. Barkay. Monrovia, 1965, 1966.

Department of State. *Annual Report*. 1966, 1970. Monrovia, 1966–70.

Department of Public Works. *Annual Report, 1966.* Monrovia, n. d.

Executive Mansion. *The Budget of the Government of Liberia.* For 1967, 1970, and 1971.

Liberian Cartographic Service. "Geographic Names." Monrovia, October 16, 1955. Mimeographed.

Liberian Code of Laws. Ithaca, N. Y.: Cornell University Press, 1957, 1958, and 1960.

Liberian Information Service. *The Plot That Failed: The Story of the Attempted Assassination of President Tubman.* Monrovia, 1959.

Liberian National Youth Organization. *Annual Report.* Monrovia, October 5, 1966.

Office of National Planning. "Industry in Liberia." Monrovia, August 1965. Mimeographed.

————. "Report on the Economic Potential of Forestry in Liberia." By G. R. Gregory. Monrovia, June 1965.

————. "Some Aspects of Recent Economic Development and Possible Implications." By Y. H. Diddens. Monrovia, March 1966. Mimeographed.

————. Transport and Communications in Liberia." By Harvey Klemmer. Monrovia, December 15, 1964.

————. Bureau of Statistics. *Census of Population, 1962.* Monrovia, 1964.

Special Commission on Government Operations. "Executive Branch Organization and Operations: A Survey Report." By Public Administration Service, Chicago, Illinois, August 1964.

Special Committee on Housing Policy. "Report of the President's Special Committee on Housing Policy." 2d draft. Monrovia, March 10, 1965.

Journals and Newspapers

Africa Report.

Bong County News. Gbarnga: Liberian Department of Information. March 31, 1967.

Daily Listener. Monrovia. 1955.

Liberia Journal of Commerce and Industry. Monrovia: Department of Interior. 1966.

Liberian Age. Monrovia. 1964–67.

Liberian Star. Monrovia. 1963–68, 1971, 1974, 1975.

Liberian Studies Journal. [Currently being published at University of Delaware, Newark, Delaware.]

New York Times. Special supplement on Liberia. New York. December 19, 1966.

Rubber Planters Bulletin. Monrovia: Rubber Planters Association of Liberia. 1965–67.

West Africa.

Index

DATE DUE

MAR 1 1981			
GAYLORD			PRINTED IN U.S.A.